AIMÉE DE JONGH

THE RETURN OF THE HONEY BUZZARD

SELF MADE HERO

For Bob, who gave me the confidence and inspiration to make this book.
With thanks to Mara, who advised and supported me from beginning to end.

First published in English in 2016
by SelfMadeHero
139-141 Pancras Road
London NW1 1UN
www.selfmadehero.com

Written and illustrated by Aimée De Jongh
Text and image copyright: © 2014 Aimée de Jongh.
Originally published by De Bezige Bij / Oog & Blik, Amsterdam
Translated from Dutch by Michele Hutchison
Translation copyright: © 2016 Michele Hutchison

Publishing Director: Emma Hayley
Sales & Marketing Manager: Sam Humphrey
Publishing Assistant: Guillaume Rater
UK Publicist: Paul Smith
US Publicist: Maya Bradford
Designer: Txabi Jones
With thanks to: Dan Lockwood

Nederlands
letterenfonds
dutch foundation
for literature

This book was published with the support of the Dutch Foundation for Literature

A CIP record for this book is available from the British Library

ISBN 978-1-910593-16-5

10 9 8 7 6 5 4 3 2 1

Printed and bound in Slovenia

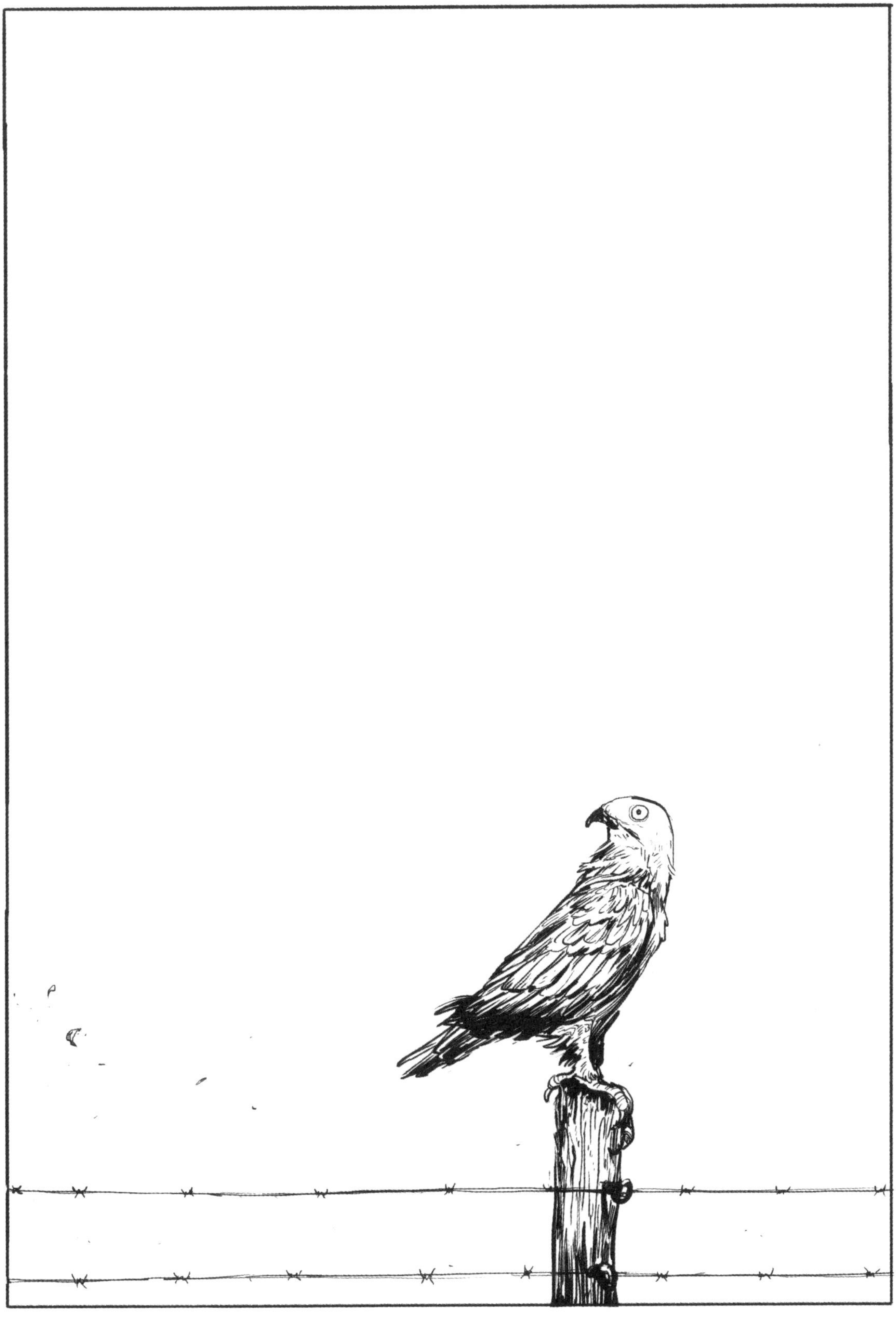

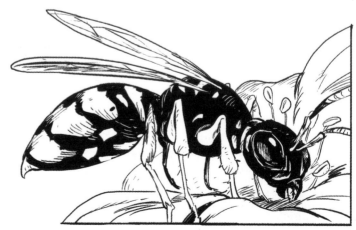

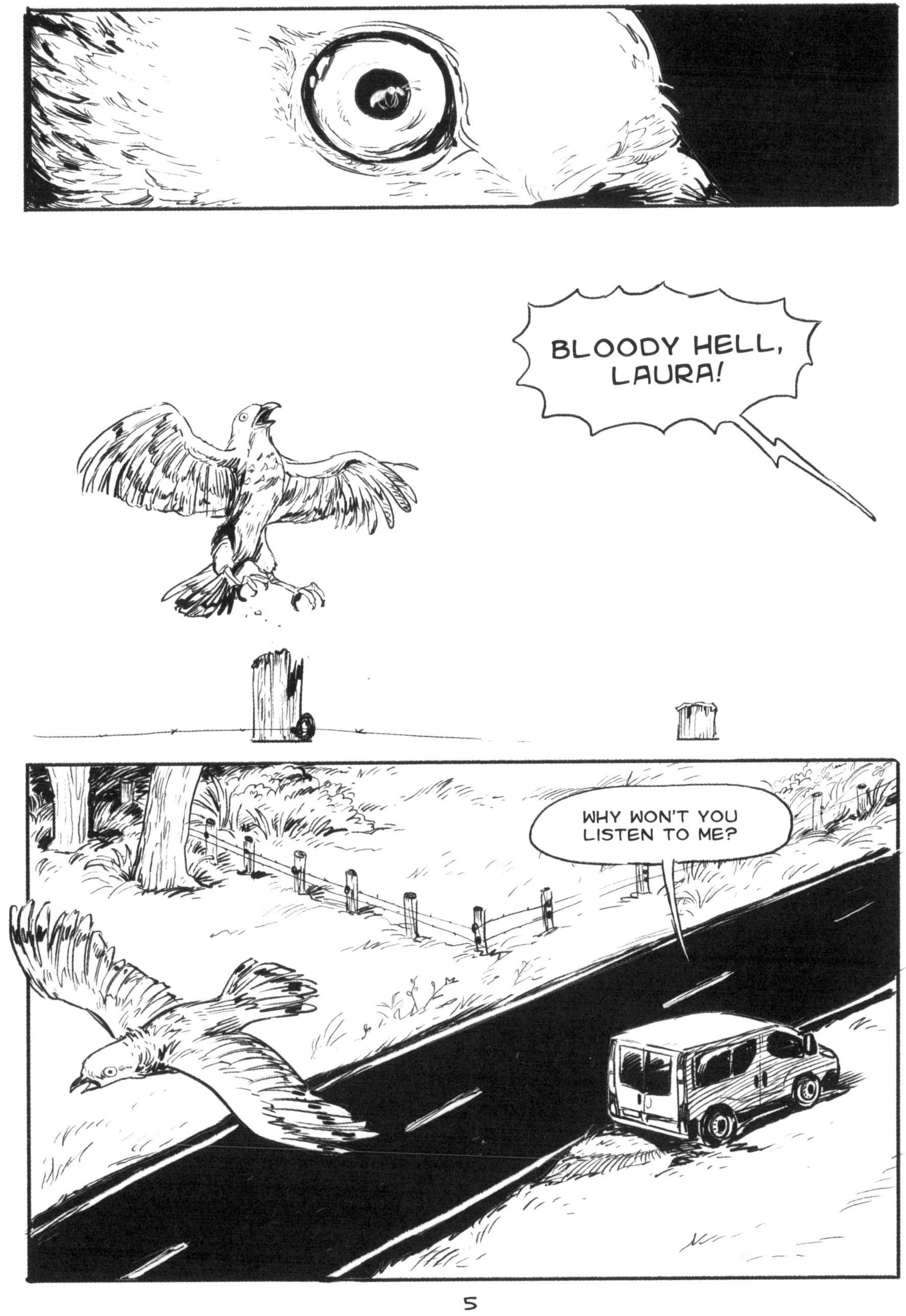
BLOODY HELL, LAURA!
WHY WON'T YOU LISTEN TO ME?

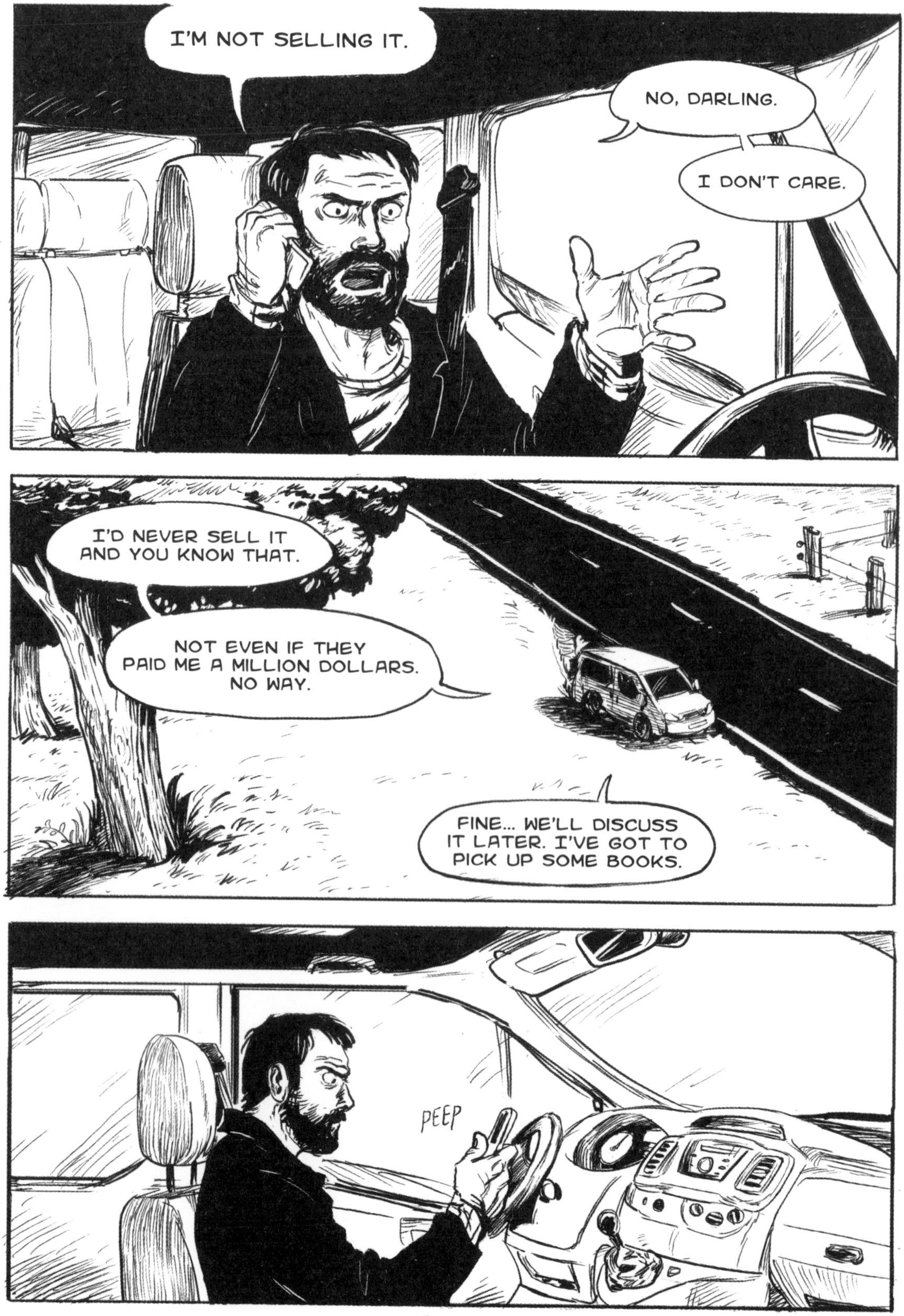
I'M NOT SELLING IT.
NO, DARLING.
I DON'T CARE.
I'D NEVER SELL IT AND YOU KNOW THAT.
NOT EVEN IF THEY PAID ME A MILLION DOLLARS. NO WAY.
FINE... WE'LL DISCUSS IT LATER. I'VE GOT TO PICK UP SOME BOOKS.
PEEP

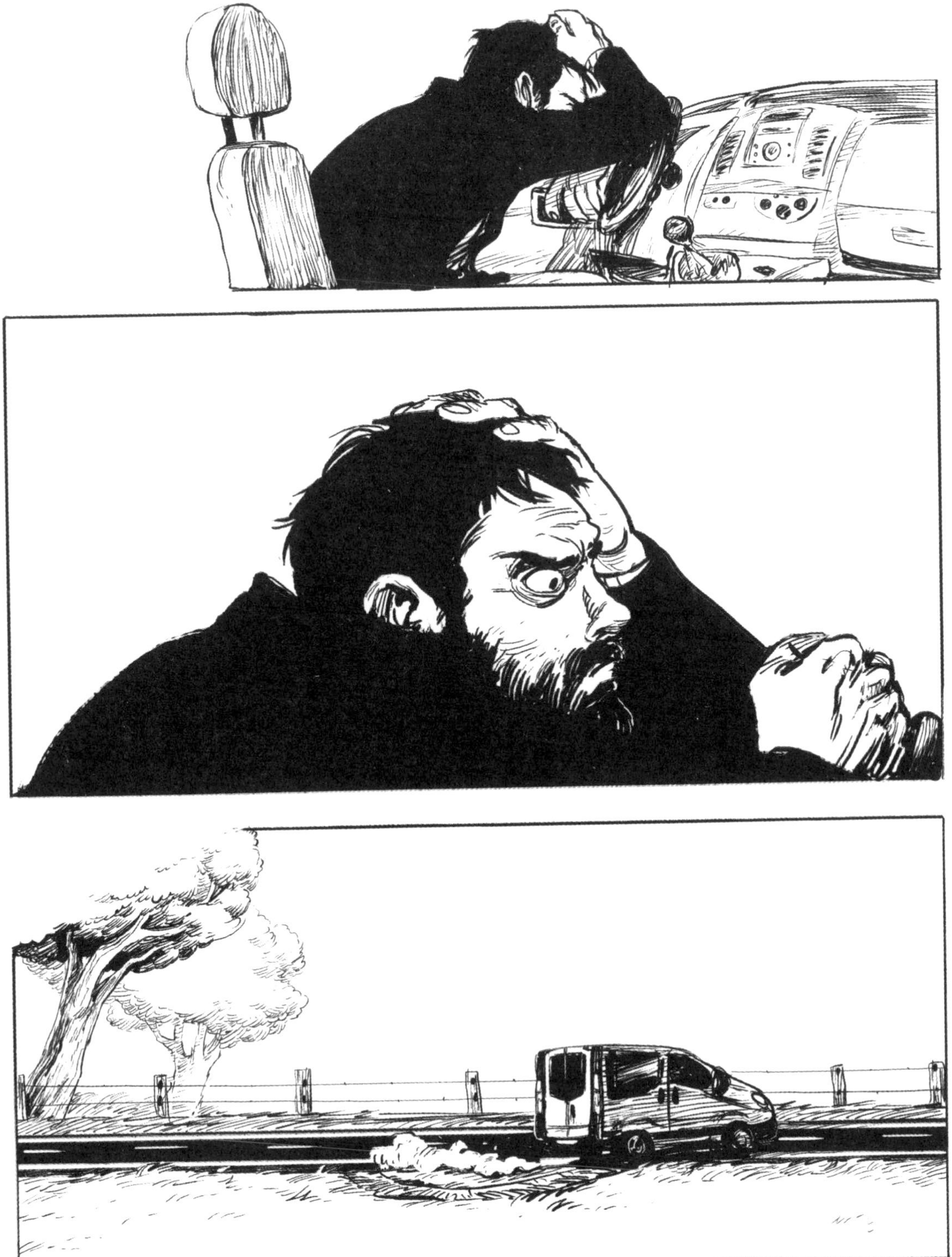

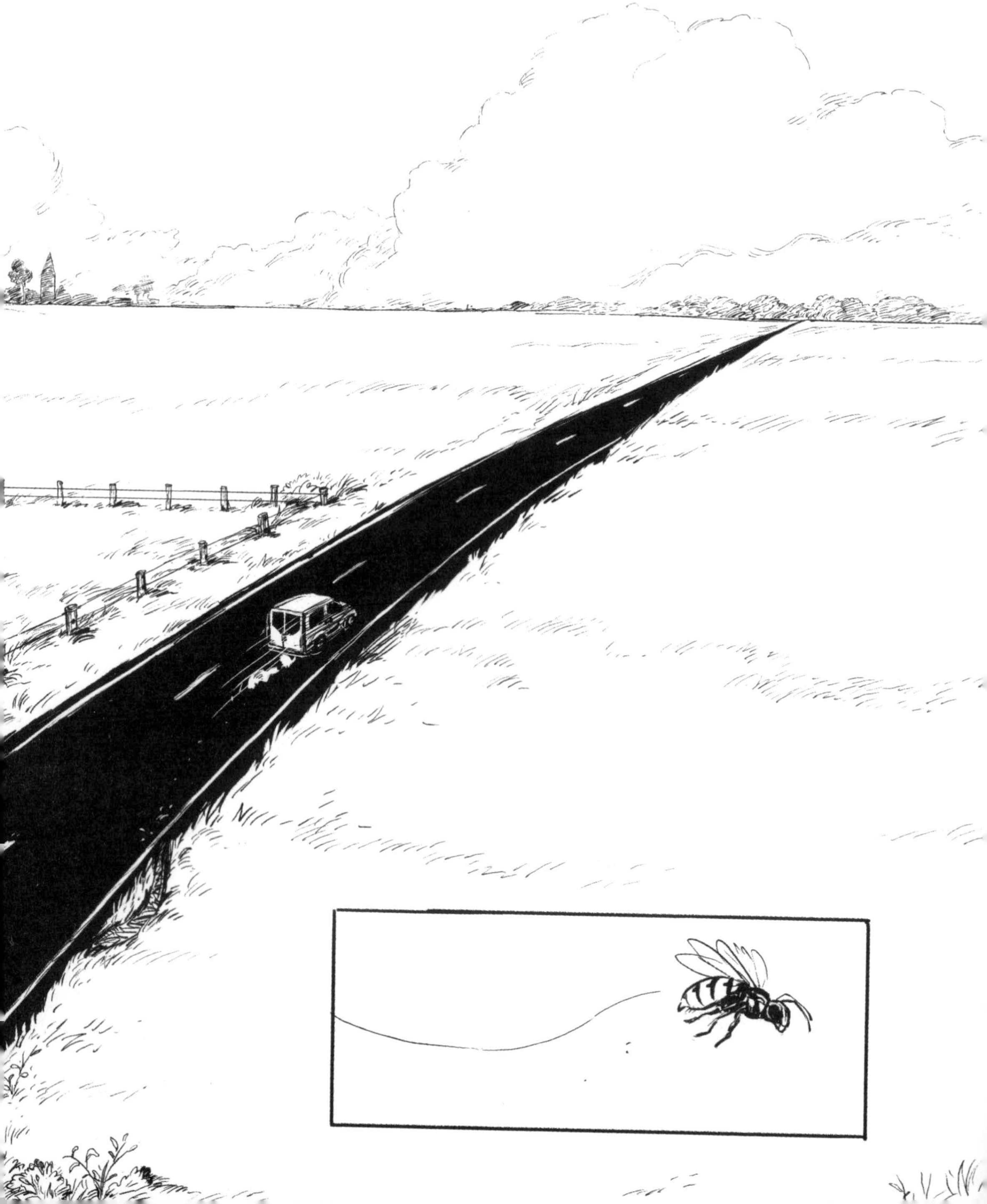

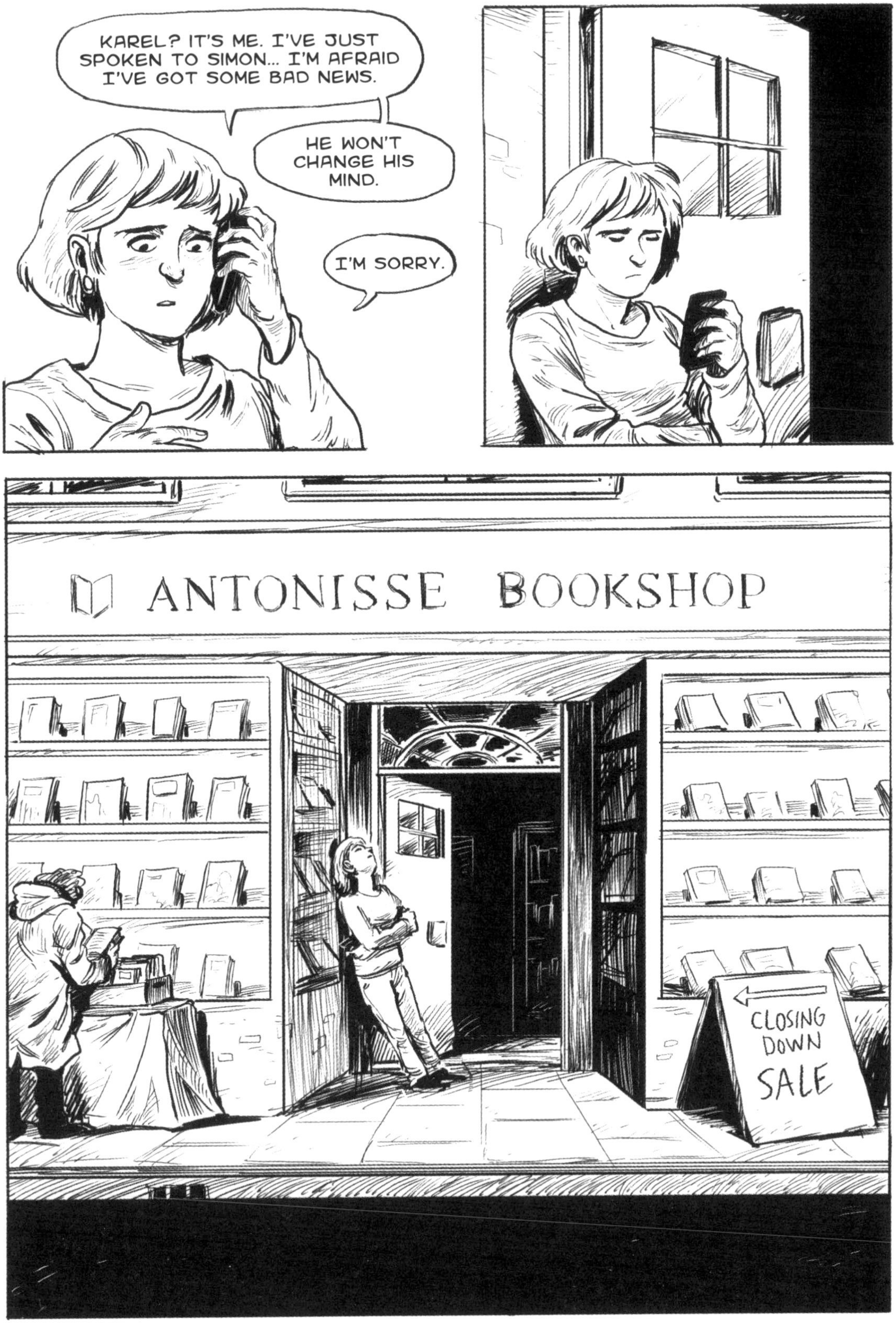
KAREL? IT'S ME. I'VE JUST SPOKEN TO SIMON... I'M AFRAID I'VE GOT SOME BAD NEWS.
HE WON'T CHANGE HIS MIND.
I'M SORRY.
ANTONISSE BOOKSHOP
CLOSING DOWN SALE

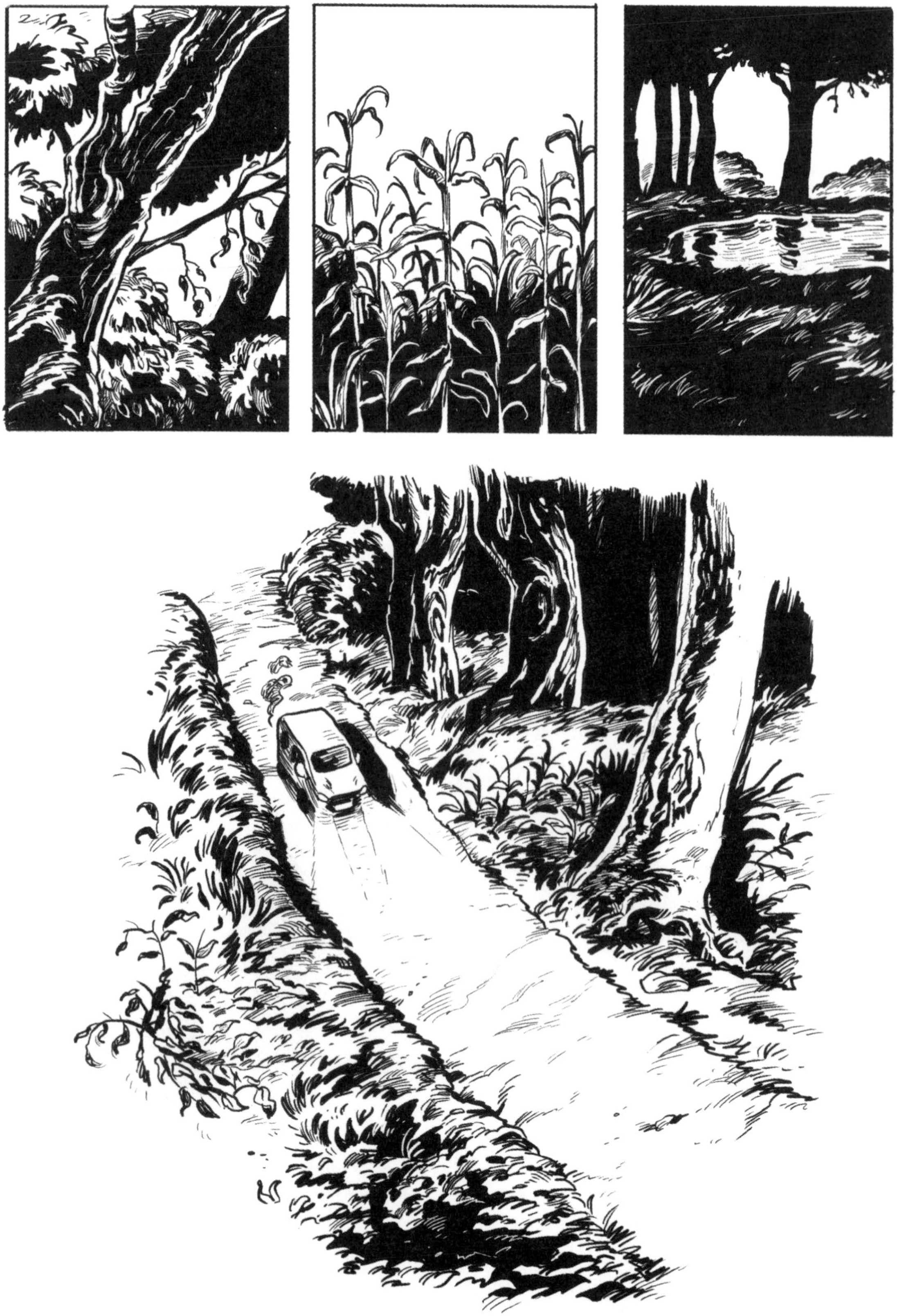

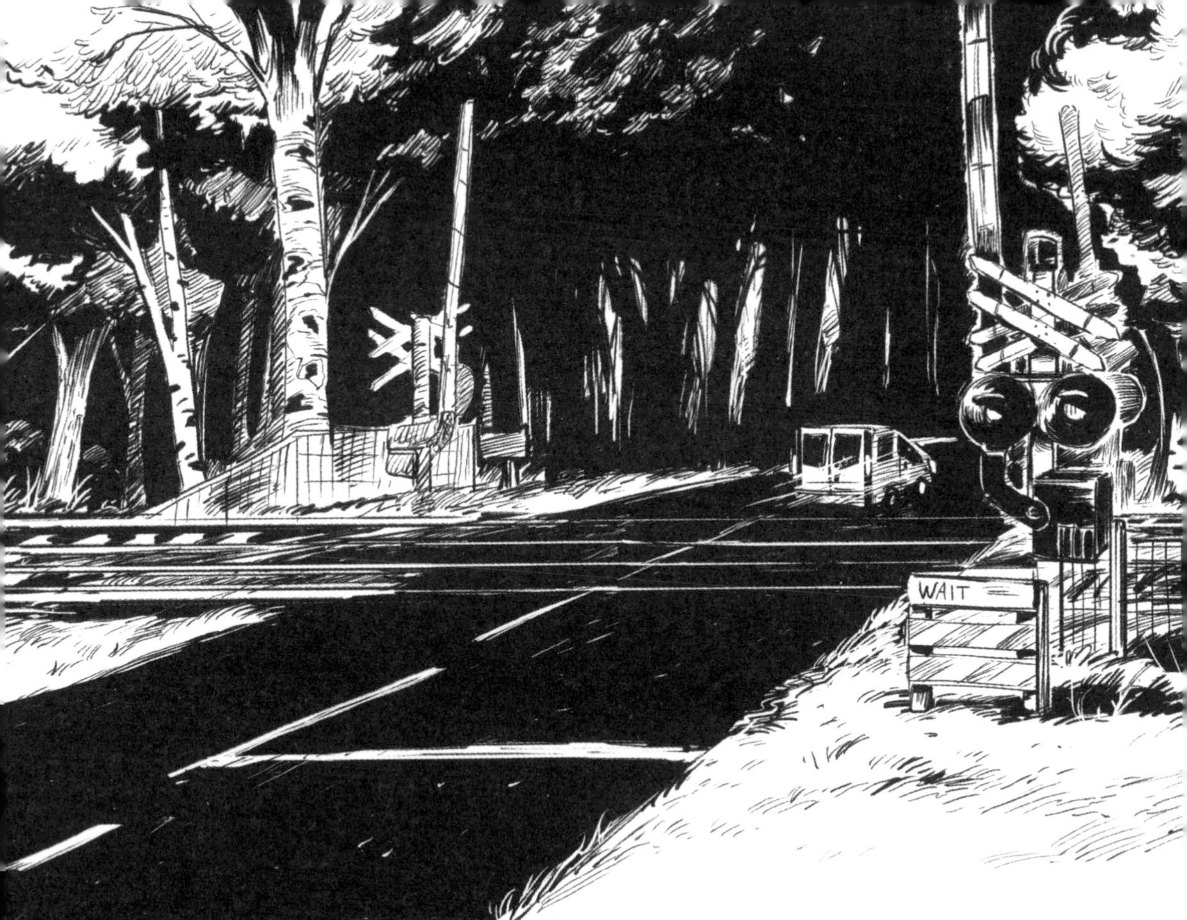
WAIT

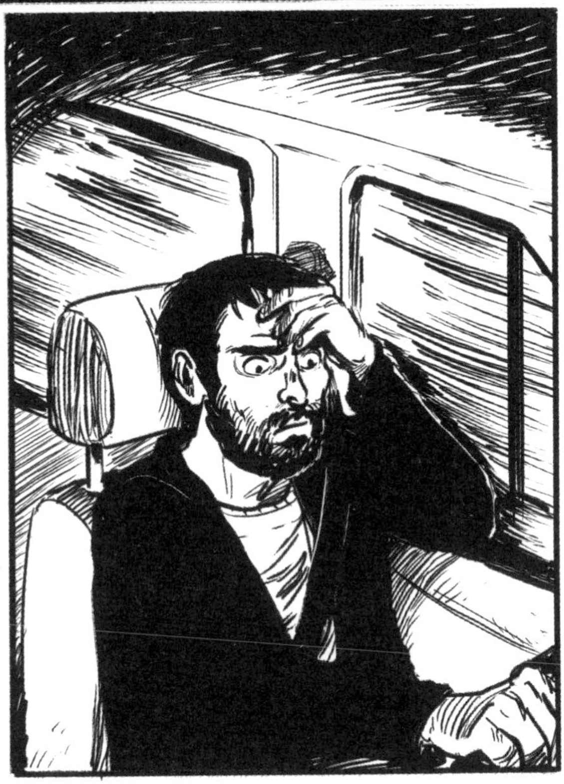

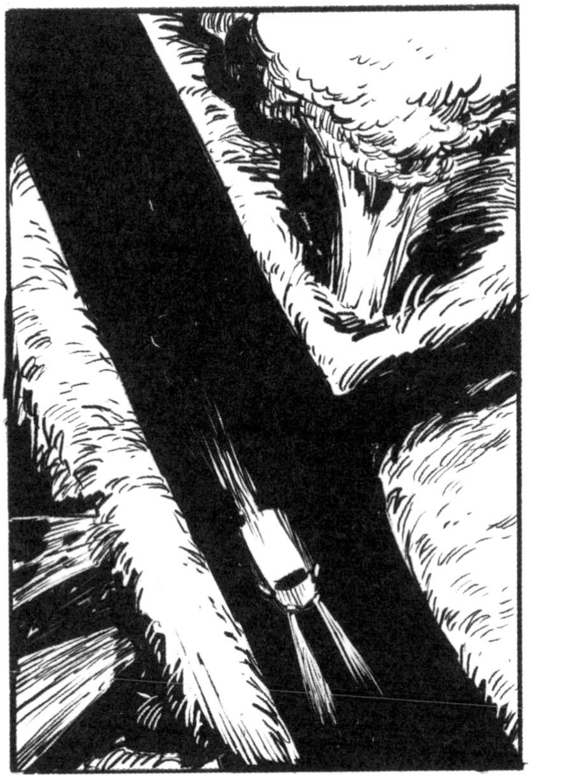

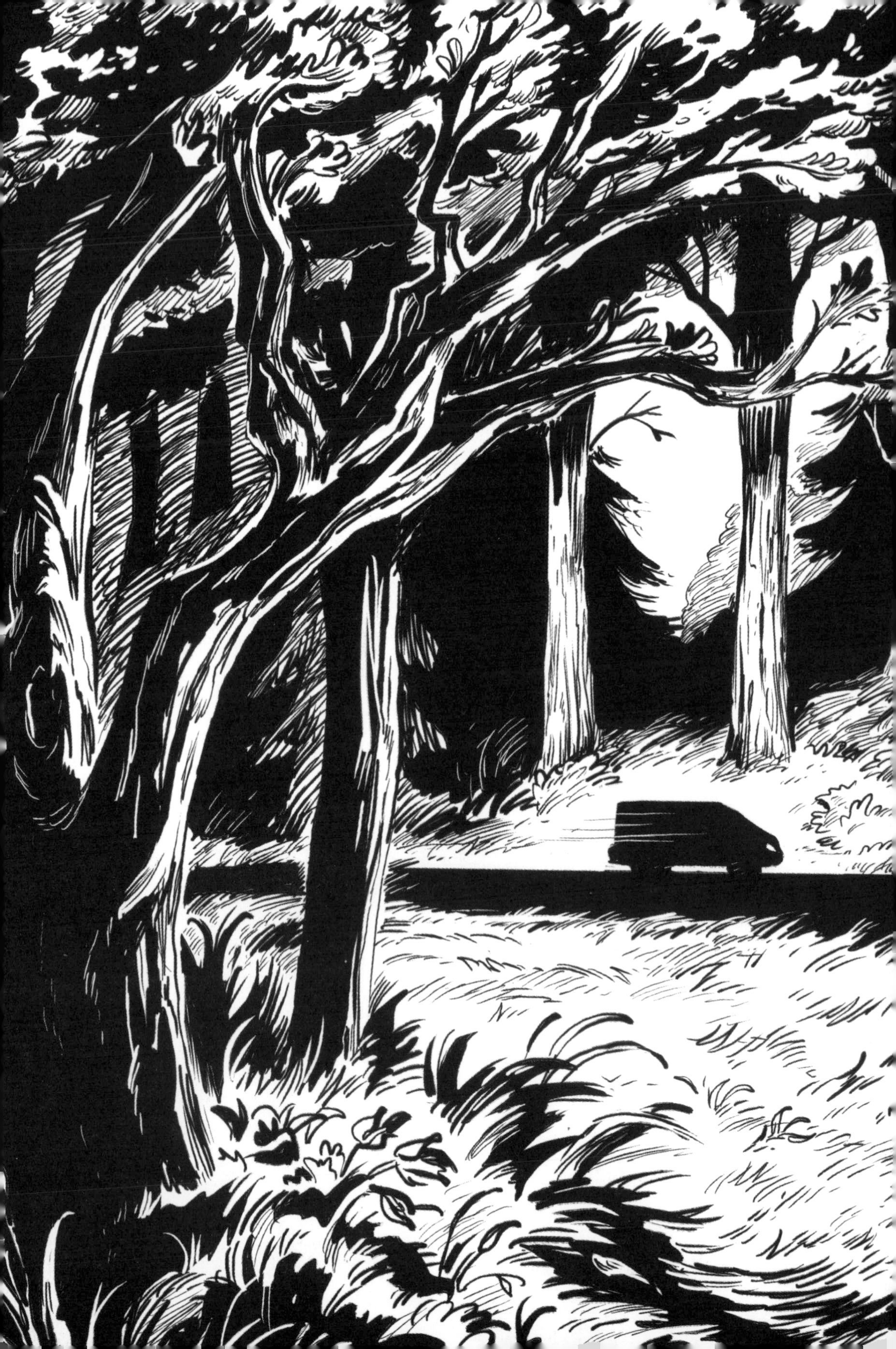

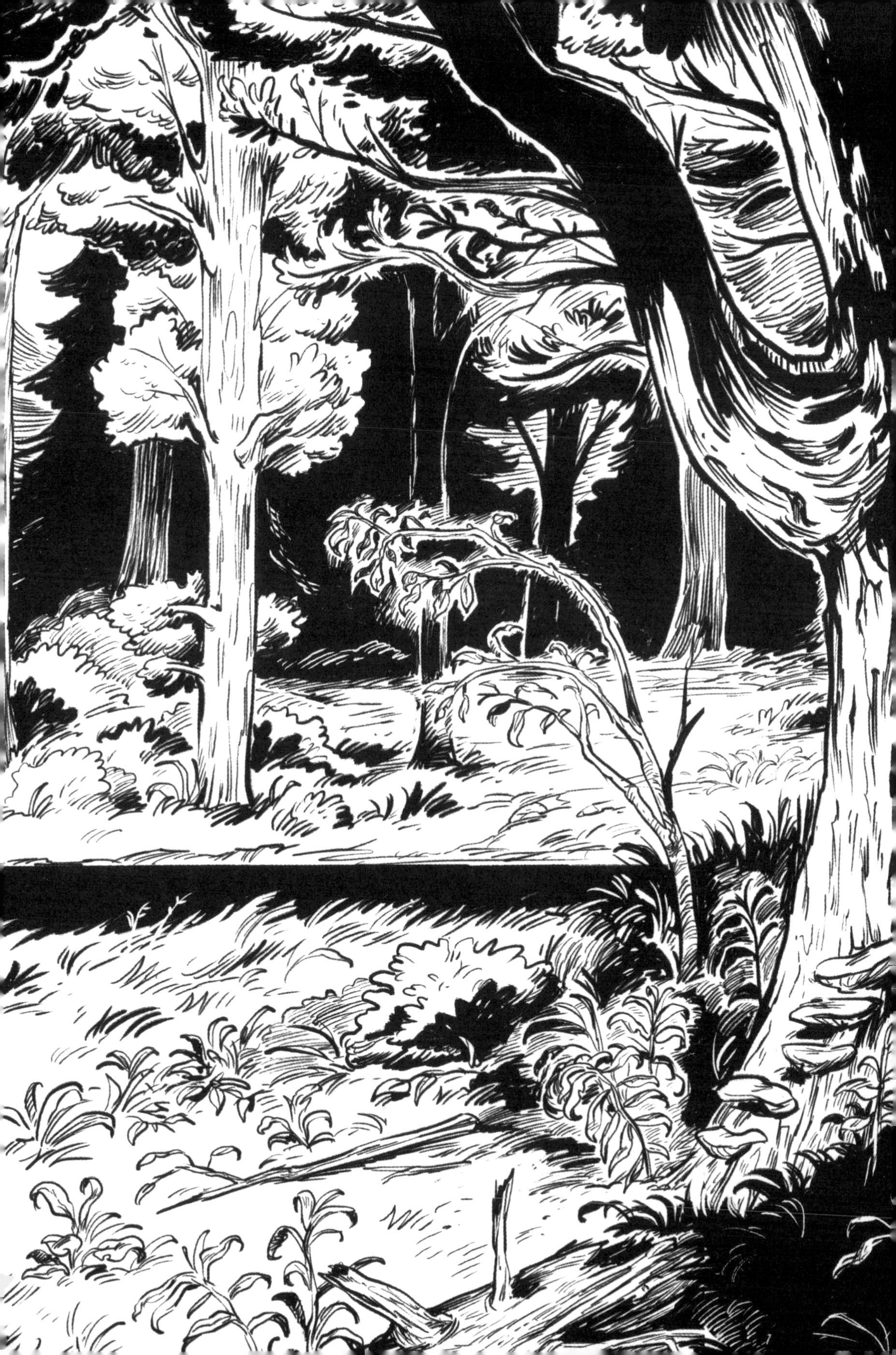

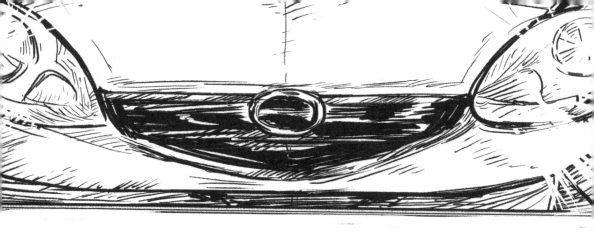

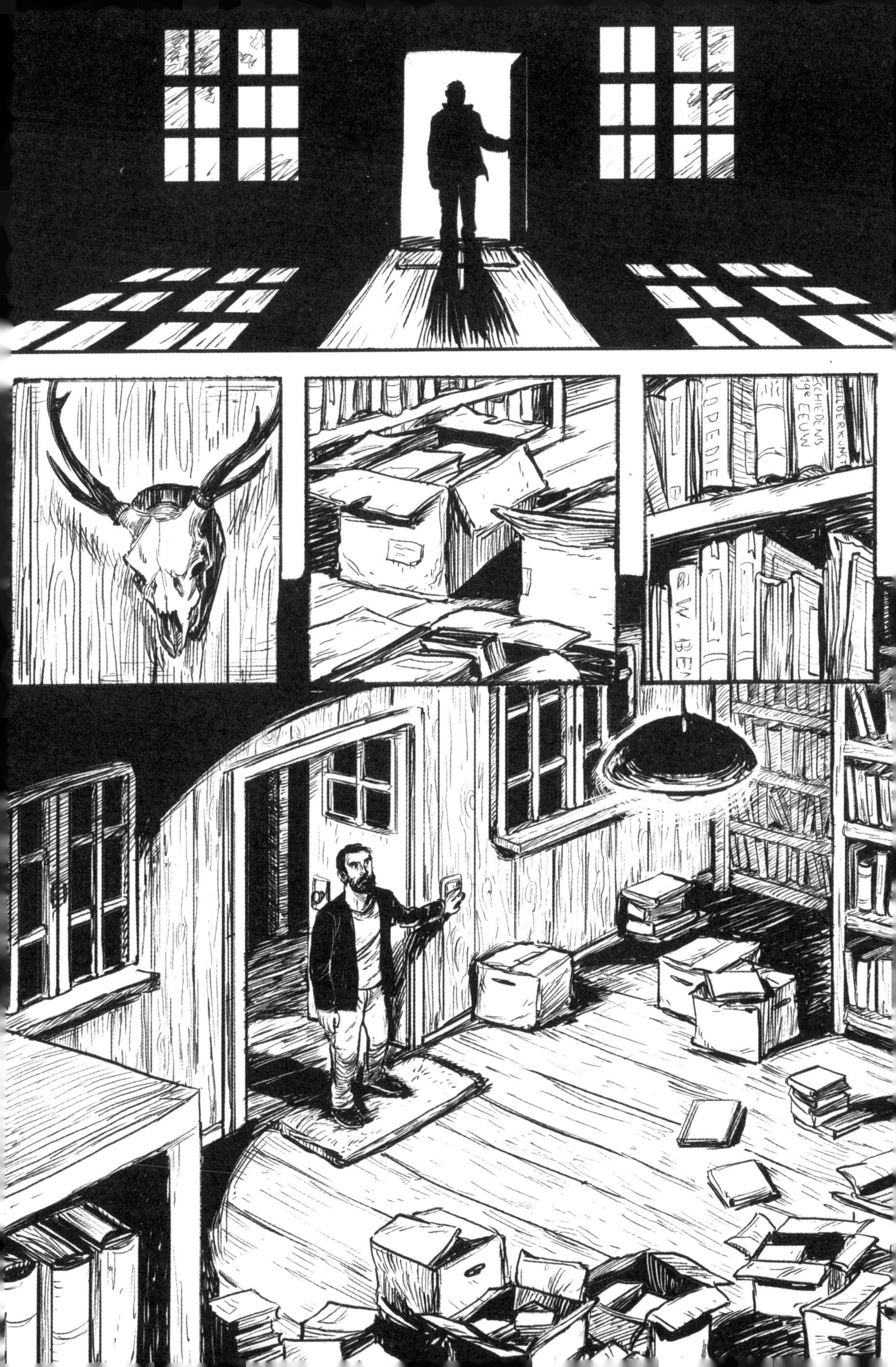

LOPEDIE
SCHIEDENIS 19e EEUW
W. BE

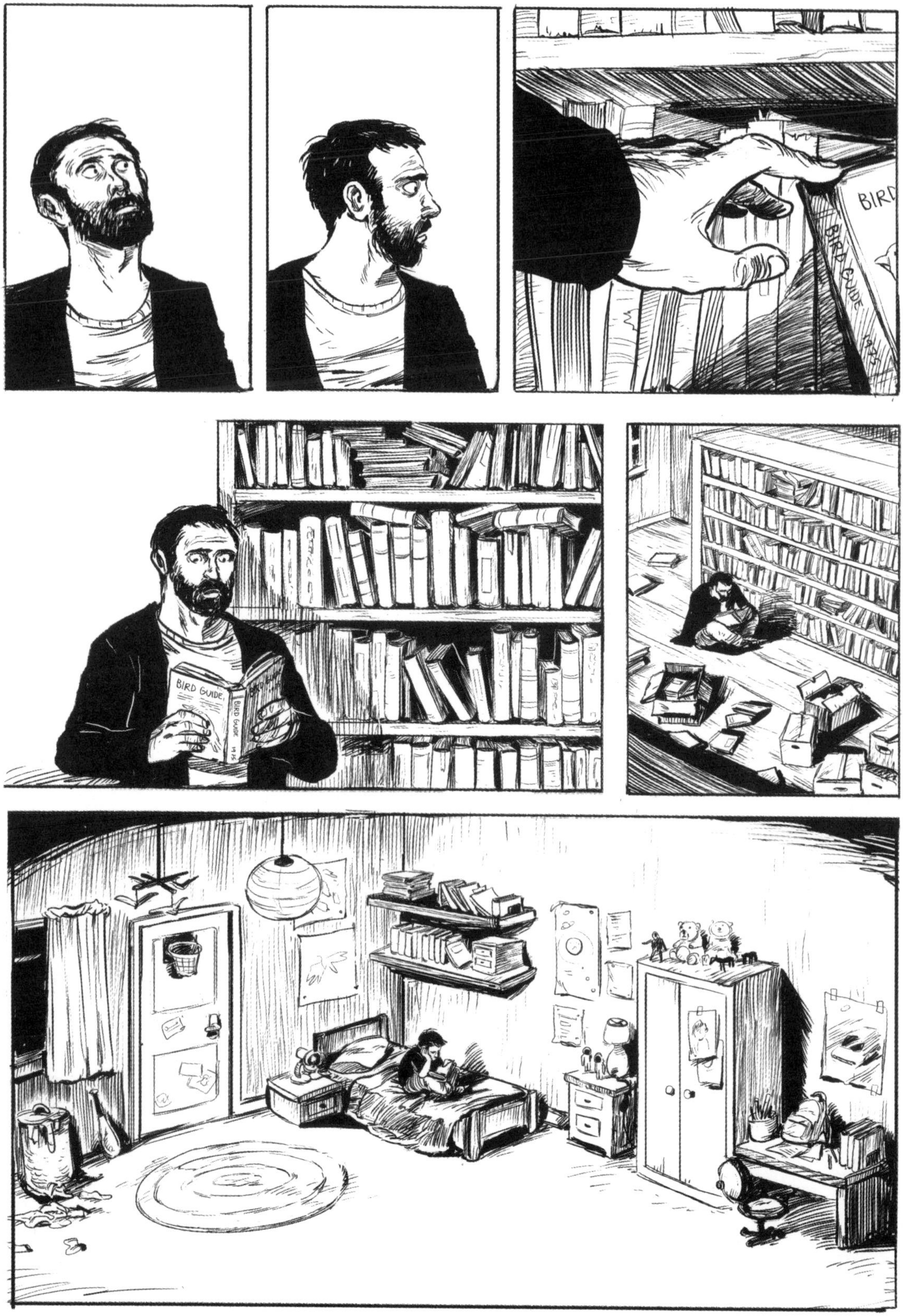
BIRD
BIRD GUIDE
BIRD GUIDE,
BIRD GUIDE

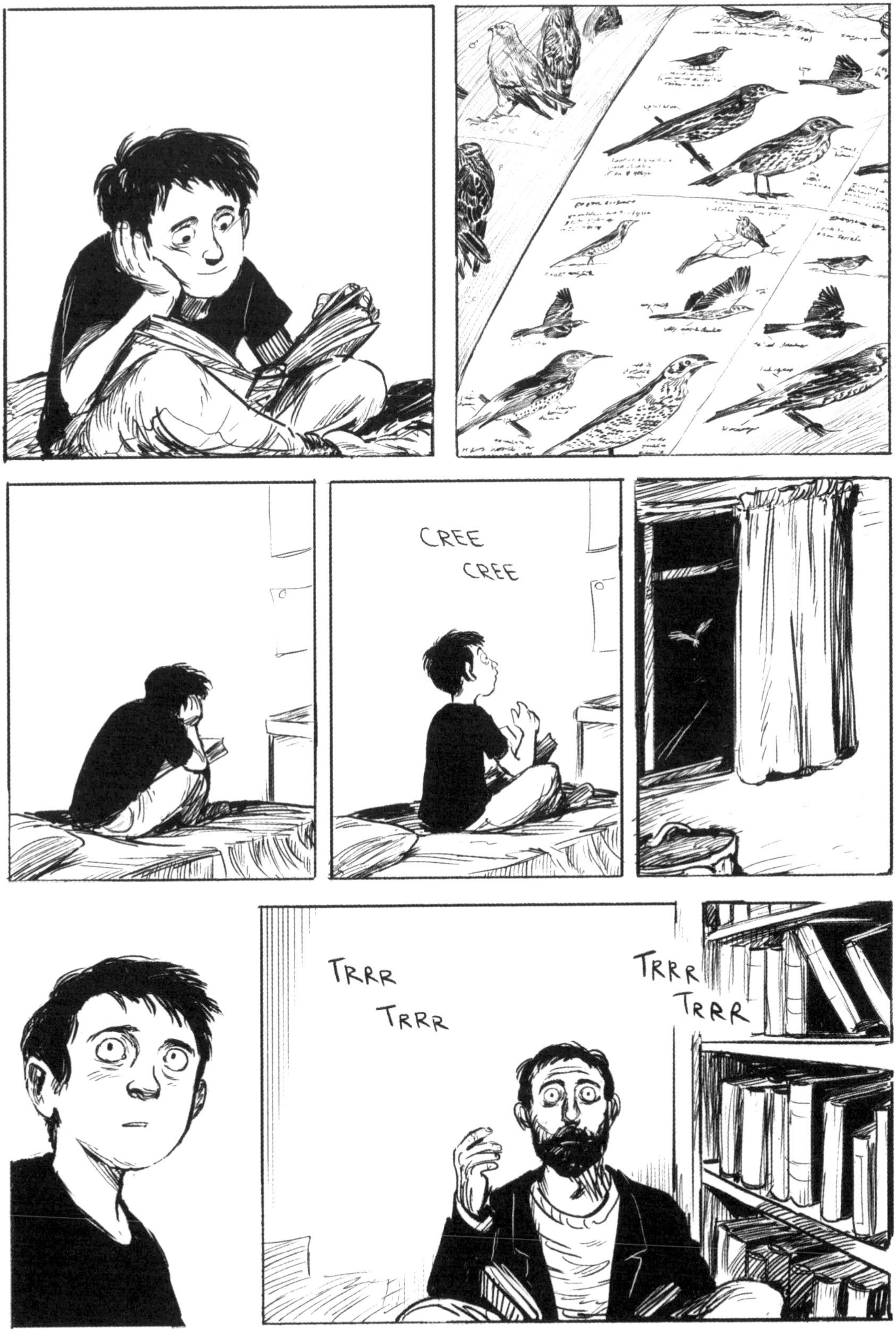
CREE
CREE
TRRR
TRRR
TRRR
TRRR

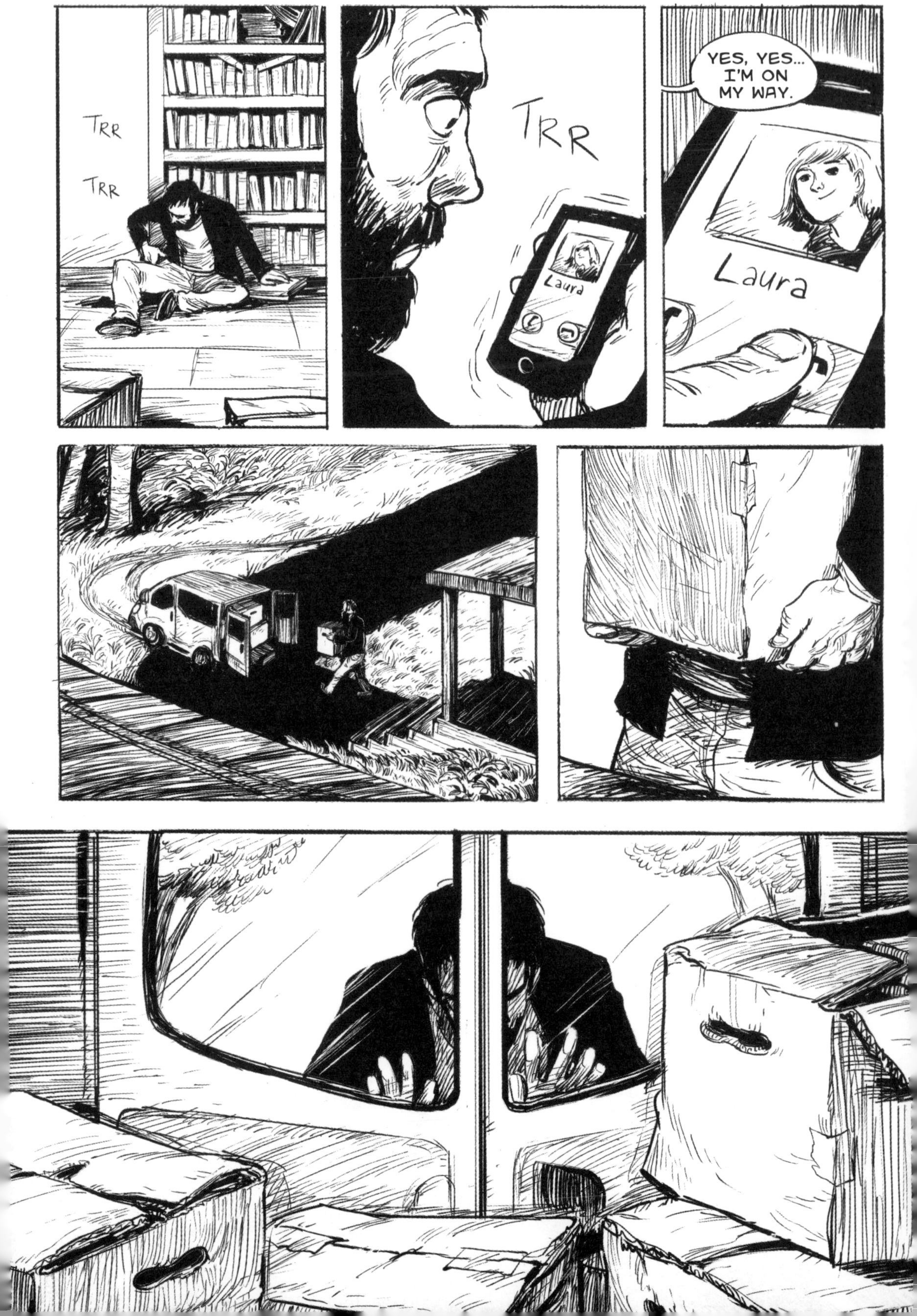
TRR
TRR
TRR
Laura
YES, YES... I'M ON MY WAY.
Laura

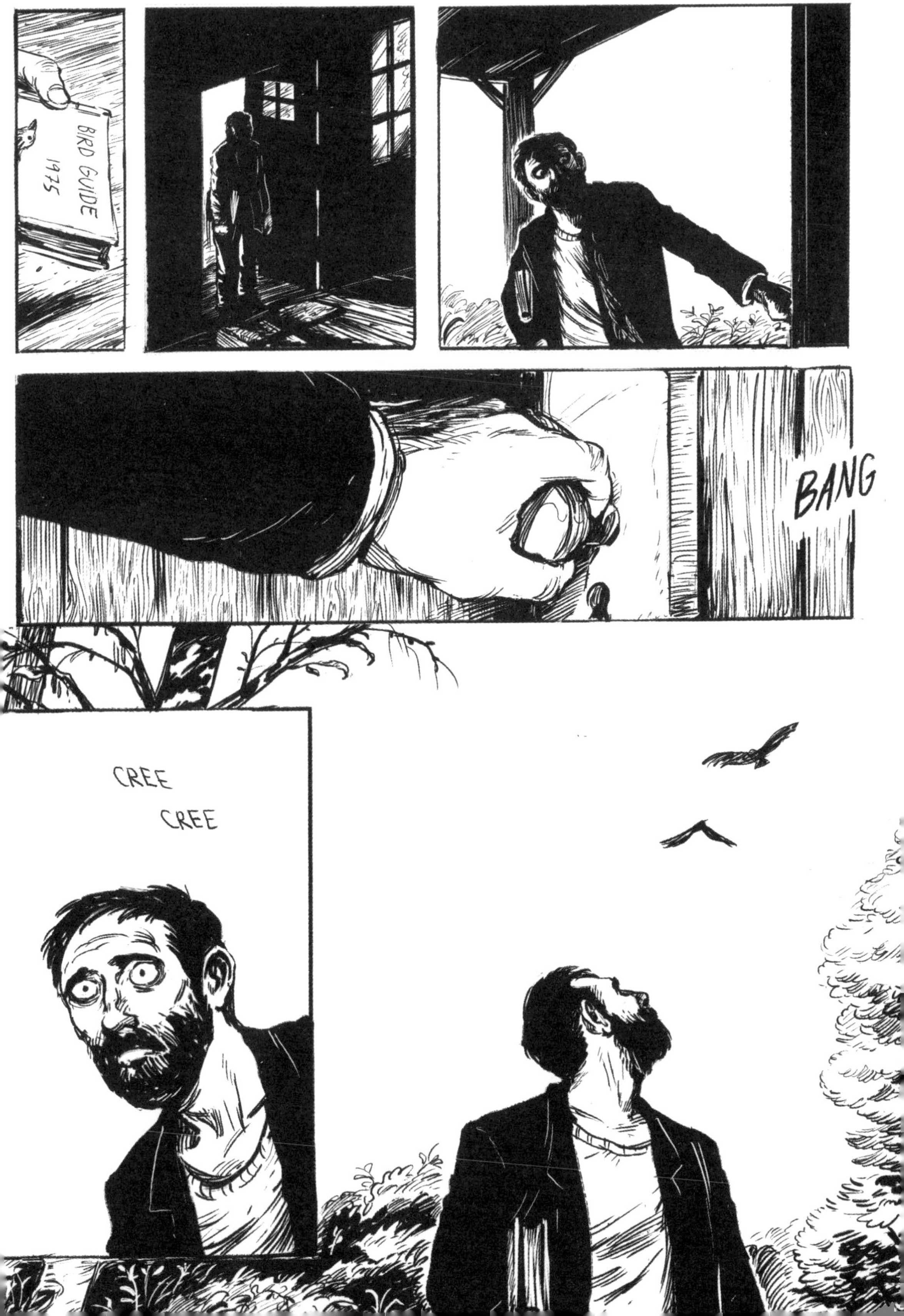
BIRD GUIDE
1975
BANG
CREE
CREE

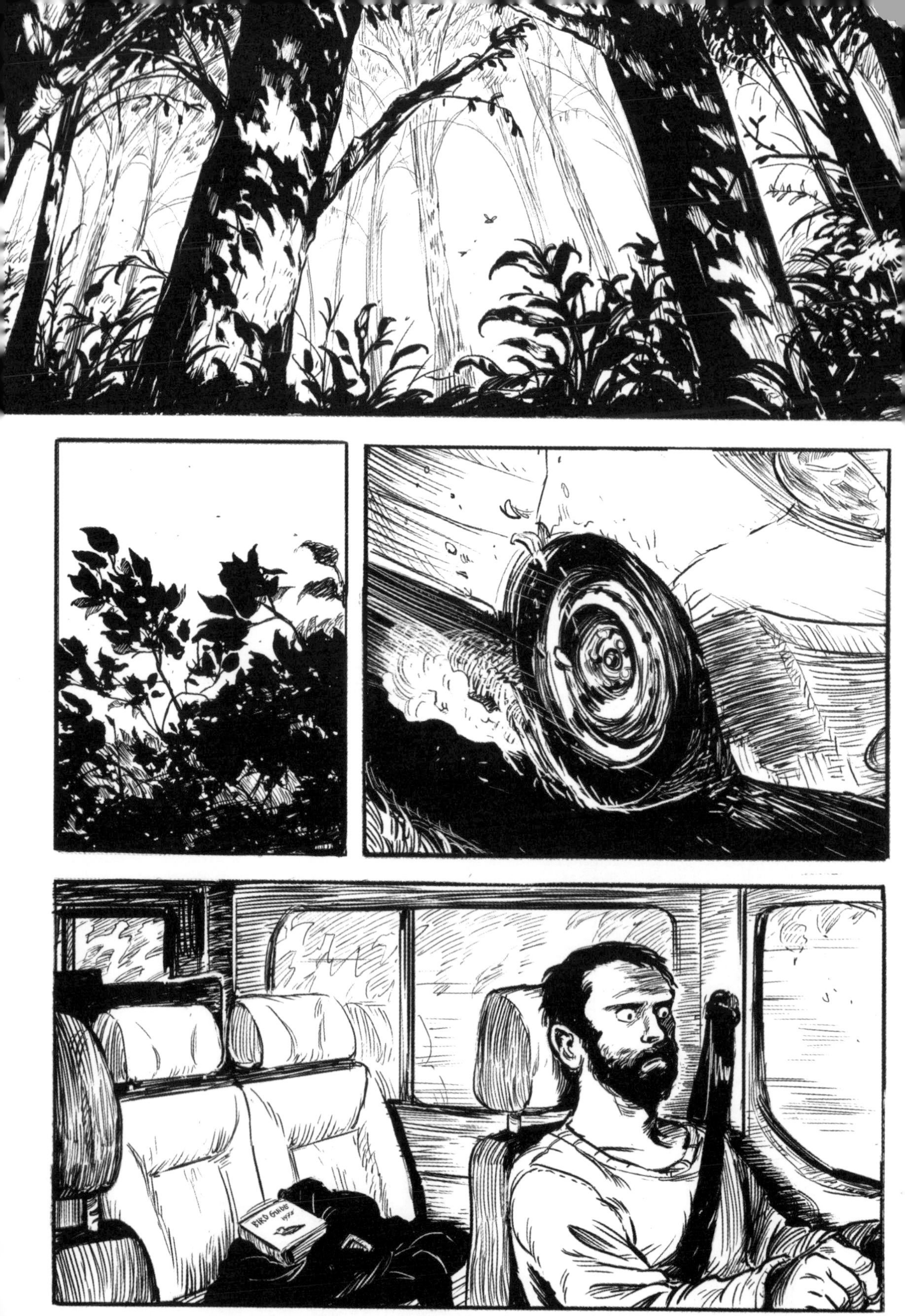
BIRD GUIDE
1975

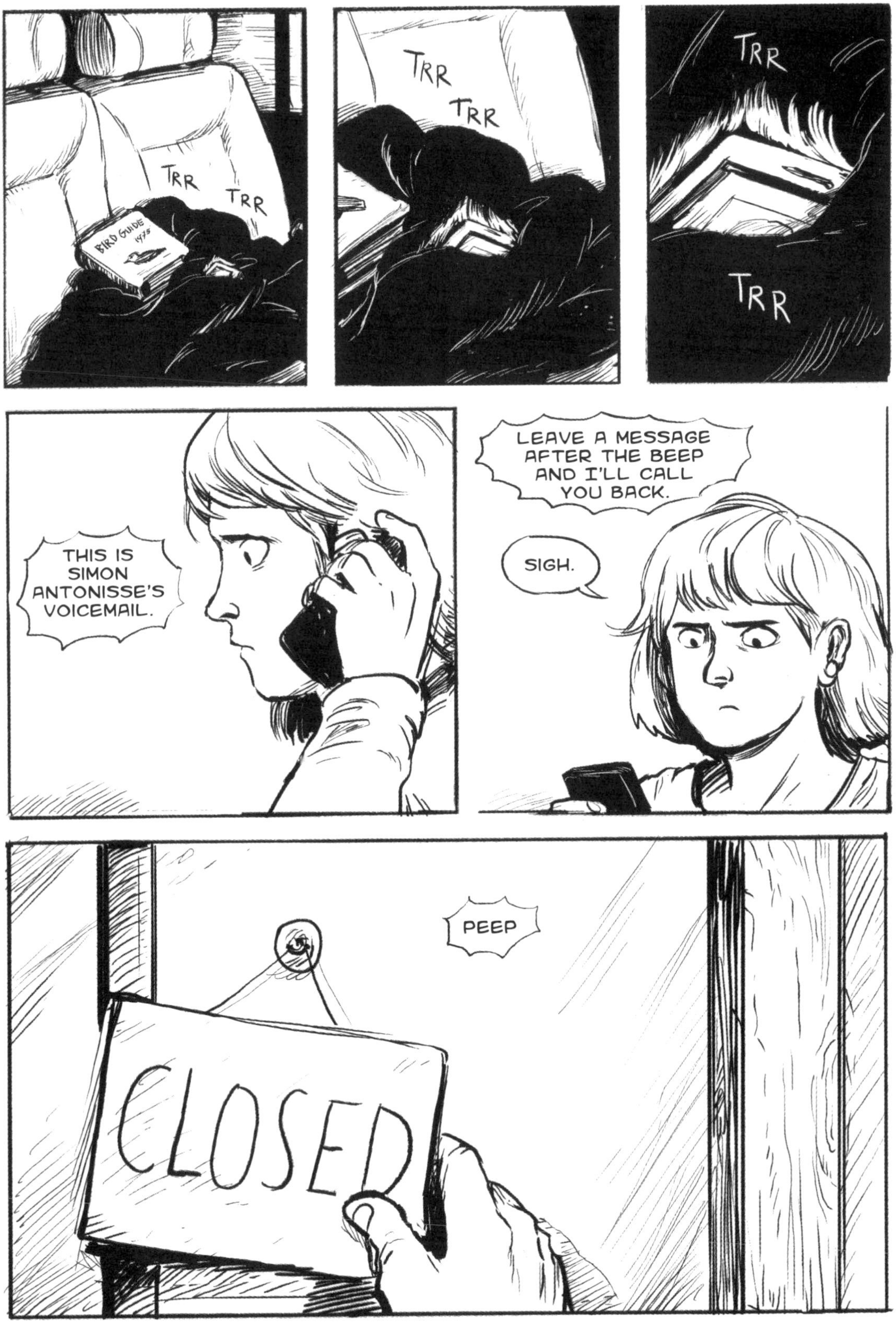
TRR
TRR
BIRD GUIDE
TRR
TRR
TRR
TRR
THIS IS SIMON ANTONISSE'S VOICEMAIL.
LEAVE A MESSAGE AFTER THE BEEP AND I'LL CALL YOU BACK.
SIGH.
PEEP
CLOSED

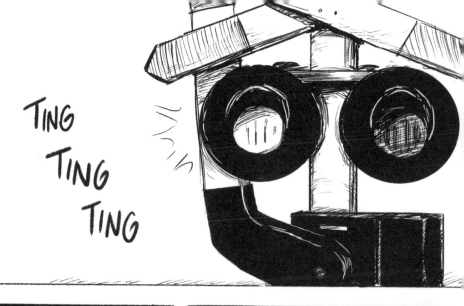

TING

TING
TING

GREAT...
AS IF I
WASN'T LATE
ENOUGH.

TING
TING
TING

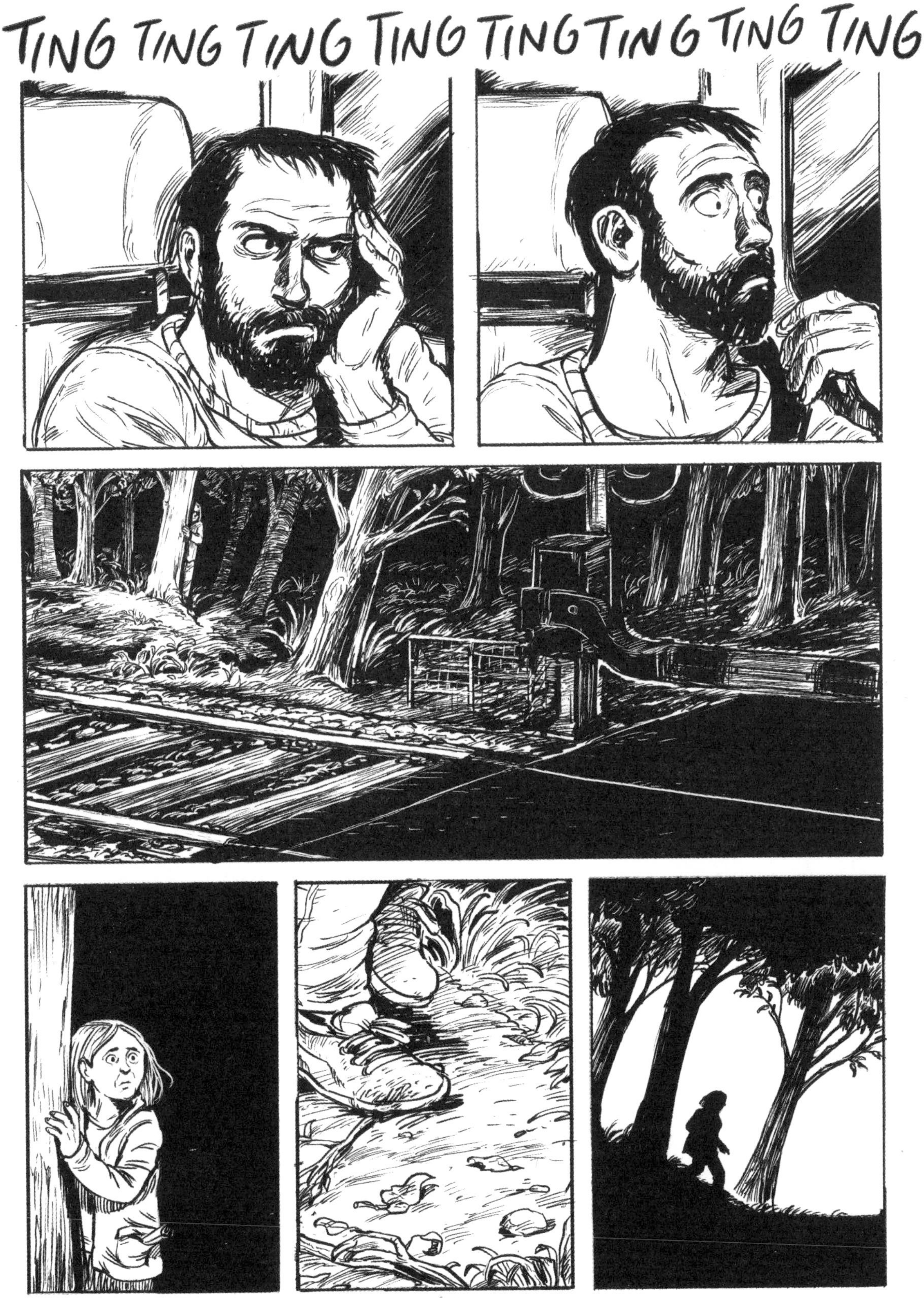
TING TING TING TING TING TING TING TING

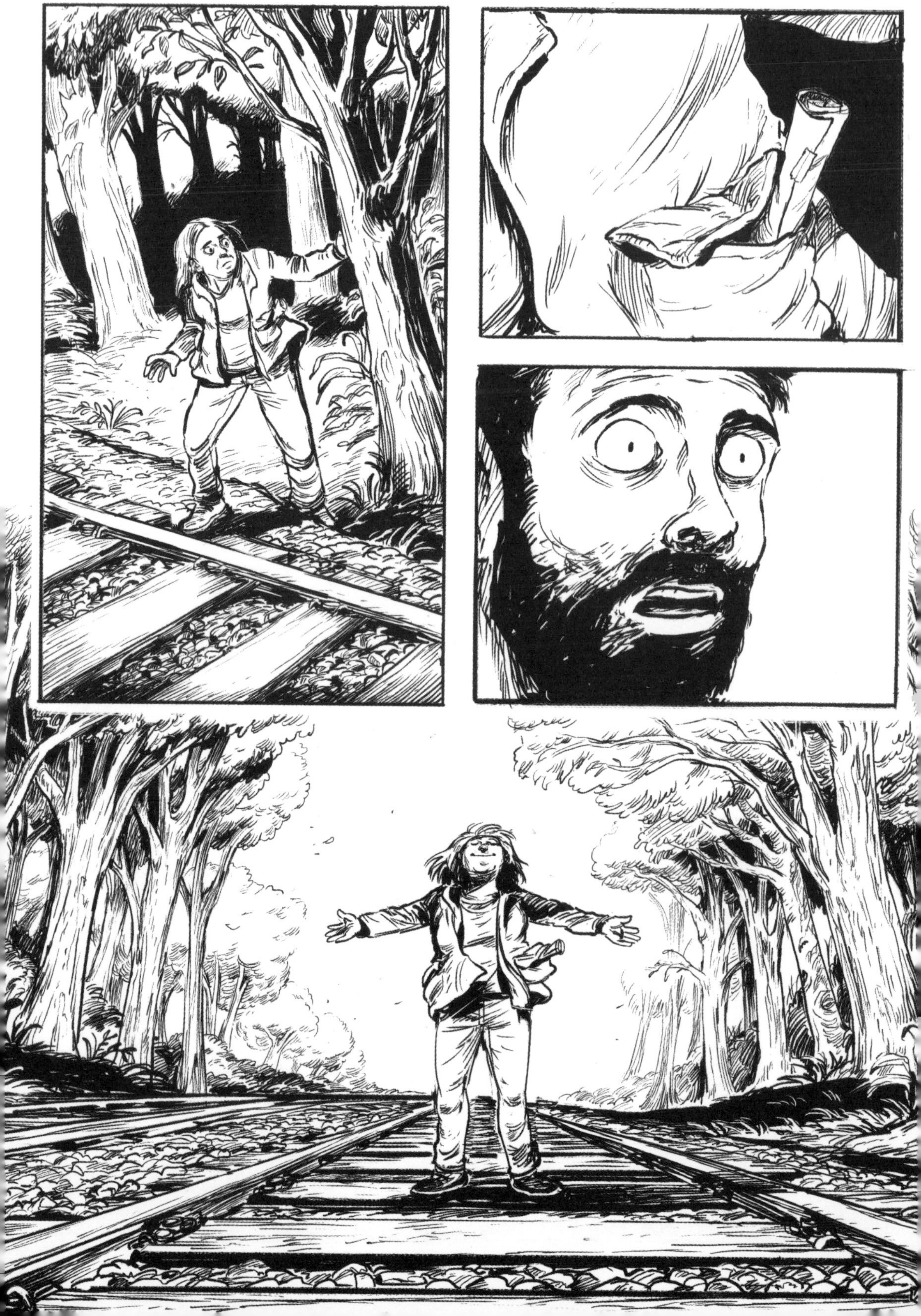

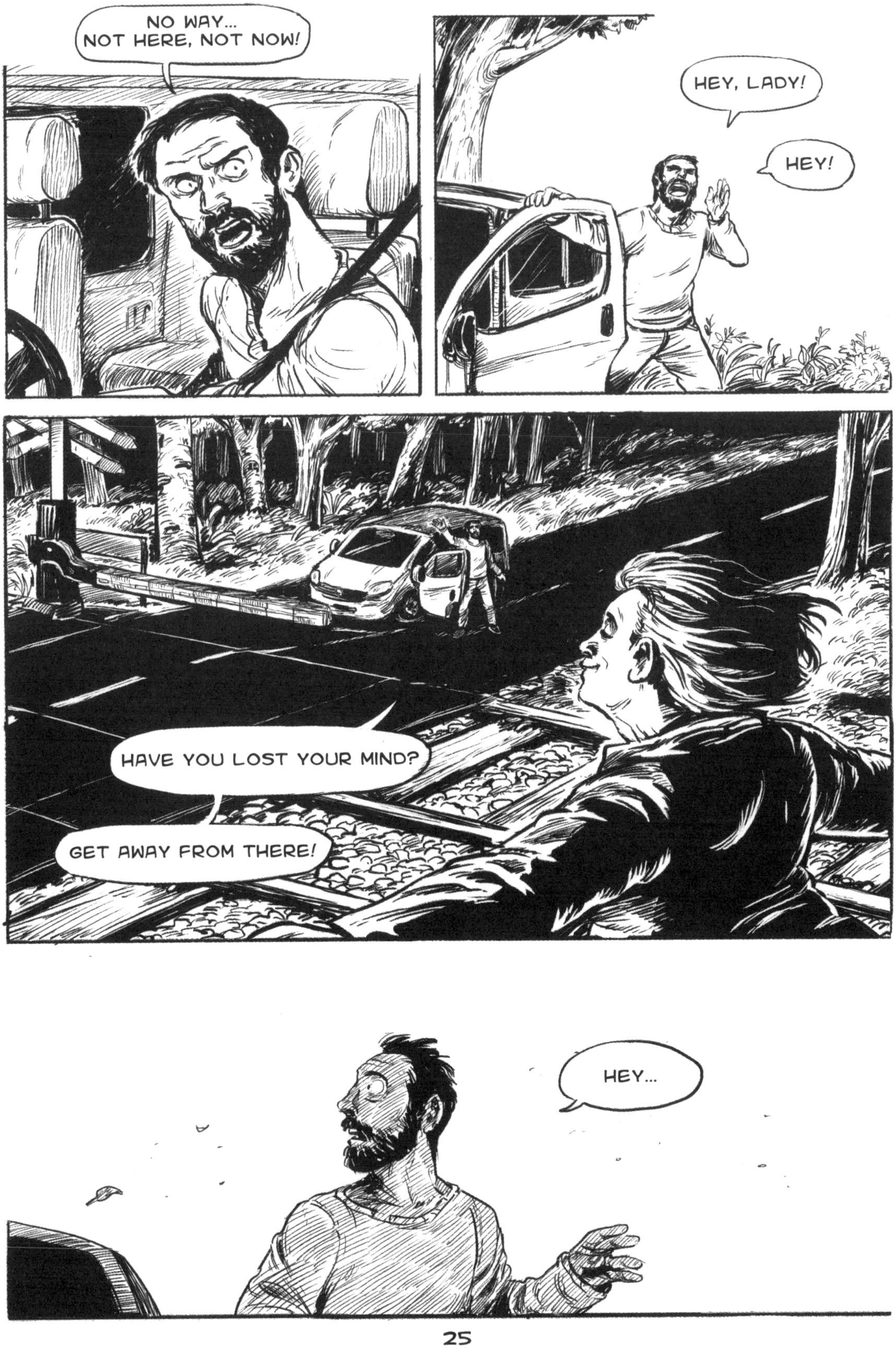
NO WAY...
NOT HERE, NOT NOW!
HEY, LADY!
HEY!
HAVE YOU LOST YOUR MIND?
GET AWAY FROM THERE!
HEY...

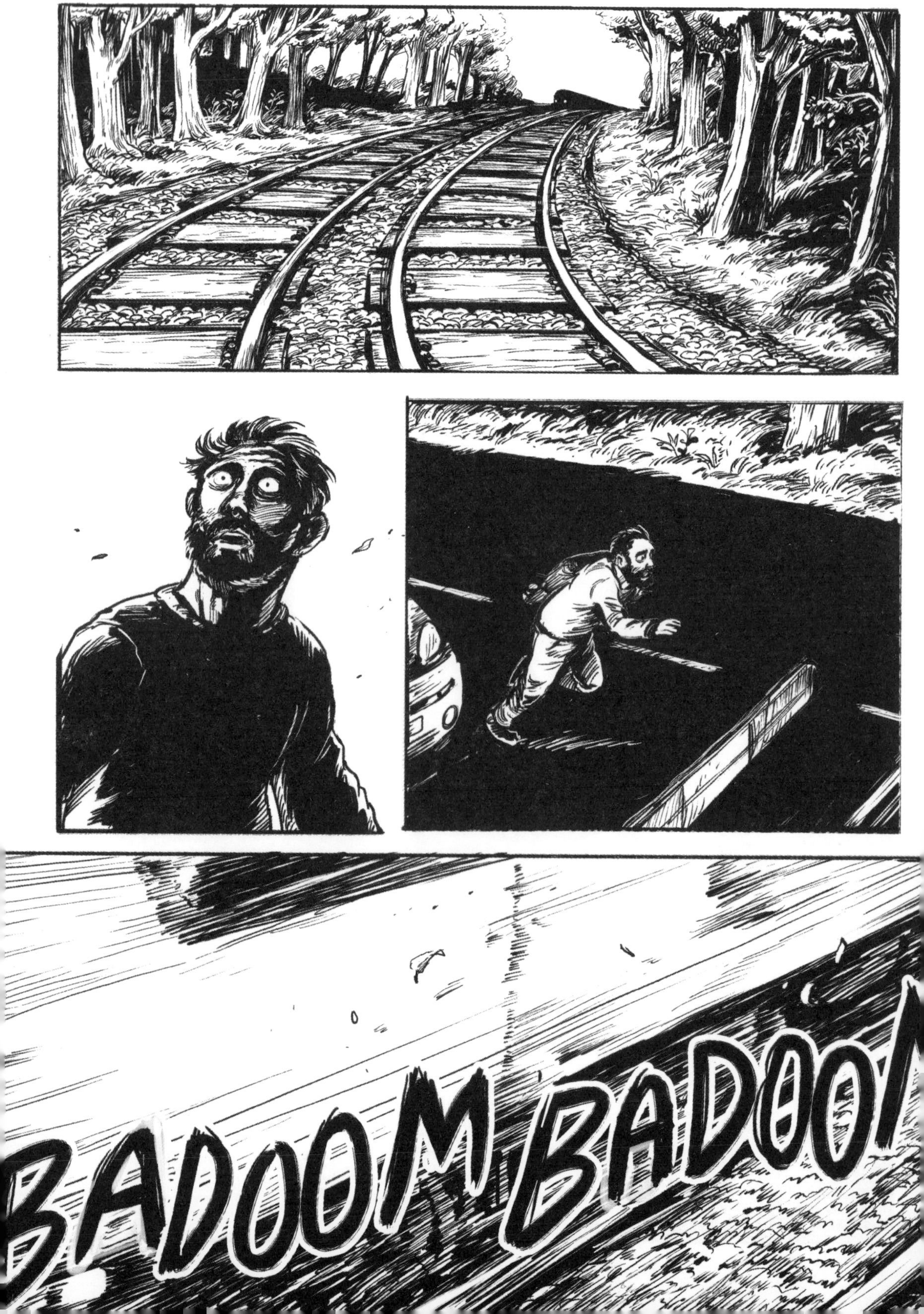
BADOOM BADOOM

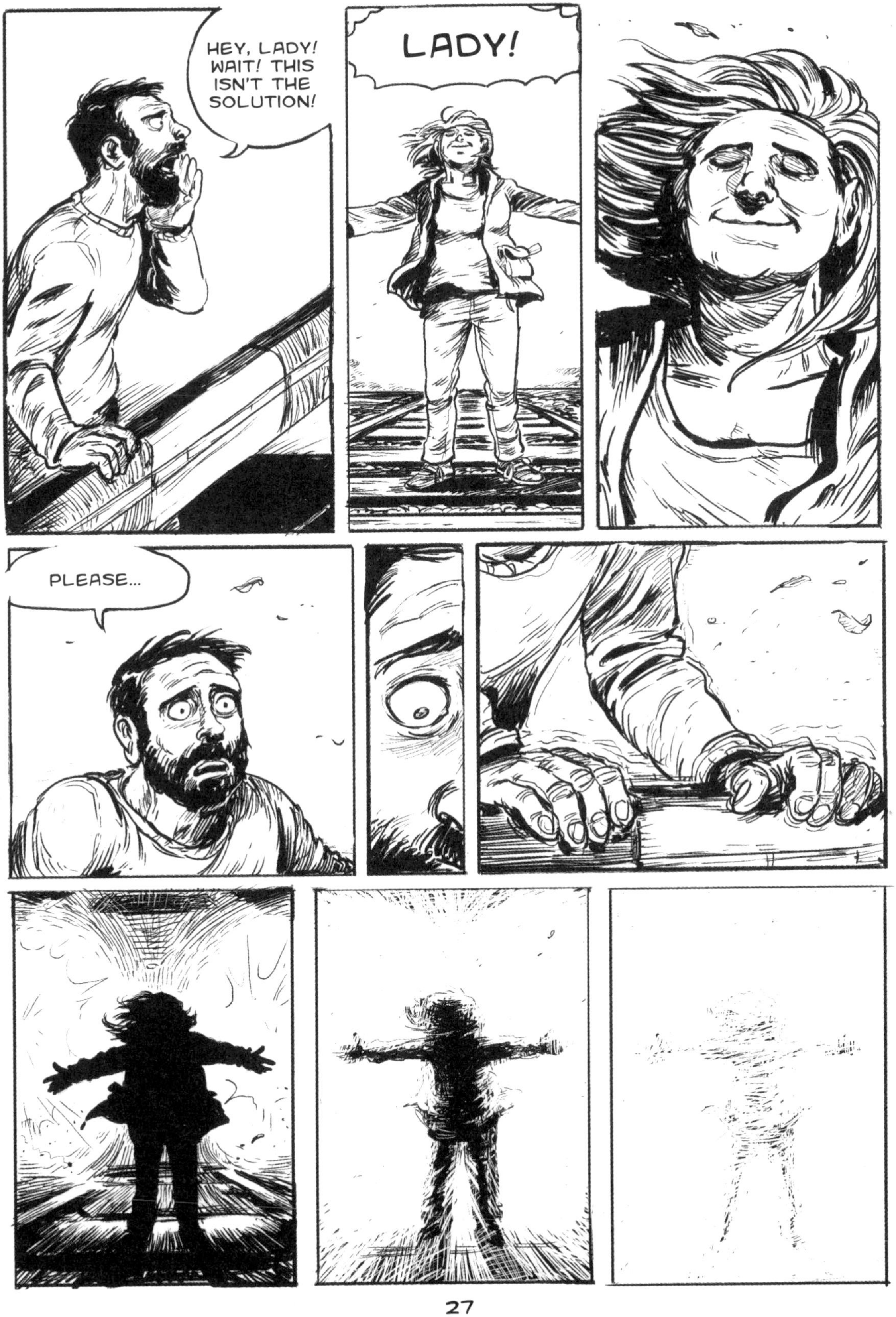
HEY, LADY! WAIT! THIS ISN'T THE SOLUTION!
LADY!
PLEASE...

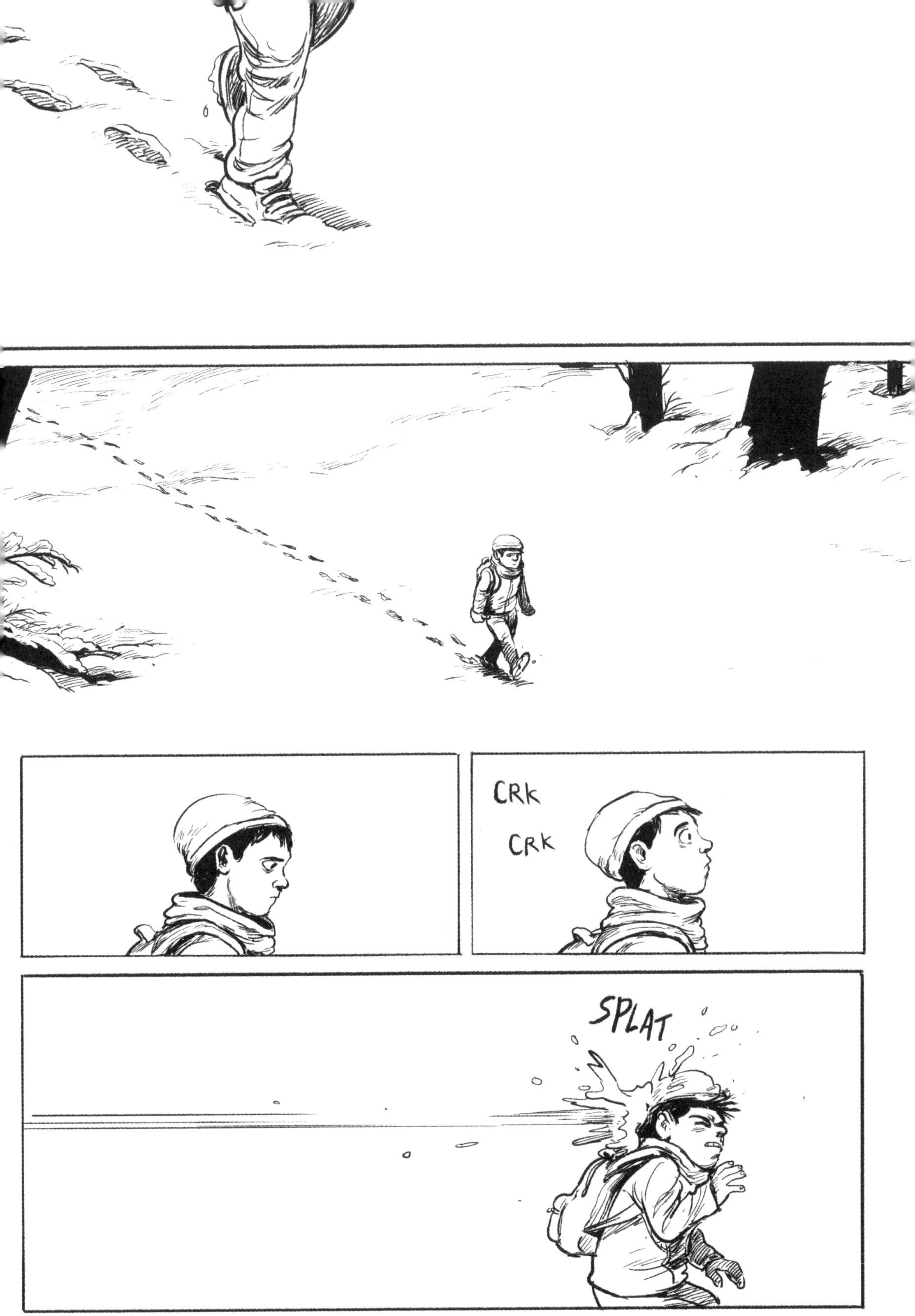
CRK
CRK
SPLAT

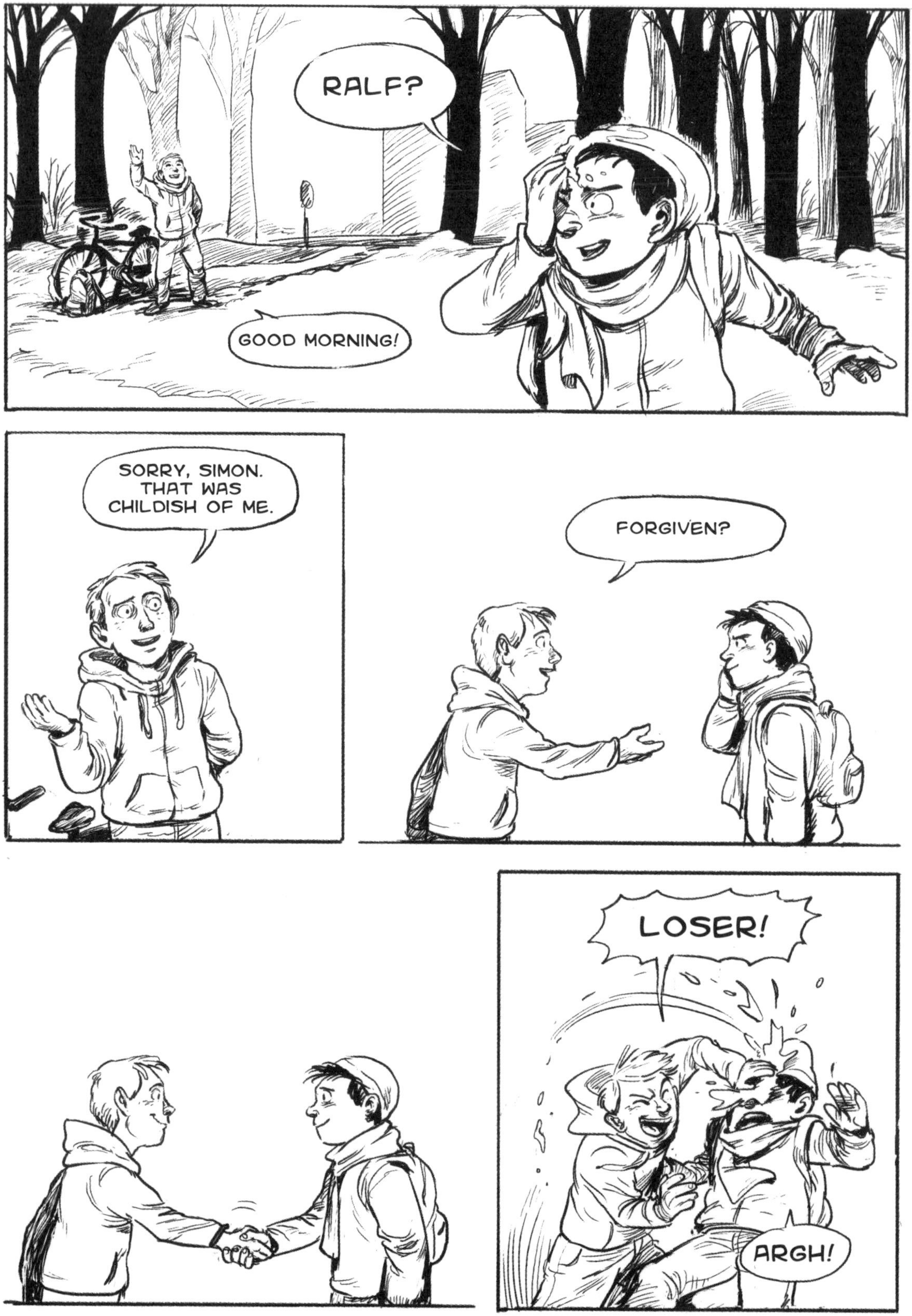
RALF?
GOOD MORNING!
SORRY, SIMON. THAT WAS CHILDISH OF ME.
FORGIVEN?
LOSER!
ARGH!

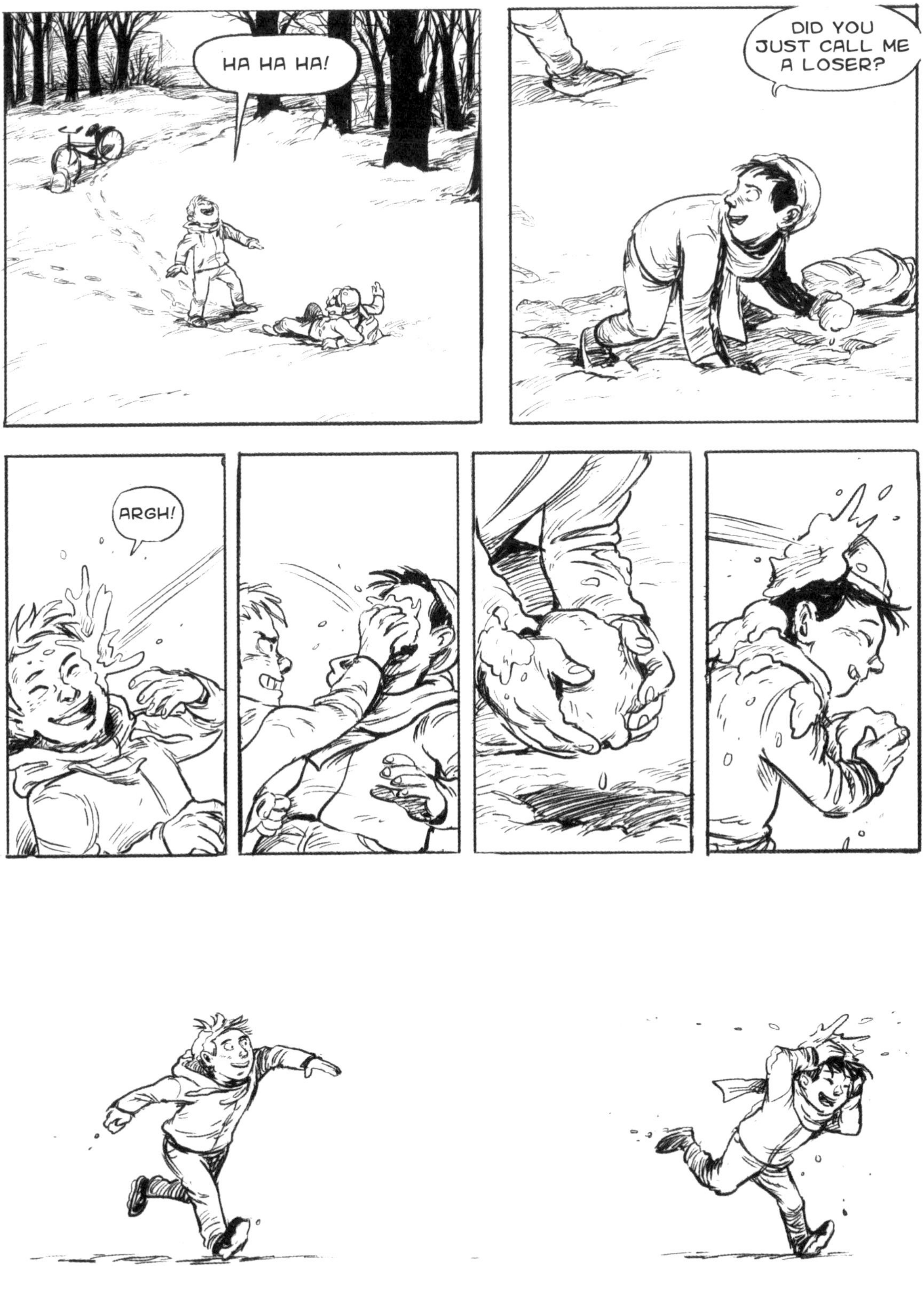
HA HA HA!
DID YOU JUST CALL ME A LOSER?
ARGH!

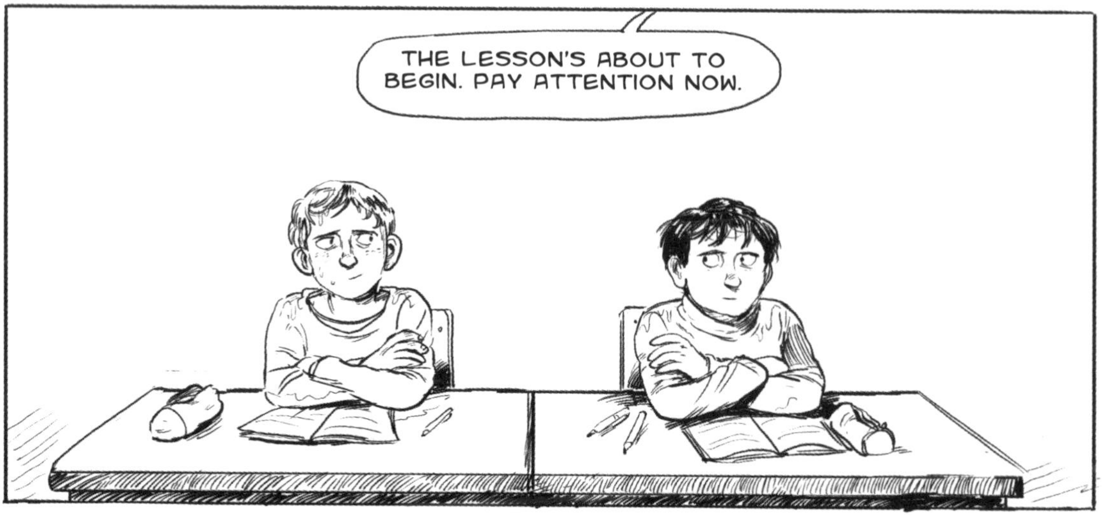
THE LESSON'S ABOUT TO BEGIN. PAY ATTENTION NOW.

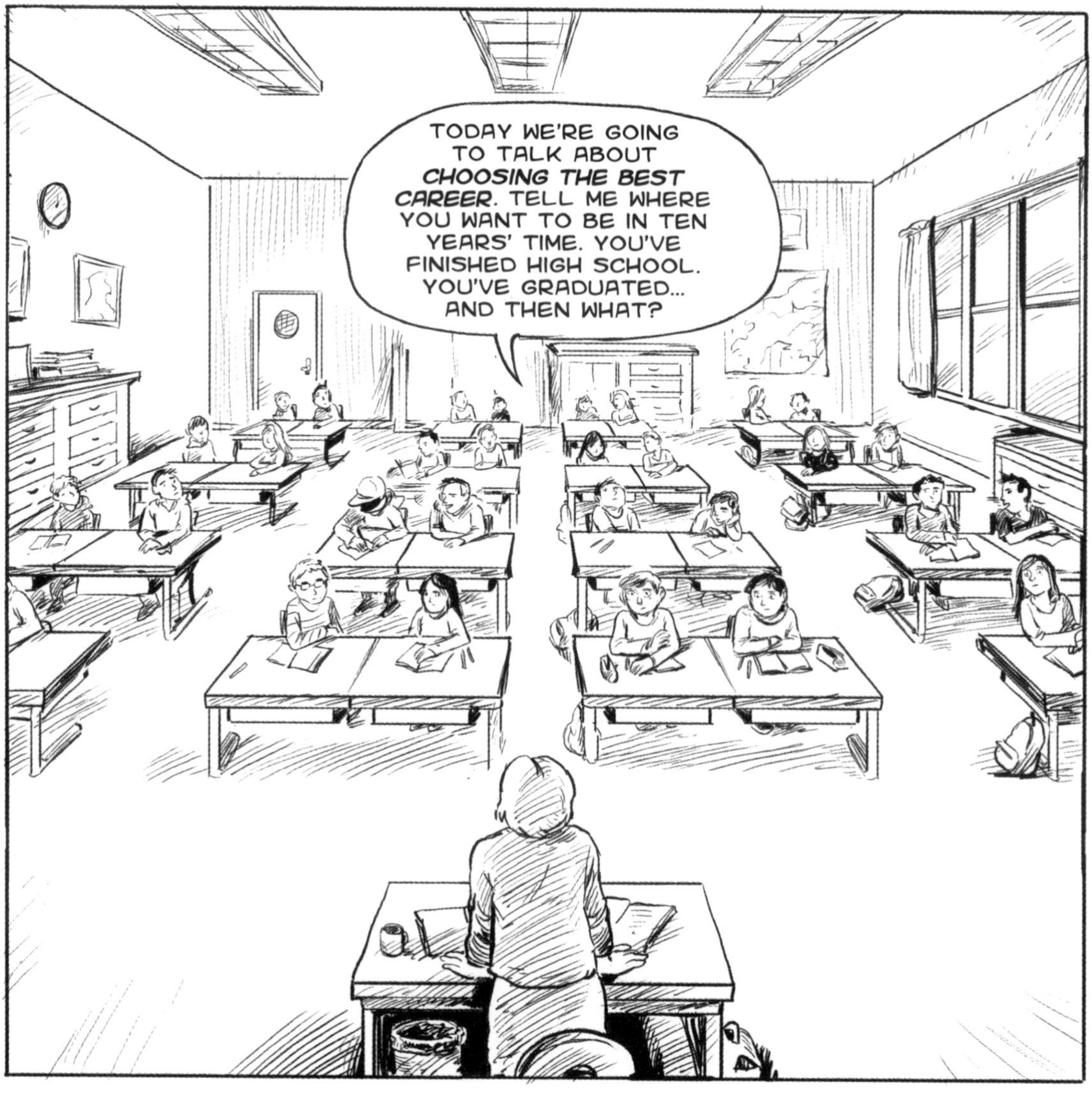
TODAY WE'RE GOING TO TALK ABOUT ***CHOOSING THE BEST CAREER***. TELL ME WHERE YOU WANT TO BE IN TEN YEARS' TIME. YOU'VE FINISHED HIGH SCHOOL. YOU'VE GRADUATED... AND THEN WHAT?

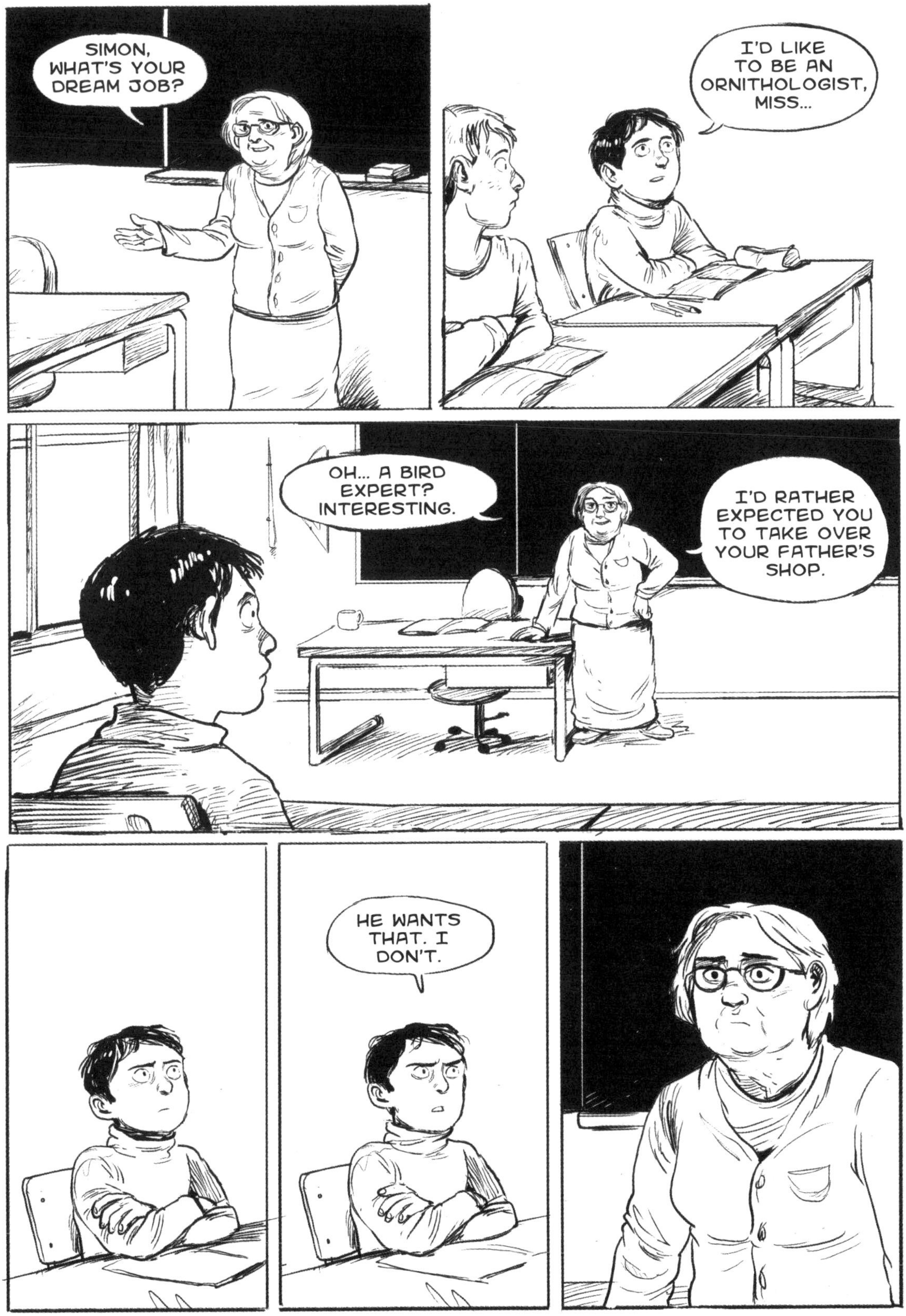
SIMON, WHAT'S YOUR DREAM JOB?
I'D LIKE TO BE AN ORNITHOLOGIST, MISS...
OH... A BIRD EXPERT? INTERESTING.
I'D RATHER EXPECTED YOU TO TAKE OVER YOUR FATHER'S SHOP.
HE WANTS THAT. I DON'T.

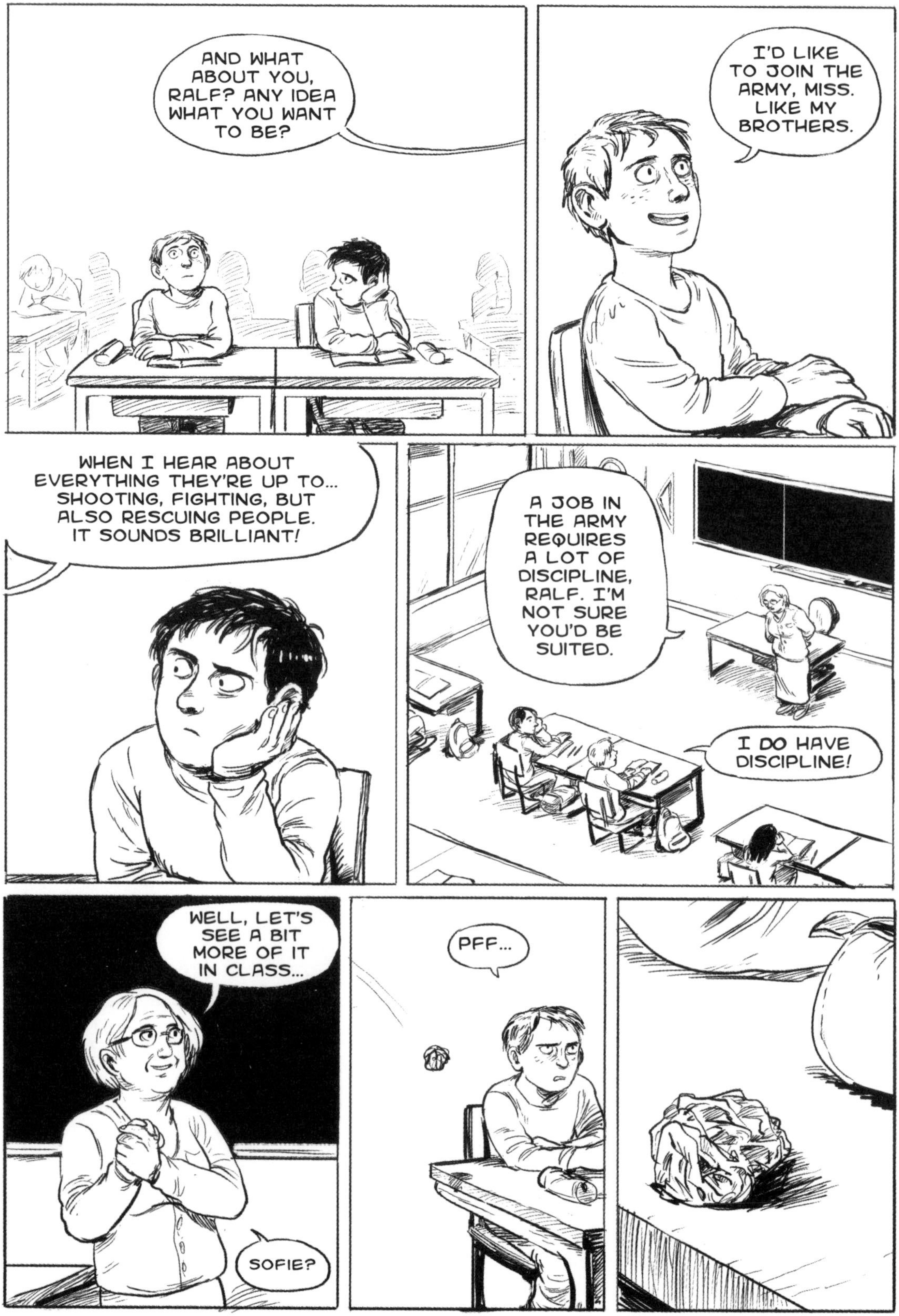
AND WHAT ABOUT YOU, RALF? ANY IDEA WHAT YOU WANT TO BE?
I'D LIKE TO JOIN THE ARMY, MISS. LIKE MY BROTHERS.
WHEN I HEAR ABOUT EVERYTHING THEY'RE UP TO... SHOOTING, FIGHTING, BUT ALSO RESCUING PEOPLE. IT SOUNDS BRILLIANT!
A JOB IN THE ARMY REQUIRES A LOT OF DISCIPLINE, RALF. I'M NOT SURE YOU'D BE SUITED.
I DO HAVE DISCIPLINE!
WELL, LET'S SEE A BIT MORE OF IT IN CLASS...
SOFIE?
PFF...

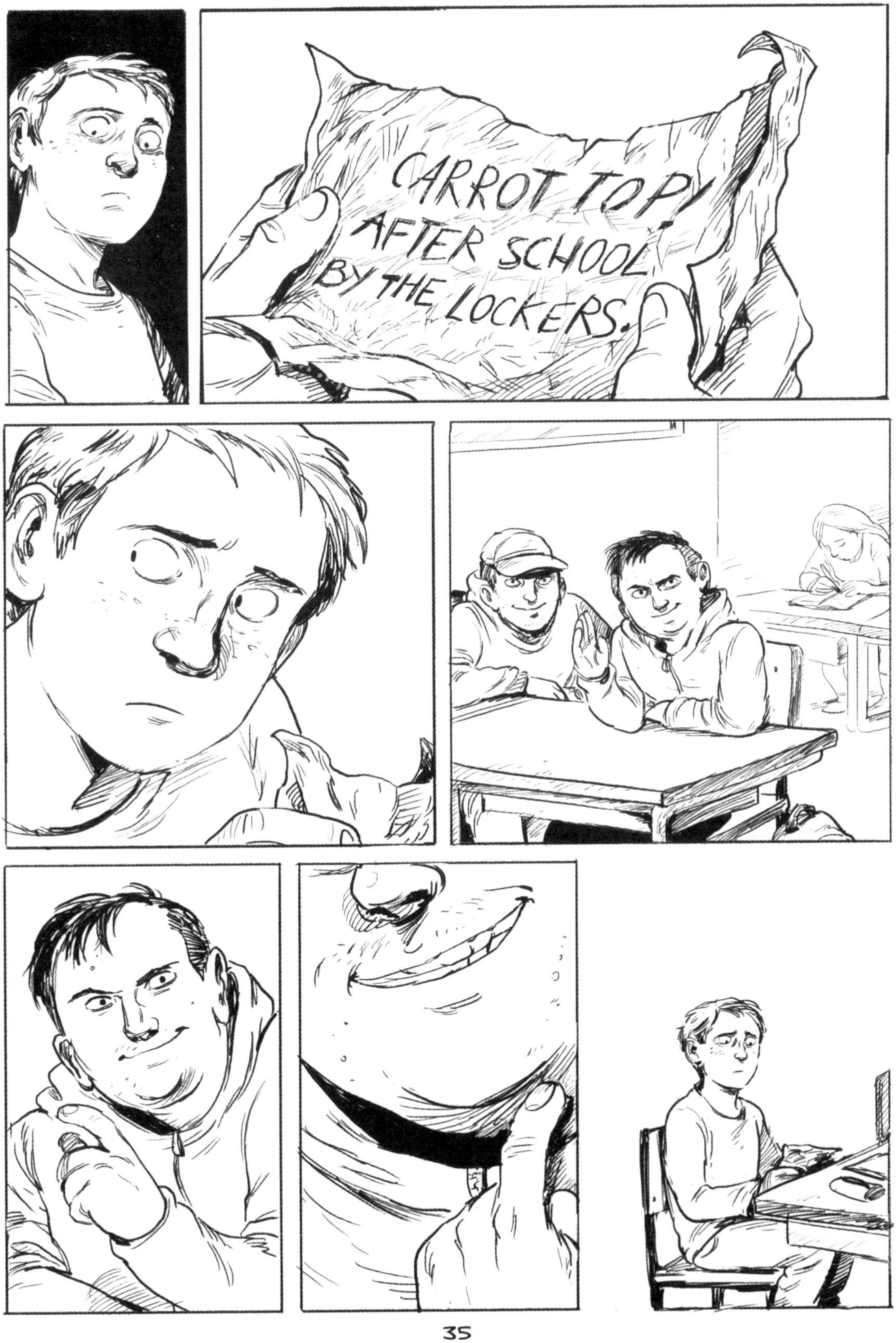
CARROT TOP!
AFTER SCHOOL
BY THE LOCKERS.

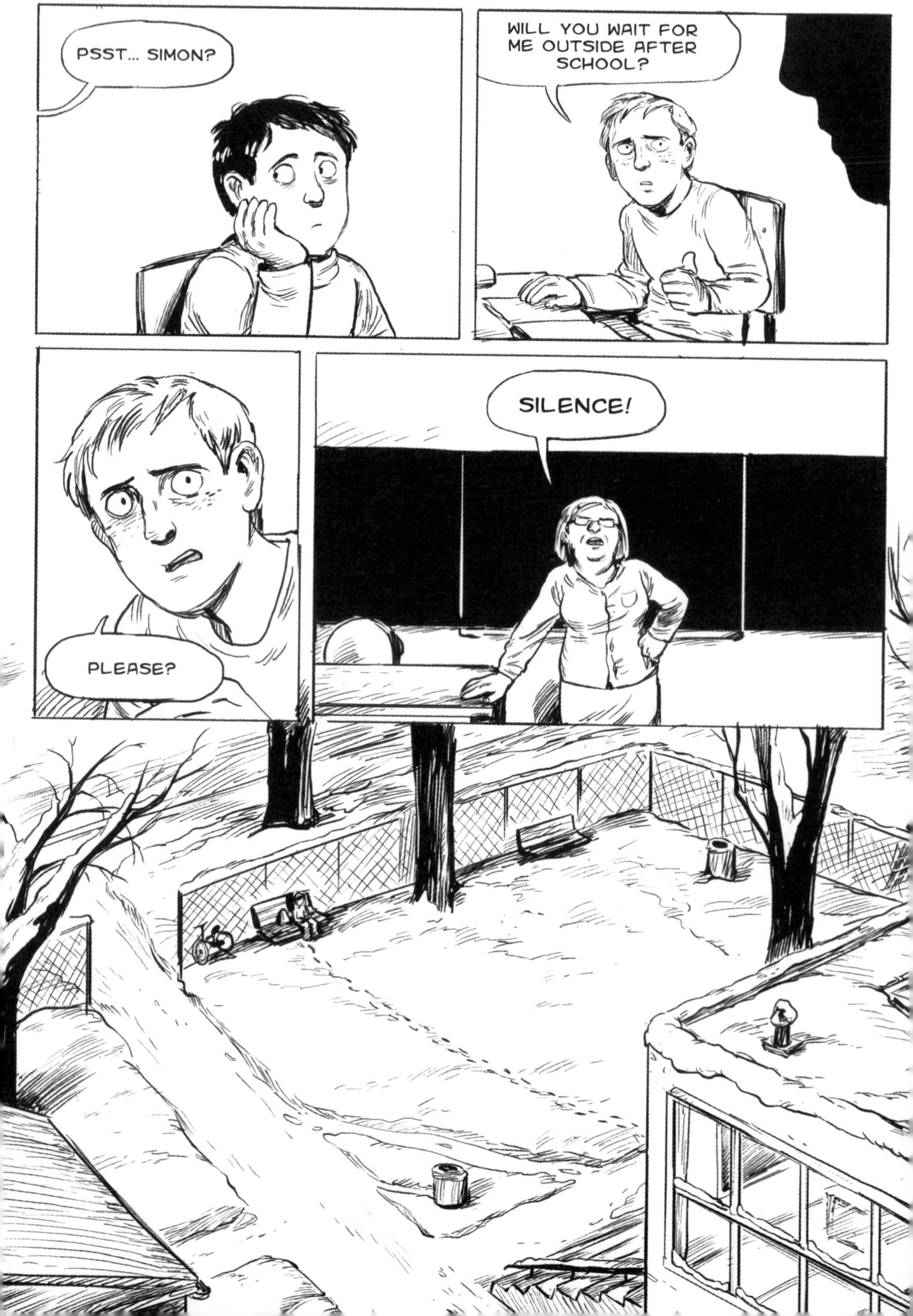
PSST... SIMON?
WILL YOU WAIT FOR ME OUTSIDE AFTER SCHOOL?
PLEASE?
SILENCE!

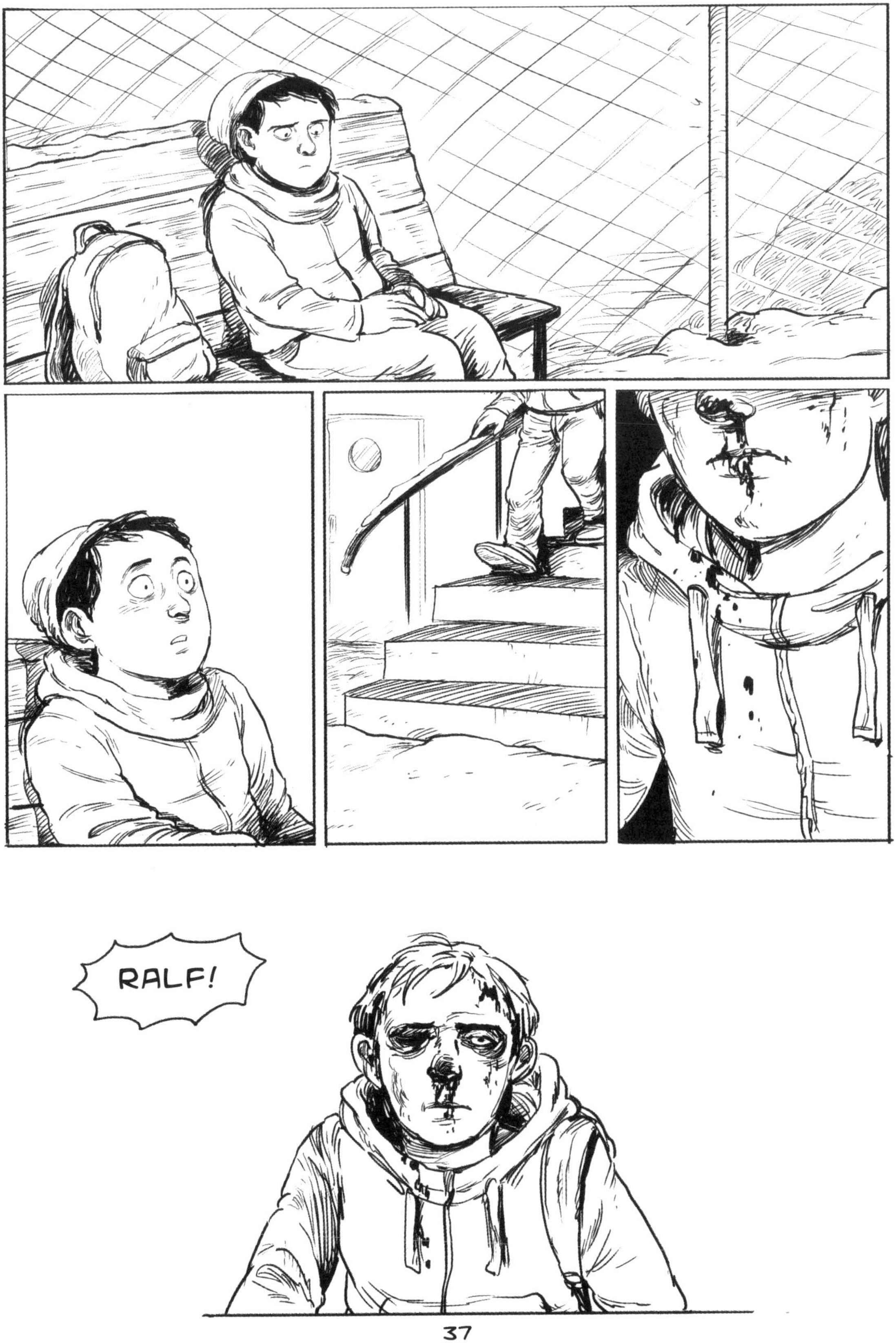
RALF!

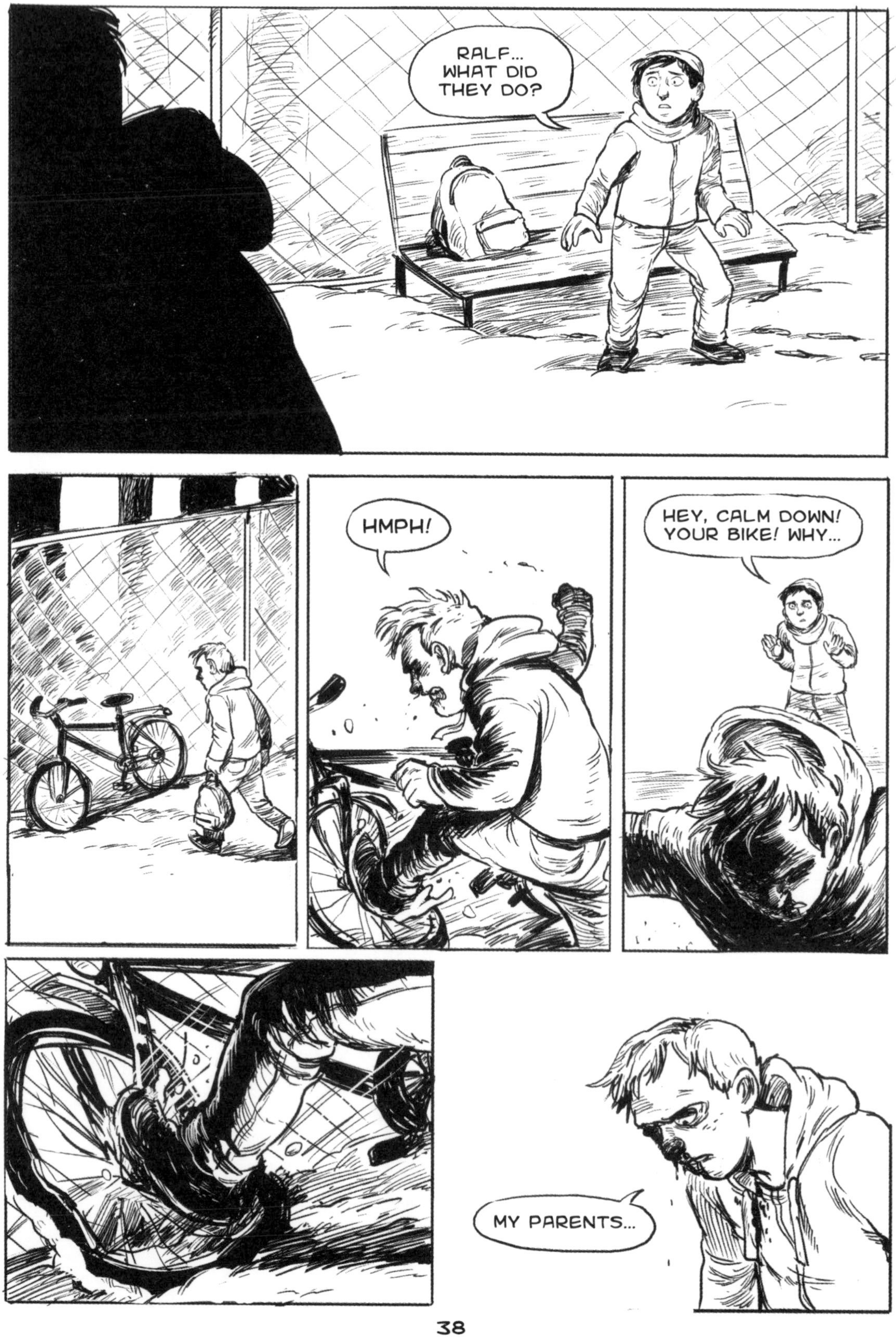
RALF...
WHAT DID
THEY DO?
HMPH!
HEY, CALM DOWN!
YOUR BIKE! WHY...
MY PARENTS...

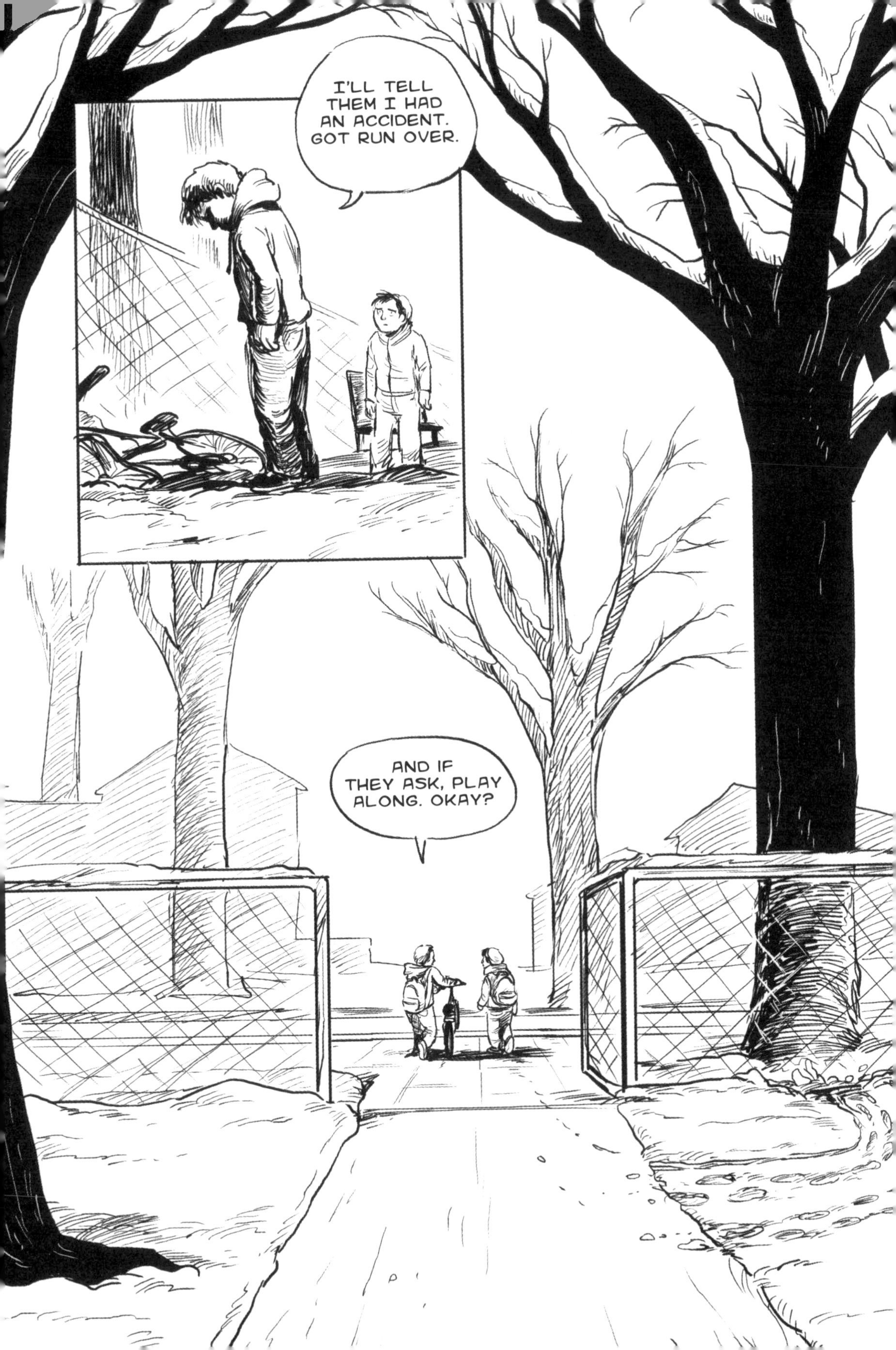
I'LL TELL THEM I HAD AN ACCIDENT. GOT RUN OVER.
AND IF THEY ASK, PLAY ALONG. OKAY?

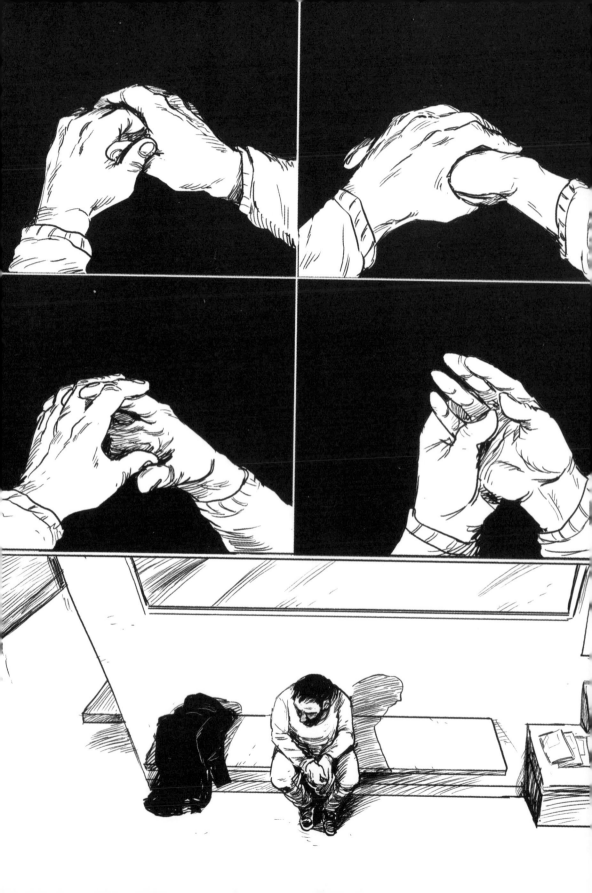

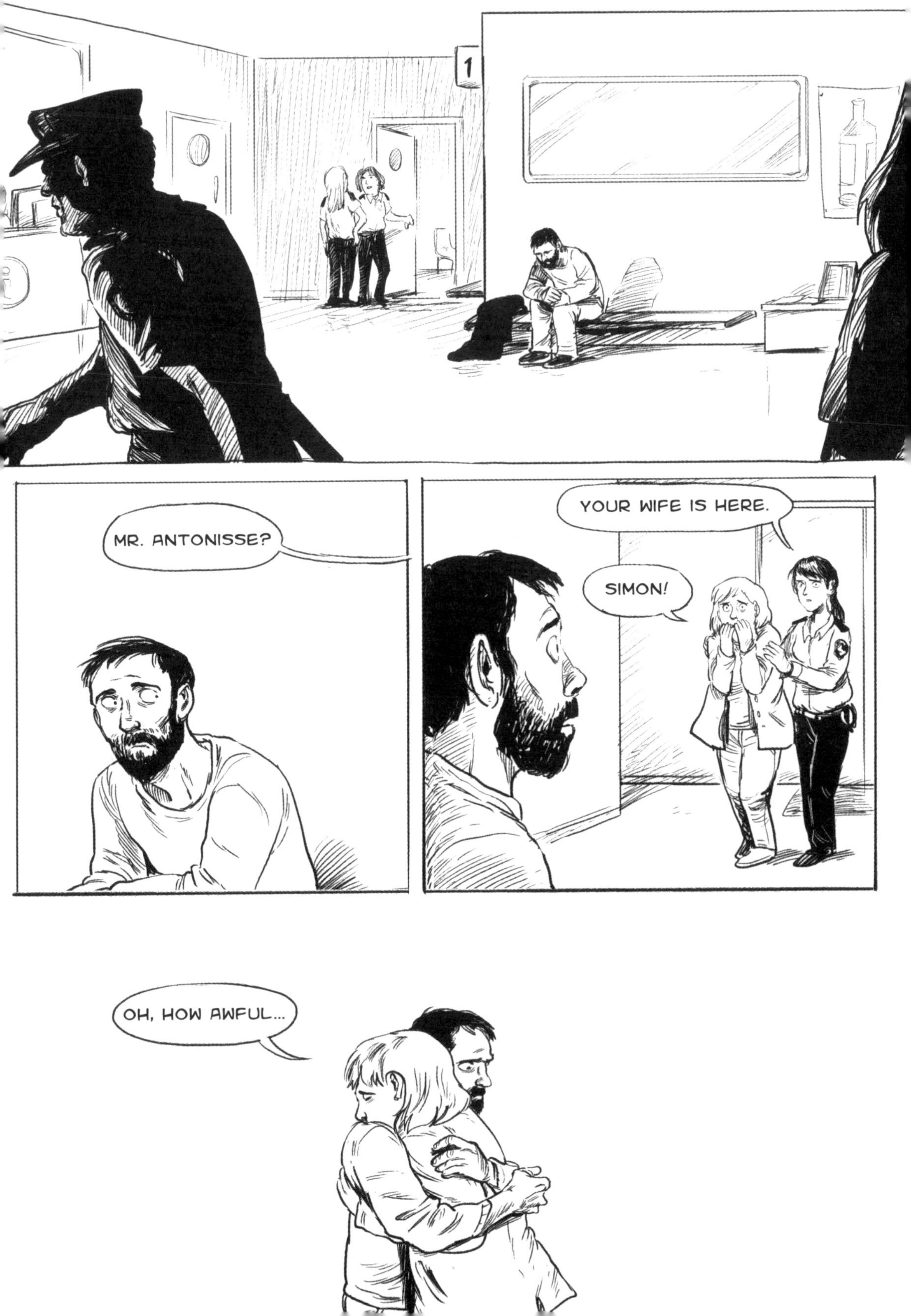
MR. ANTONISSE?
YOUR WIFE IS HERE.
SIMON!
OH, HOW AWFUL...

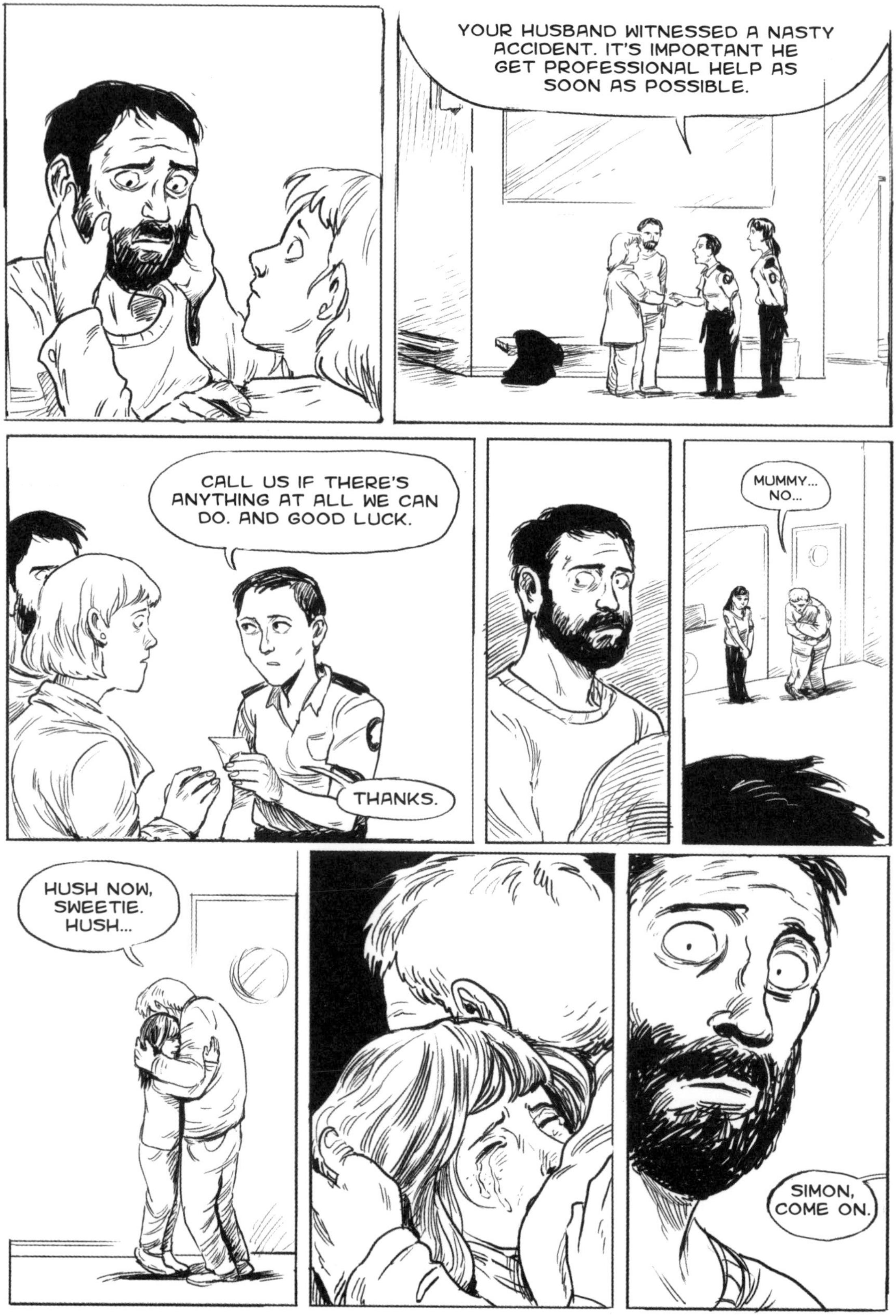
YOUR HUSBAND WITNESSED A NASTY ACCIDENT. IT'S IMPORTANT HE GET PROFESSIONAL HELP AS SOON AS POSSIBLE.
CALL US IF THERE'S ANYTHING AT ALL WE CAN DO. AND GOOD LUCK.
THANKS.
MUMMY... NO...
HUSH NOW, SWEETIE. HUSH...
SIMON, COME ON.

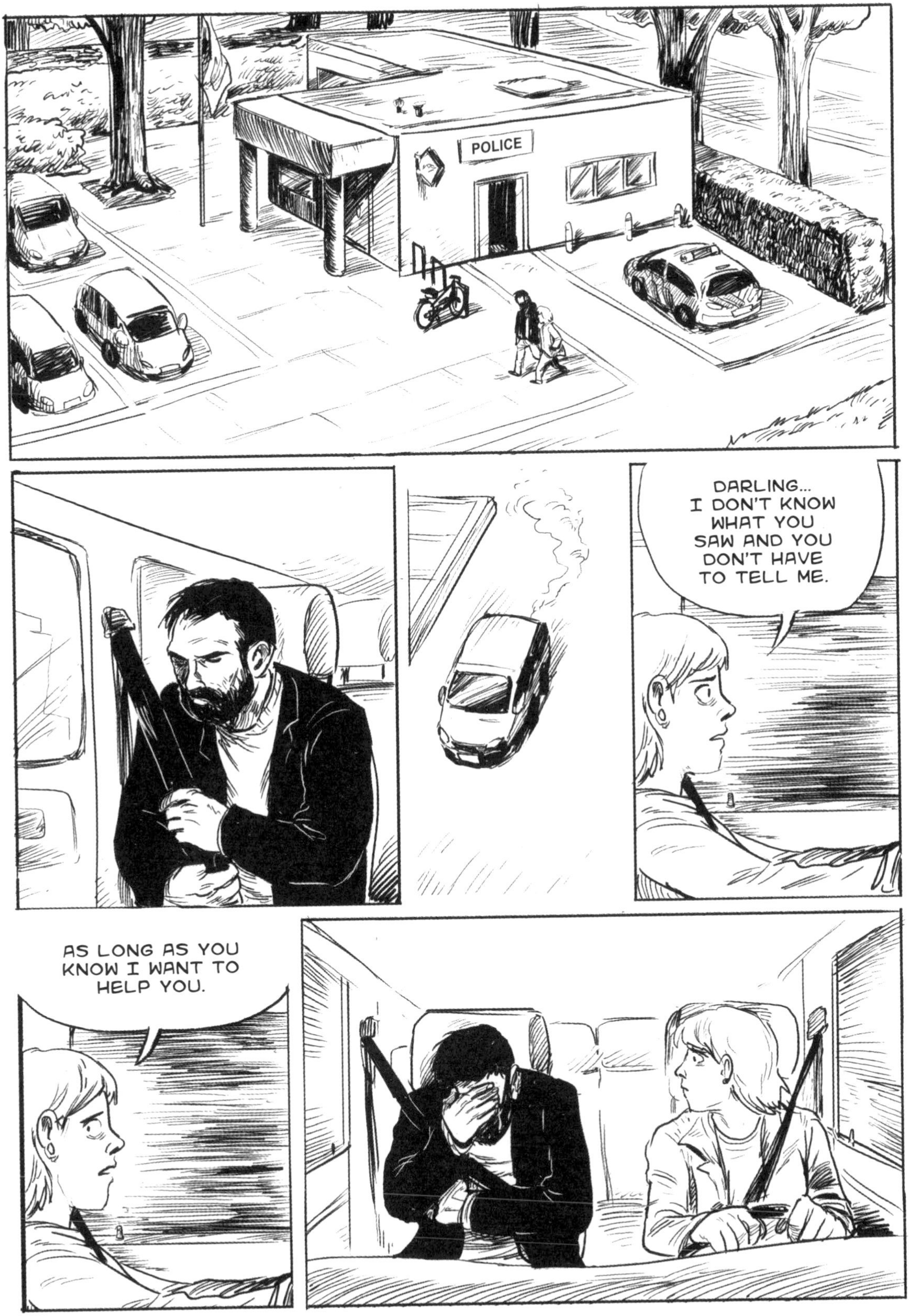
POLICE
DARLING... I DON'T KNOW WHAT YOU SAW AND YOU DON'T HAVE TO TELL ME.
AS LONG AS YOU KNOW I WANT TO HELP YOU.

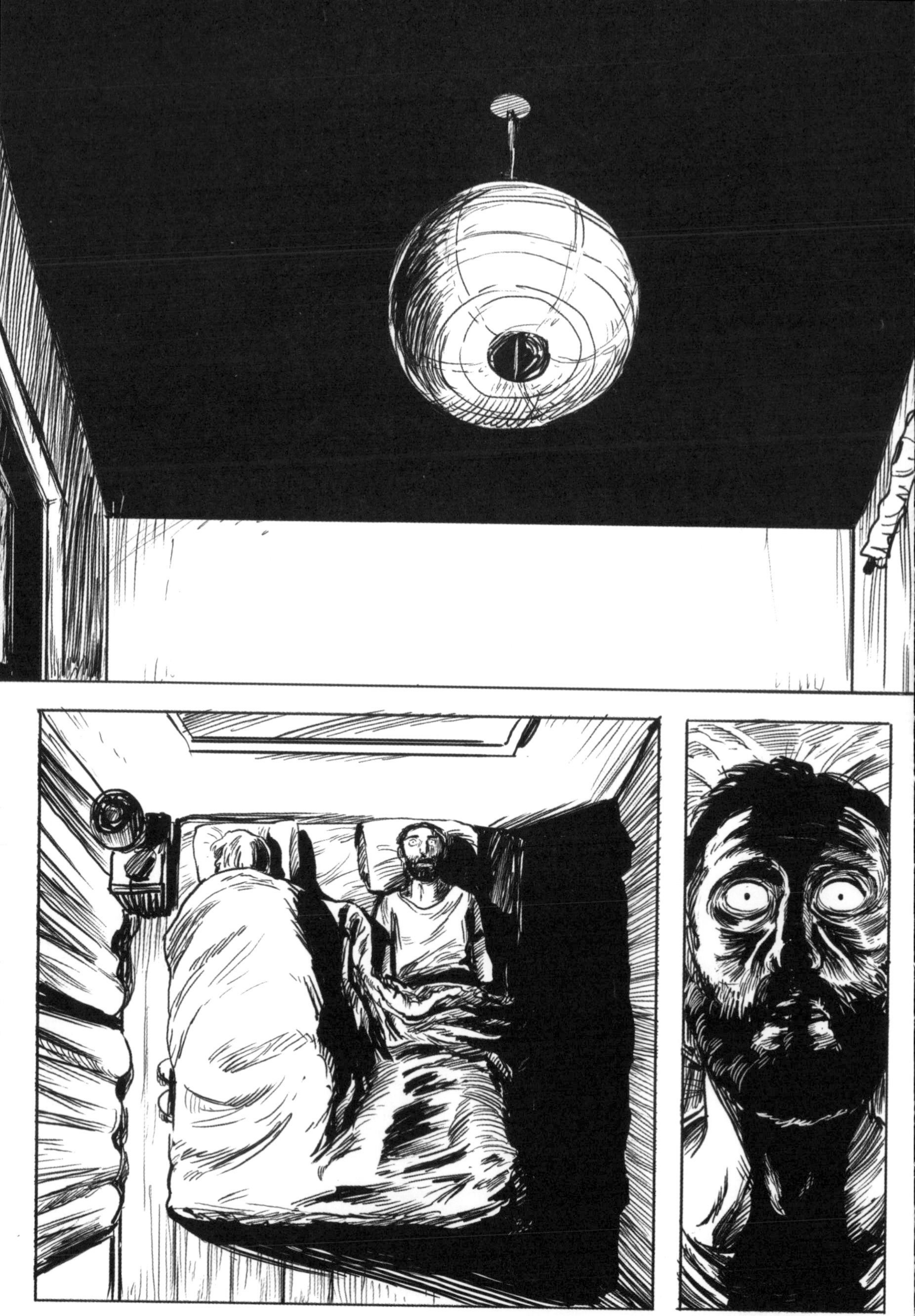

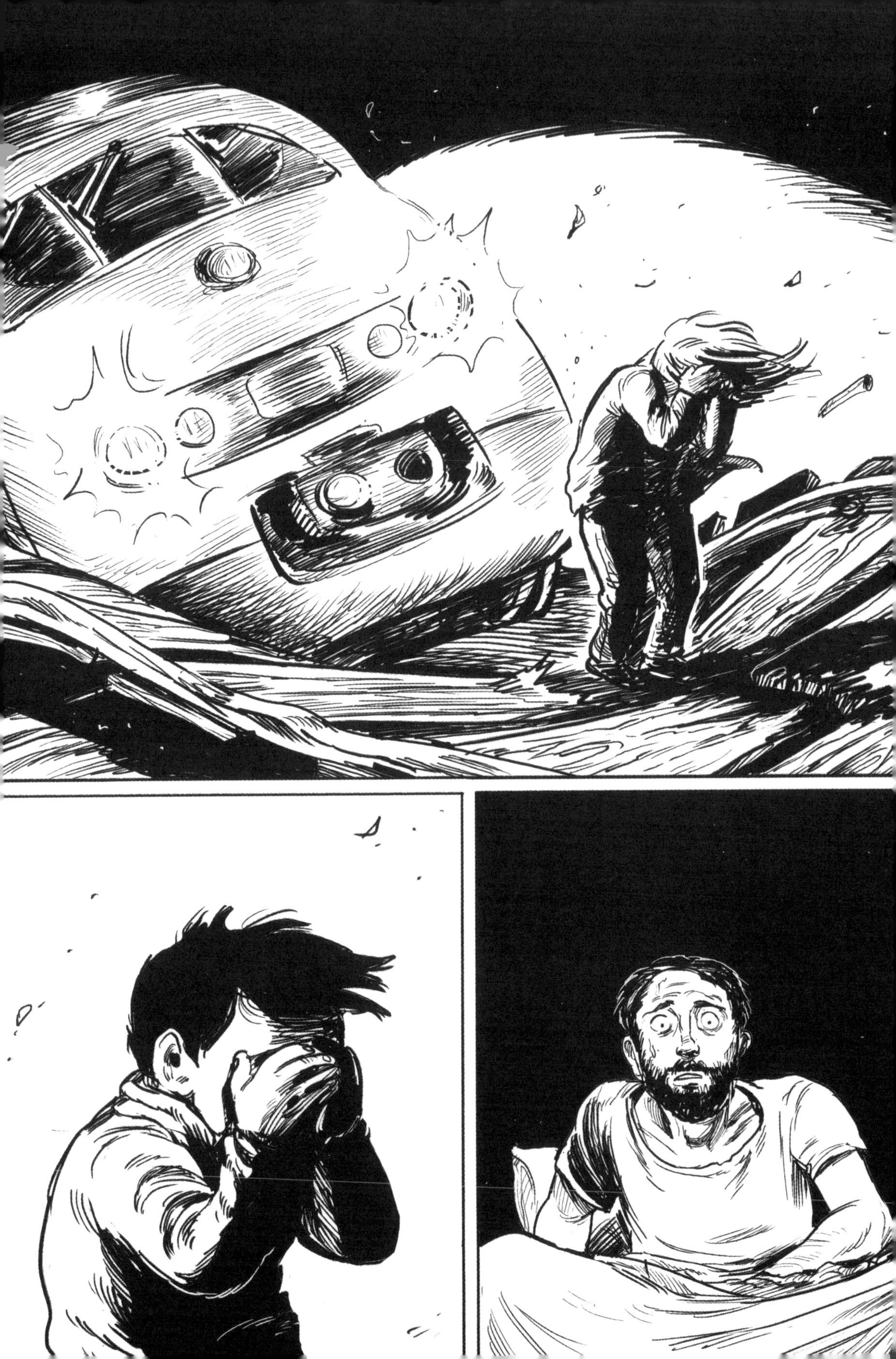

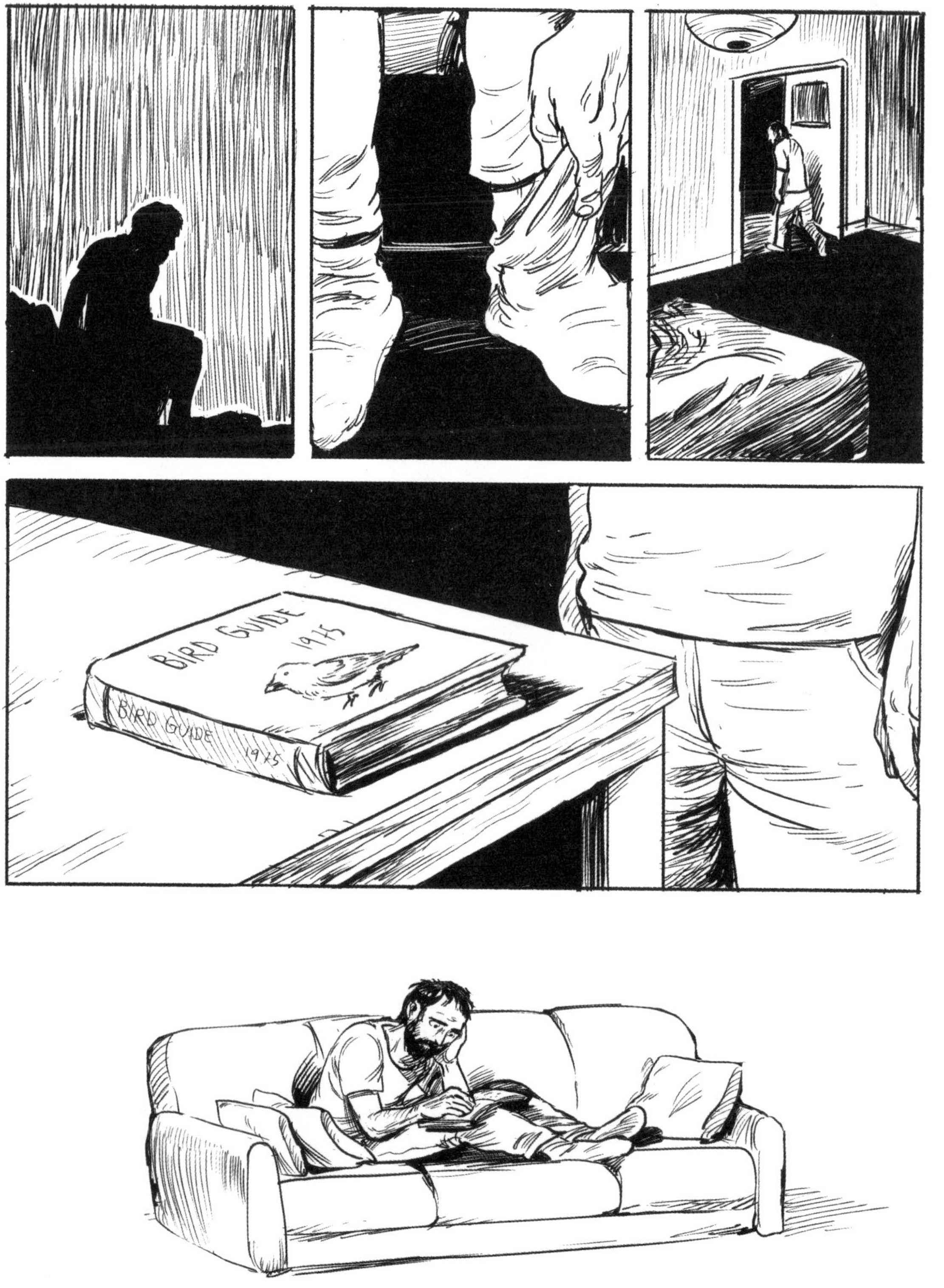
BIRD GUIDE
1975
BIRD GUIDE
1975

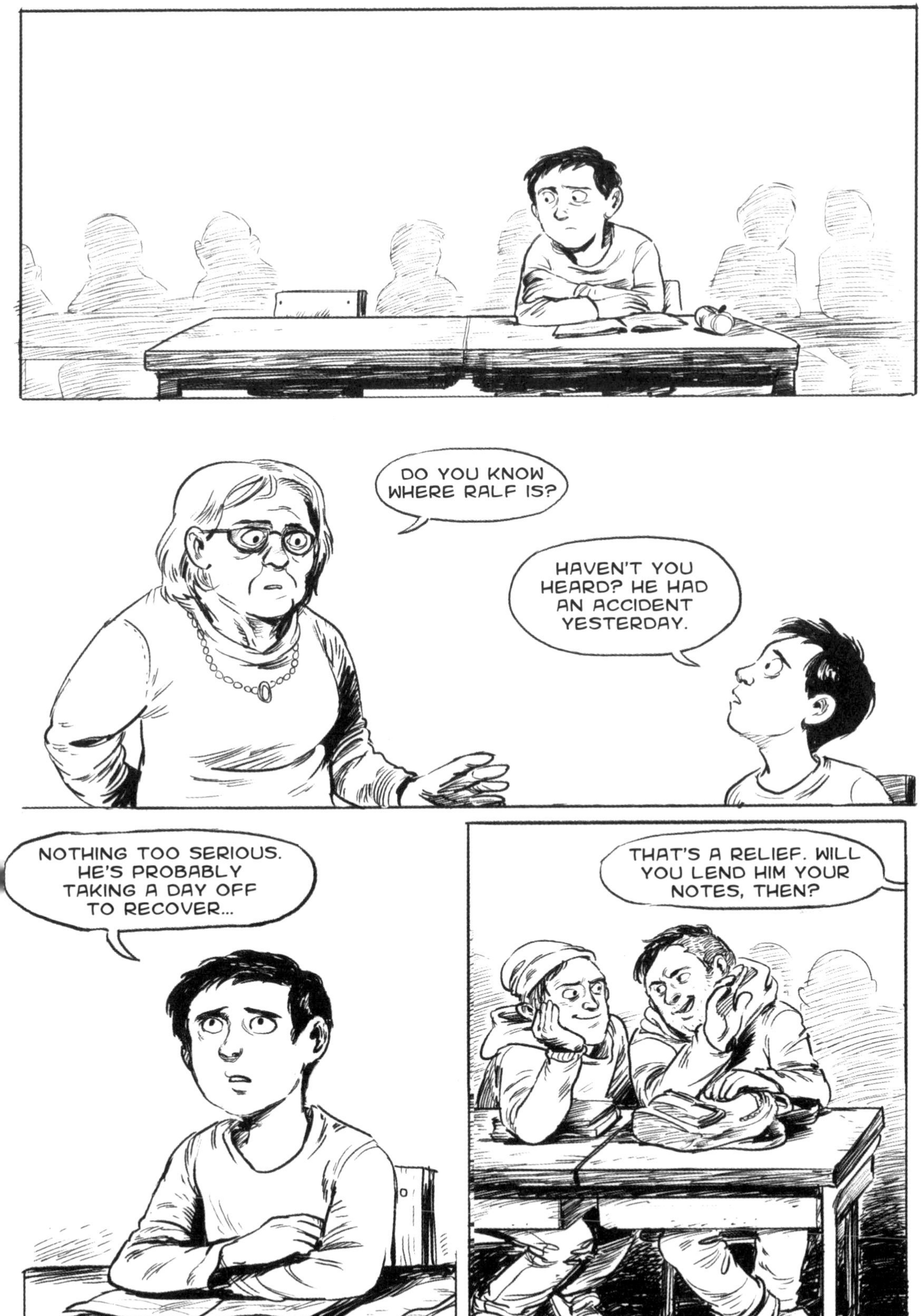
DO YOU KNOW WHERE RALF IS?
HAVEN'T YOU HEARD? HE HAD AN ACCIDENT YESTERDAY.
NOTHING TOO SERIOUS. HE'S PROBABLY TAKING A DAY OFF TO RECOVER...
THAT'S A RELIEF. WILL YOU LEND HIM YOUR NOTES, THEN?

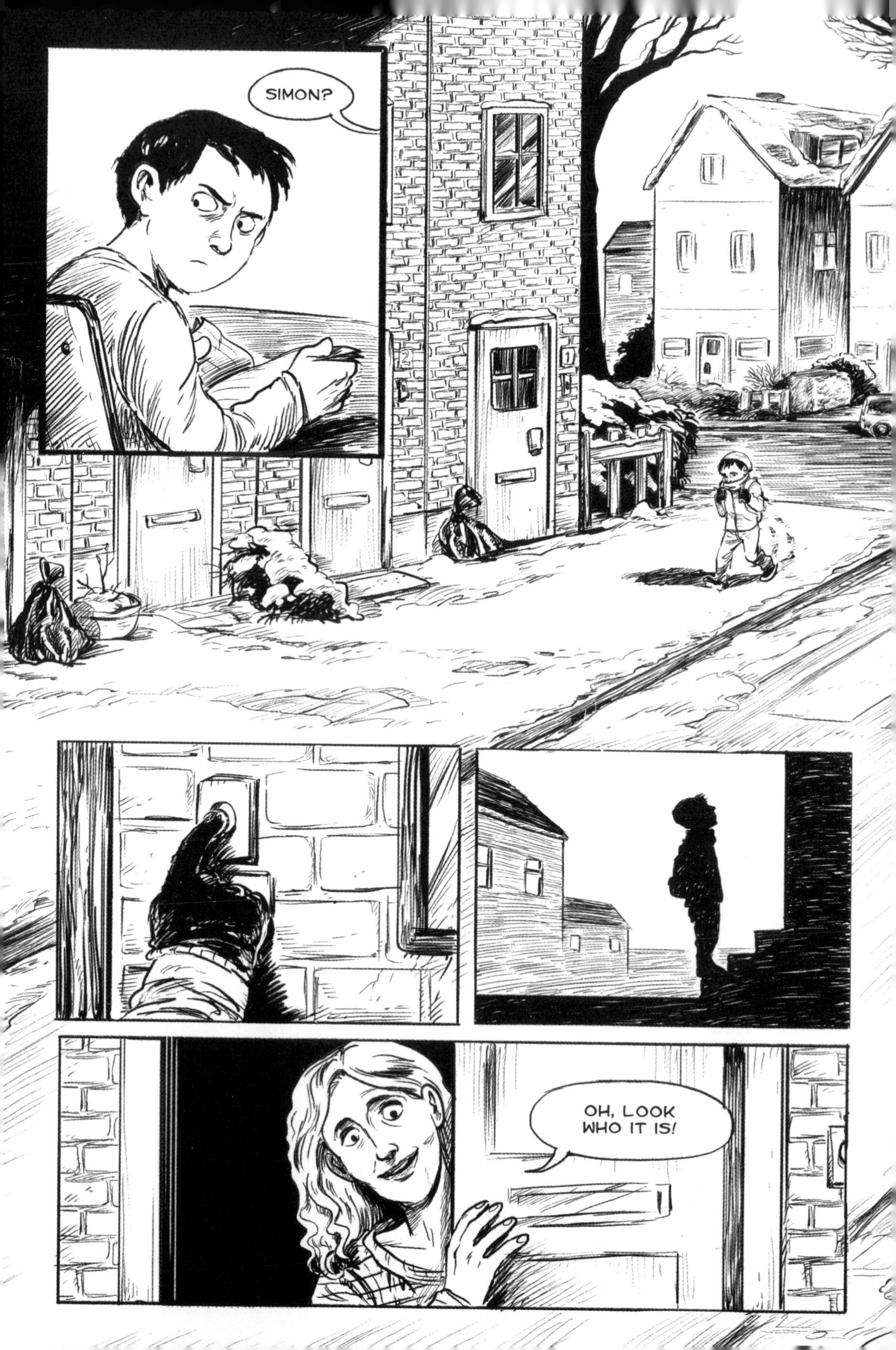
SIMON?
OH, LOOK WHO IT IS!

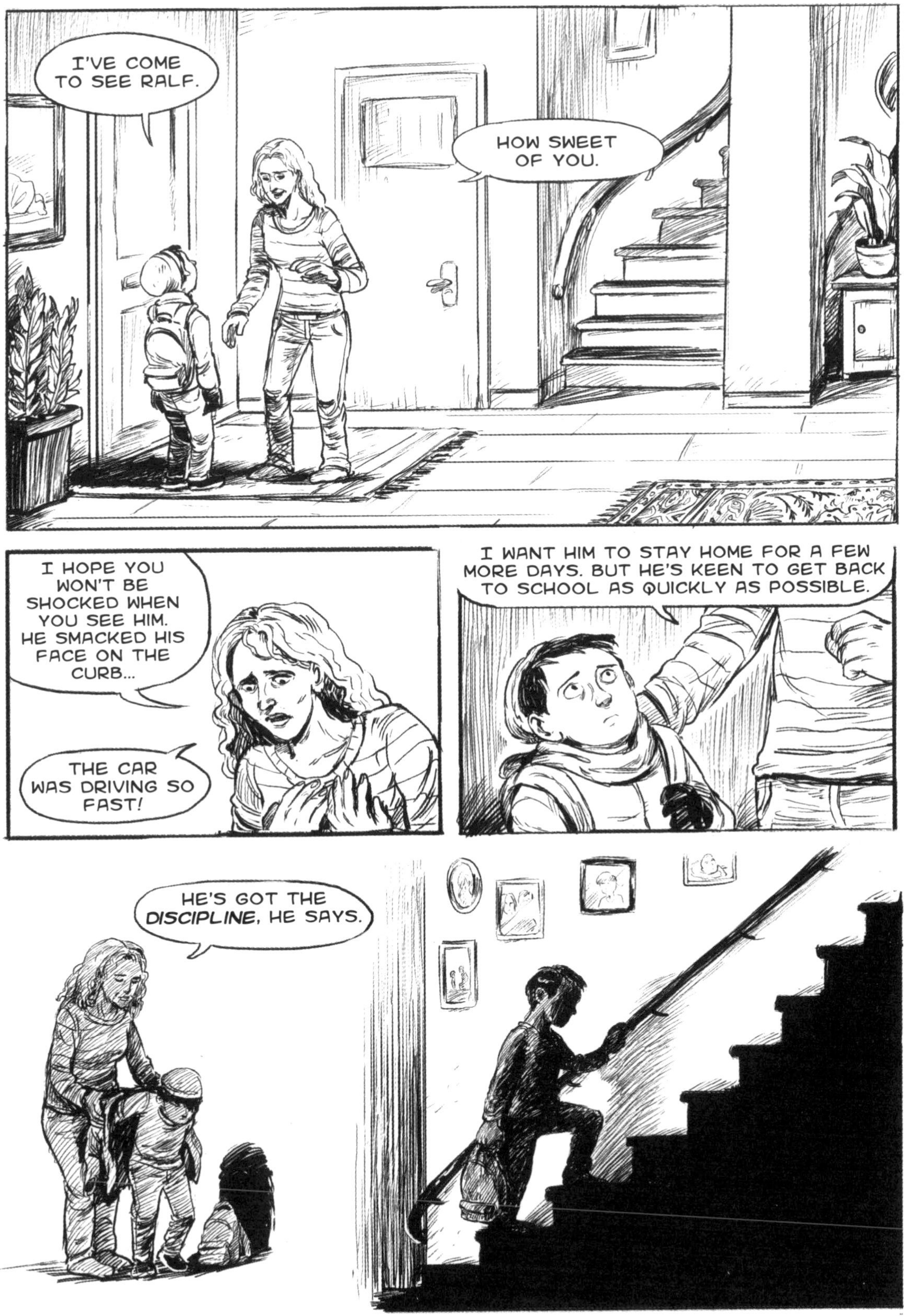
I'VE COME TO SEE RALF.
HOW SWEET OF YOU.
I HOPE YOU WON'T BE SHOCKED WHEN YOU SEE HIM. HE SMACKED HIS FACE ON THE CURB...
THE CAR WAS DRIVING SO FAST!
I WANT HIM TO STAY HOME FOR A FEW MORE DAYS. BUT HE'S KEEN TO GET BACK TO SCHOOL AS QUICKLY AS POSSIBLE.
HE'S GOT THE *DISCIPLINE*, HE SAYS.

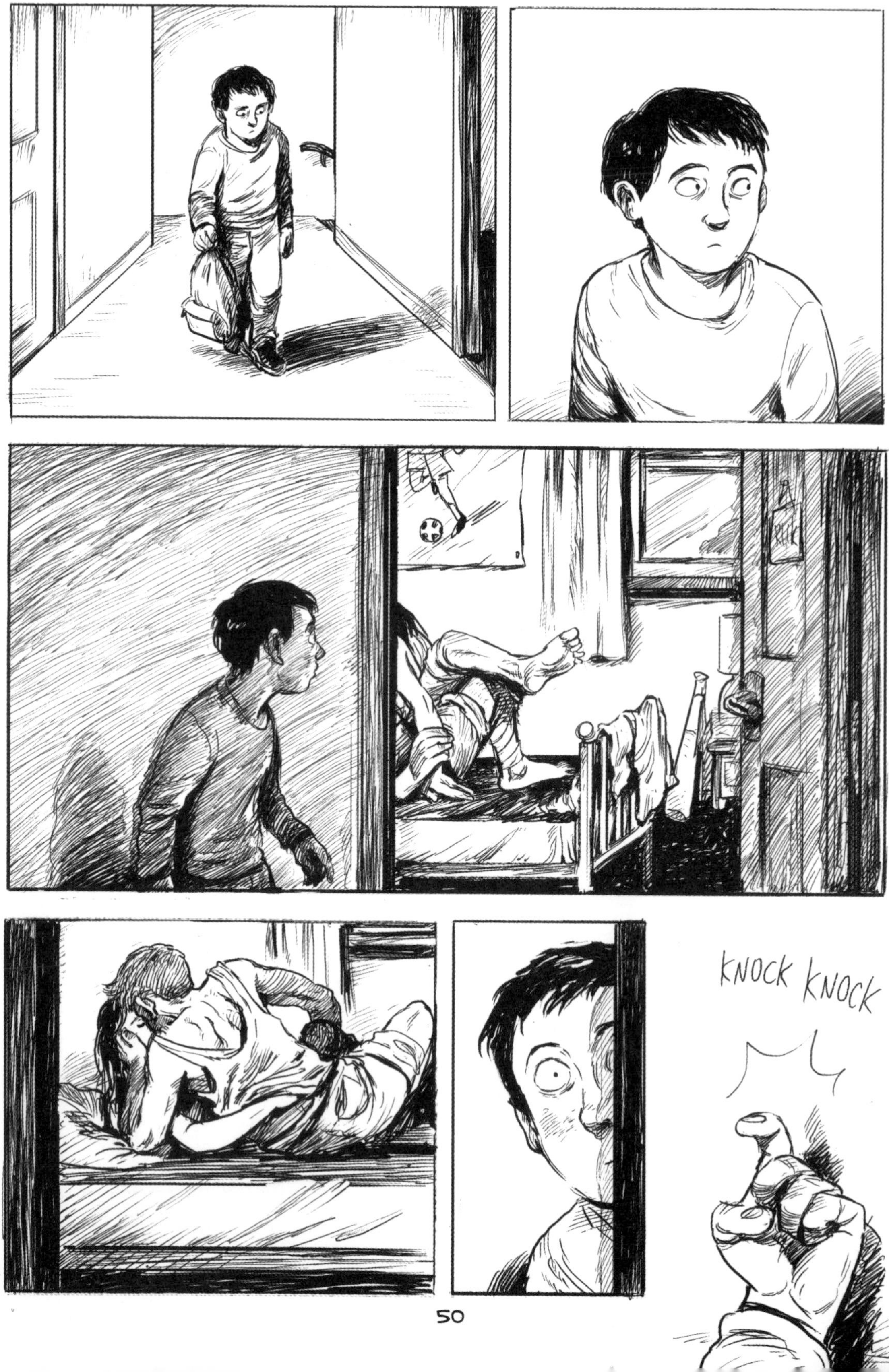
KNOCK KNOCK

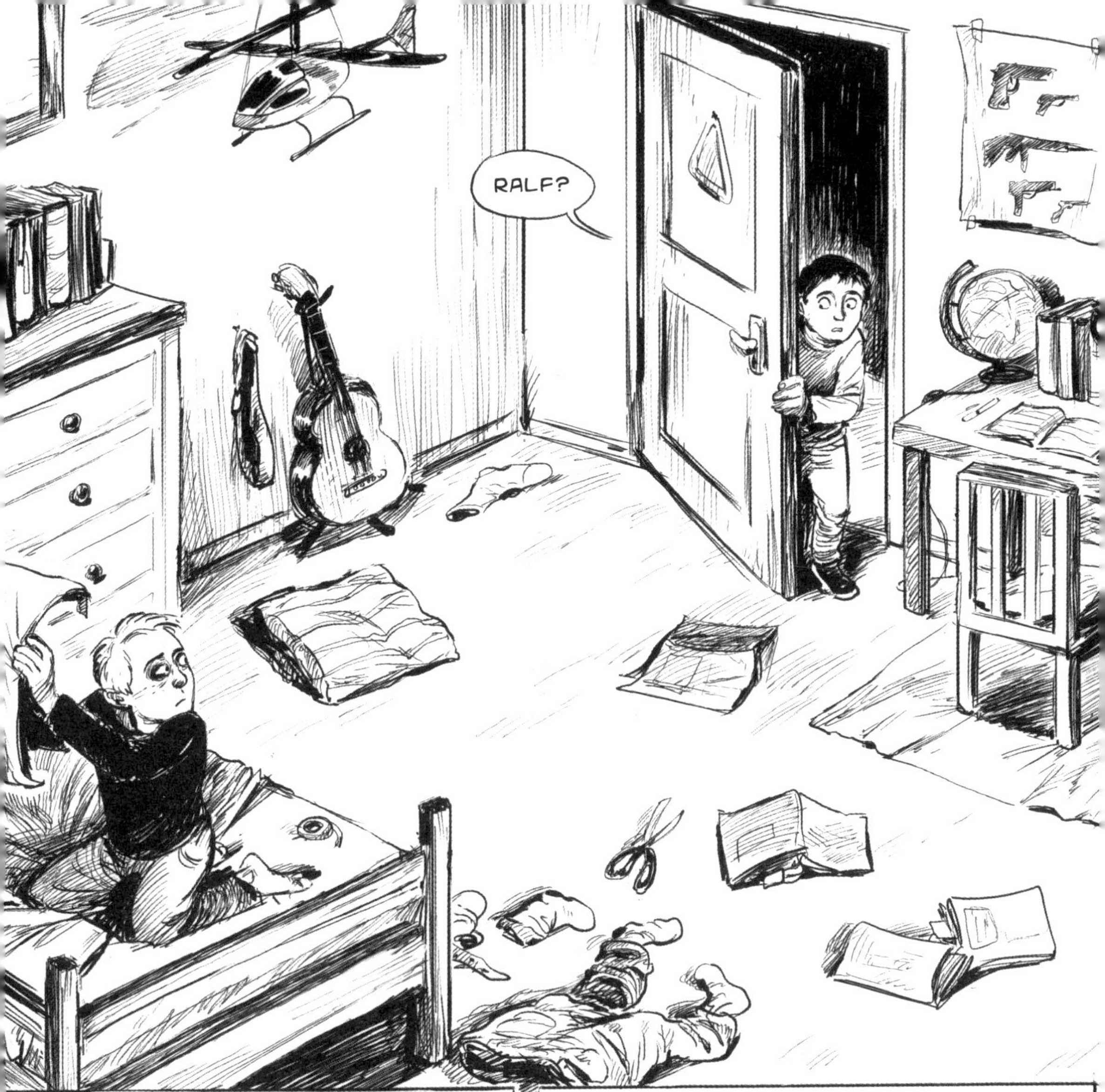
RALF?

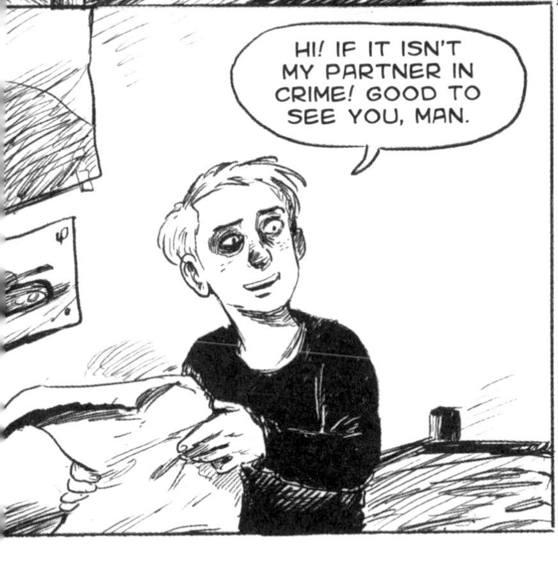
HI! IF IT ISN'T MY PARTNER IN CRIME! GOOD TO SEE YOU, MAN.

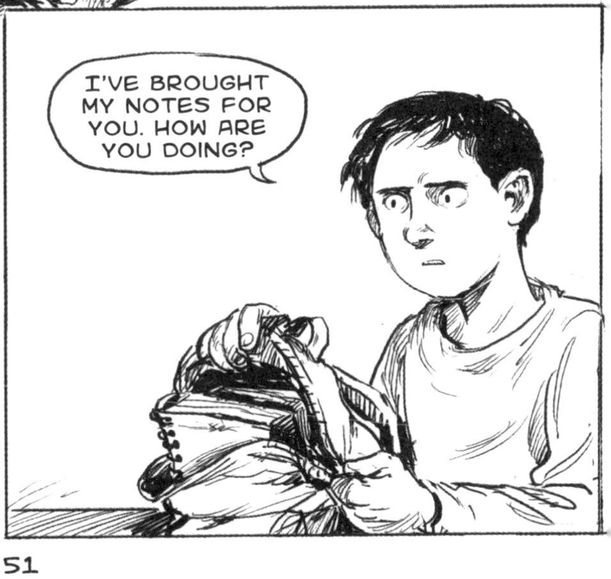
I'VE BROUGHT MY NOTES FOR YOU. HOW ARE YOU DOING?

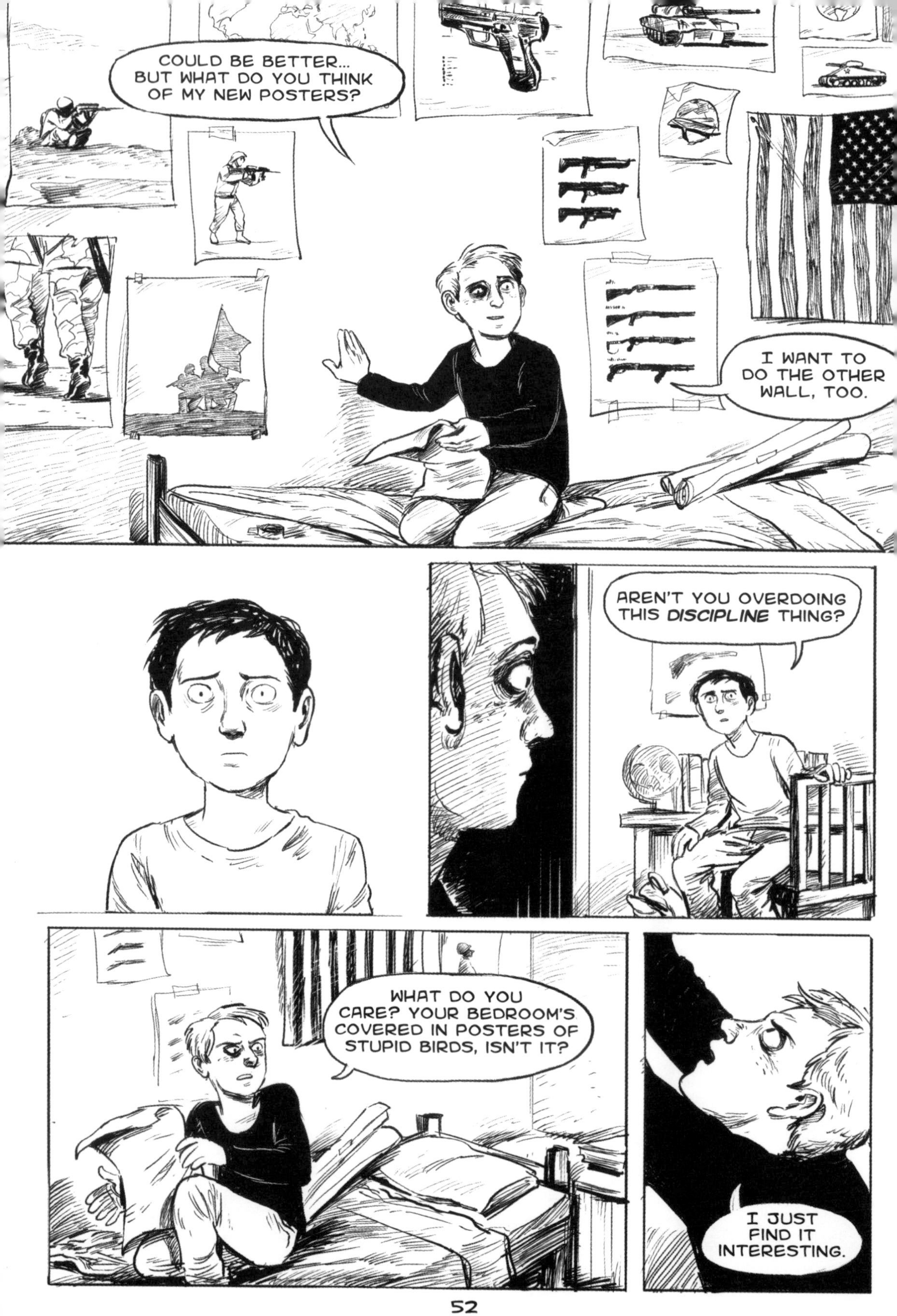
COULD BE BETTER... BUT WHAT DO YOU THINK OF MY NEW POSTERS?
I WANT TO DO THE OTHER WALL, TOO.
AREN'T YOU OVERDOING THIS *DISCIPLINE* THING?
WHAT DO YOU CARE? YOUR BEDROOM'S COVERED IN POSTERS OF STUPID BIRDS, ISN'T IT?
I JUST FIND IT INTERESTING.

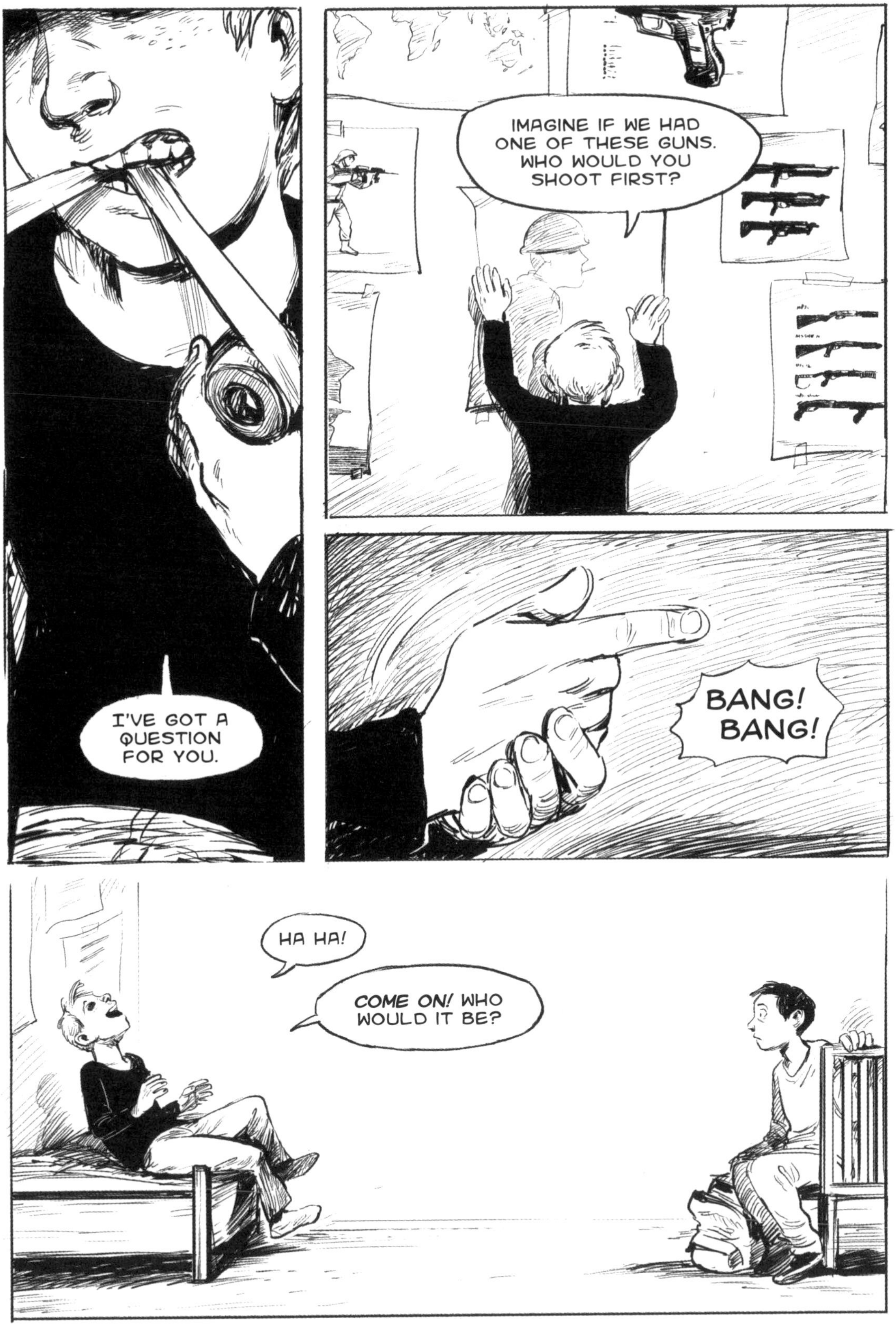
I'VE GOT A QUESTION FOR YOU.
IMAGINE IF WE HAD ONE OF THESE GUNS. WHO WOULD YOU SHOOT FIRST?
BANG! BANG!
HA HA!
COME ON! WHO WOULD IT BE?

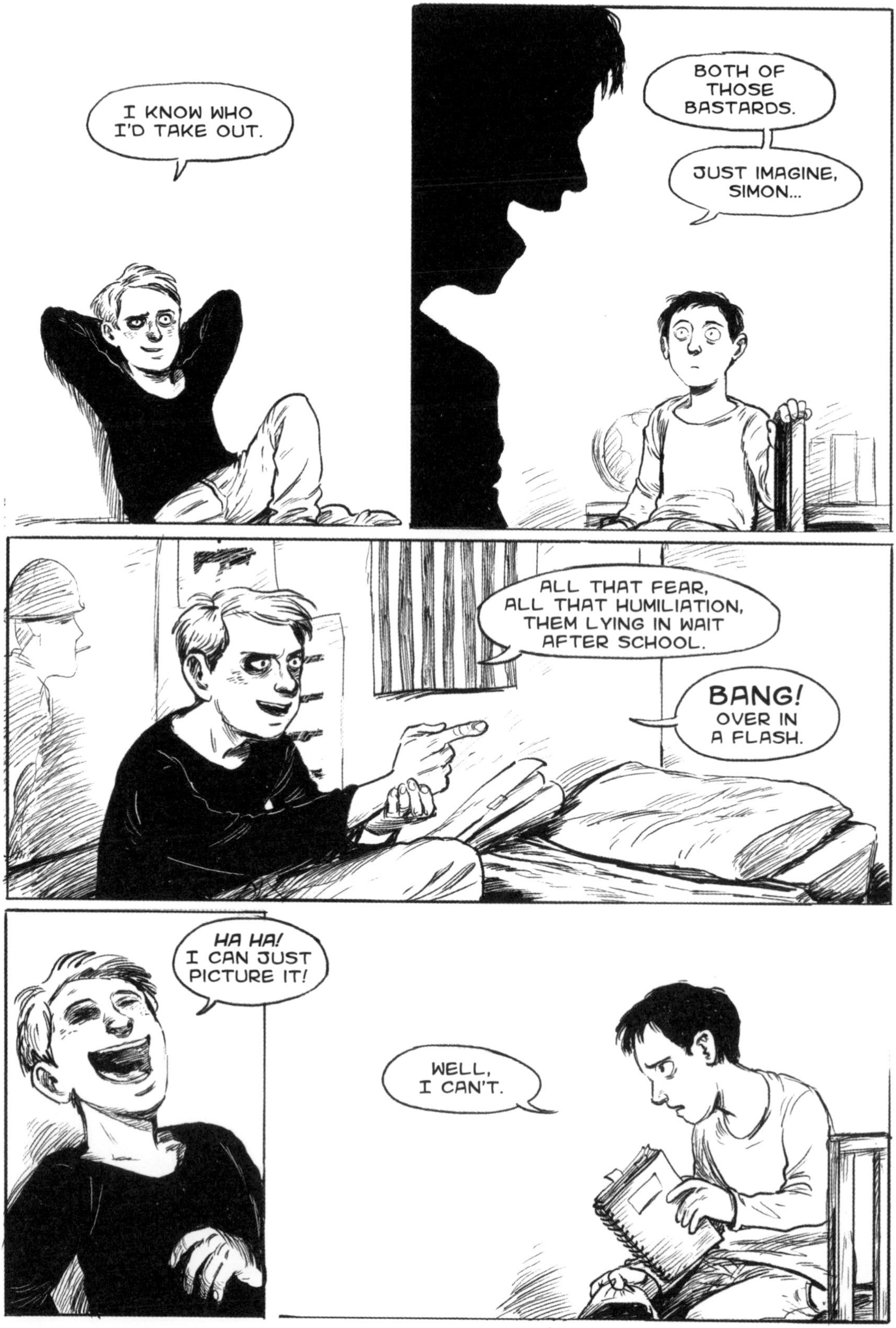
I KNOW WHO I'D TAKE OUT.
BOTH OF THOSE BASTARDS.
JUST IMAGINE, SIMON...
ALL THAT FEAR, ALL THAT HUMILIATION, THEM LYING IN WAIT AFTER SCHOOL.
BANG! OVER IN A FLASH.
HA HA! I CAN JUST PICTURE IT!
WELL, I CAN'T.

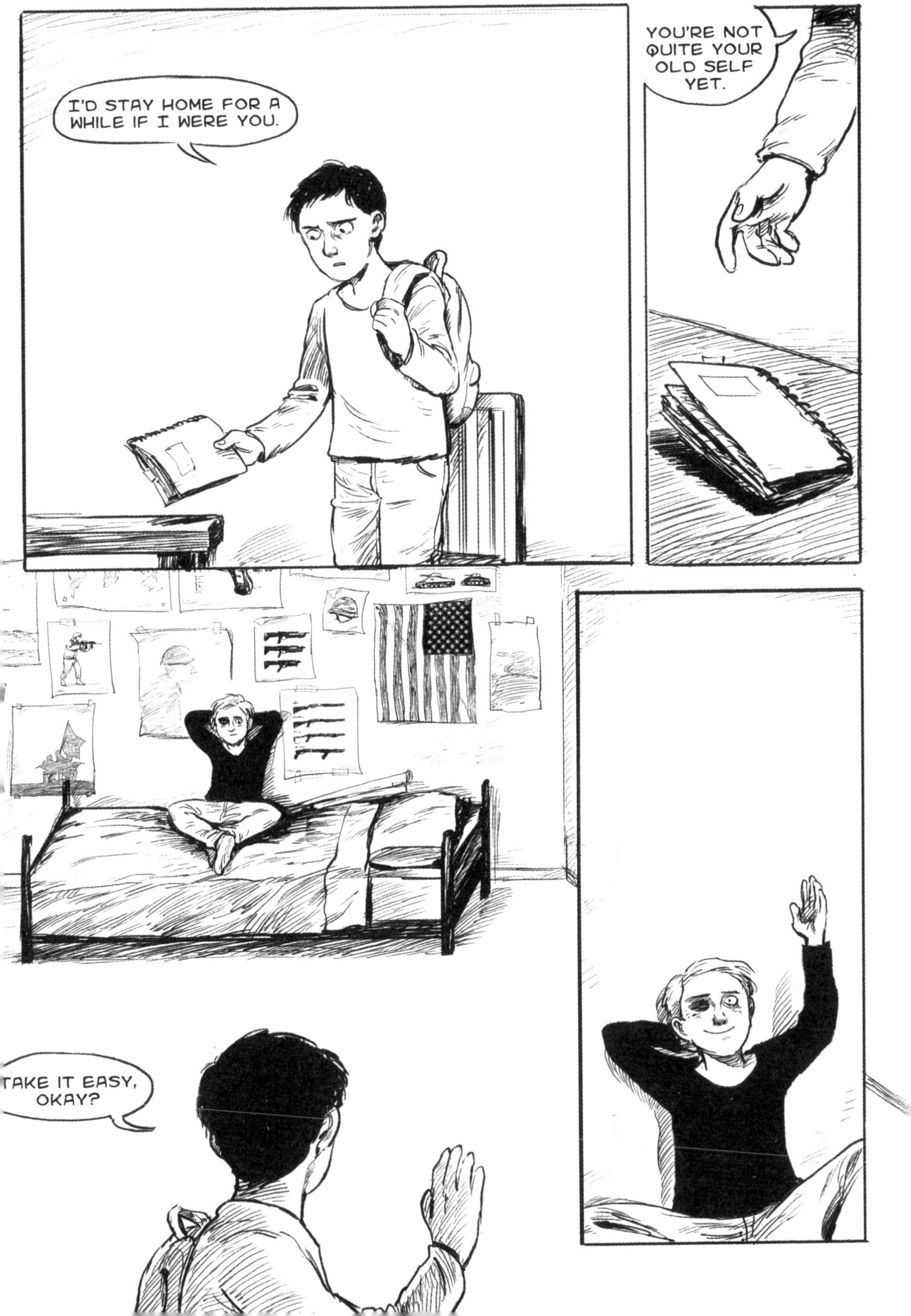
I'D STAY HOME FOR A WHILE IF I WERE YOU.
YOU'RE NOT QUITE YOUR OLD SELF YET.
TAKE IT EASY, OKAY?

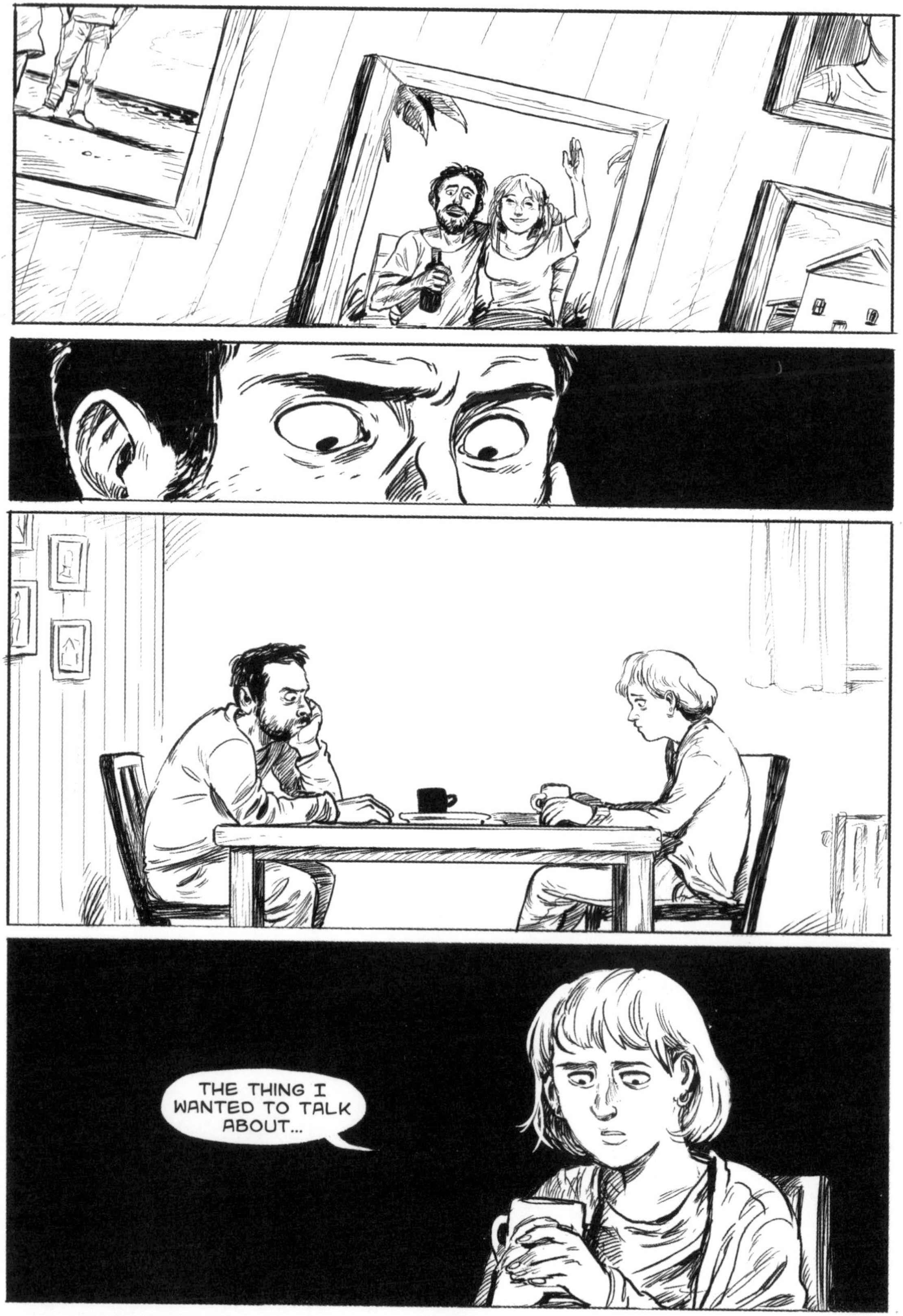
THE THING I WANTED TO TALK ABOUT...

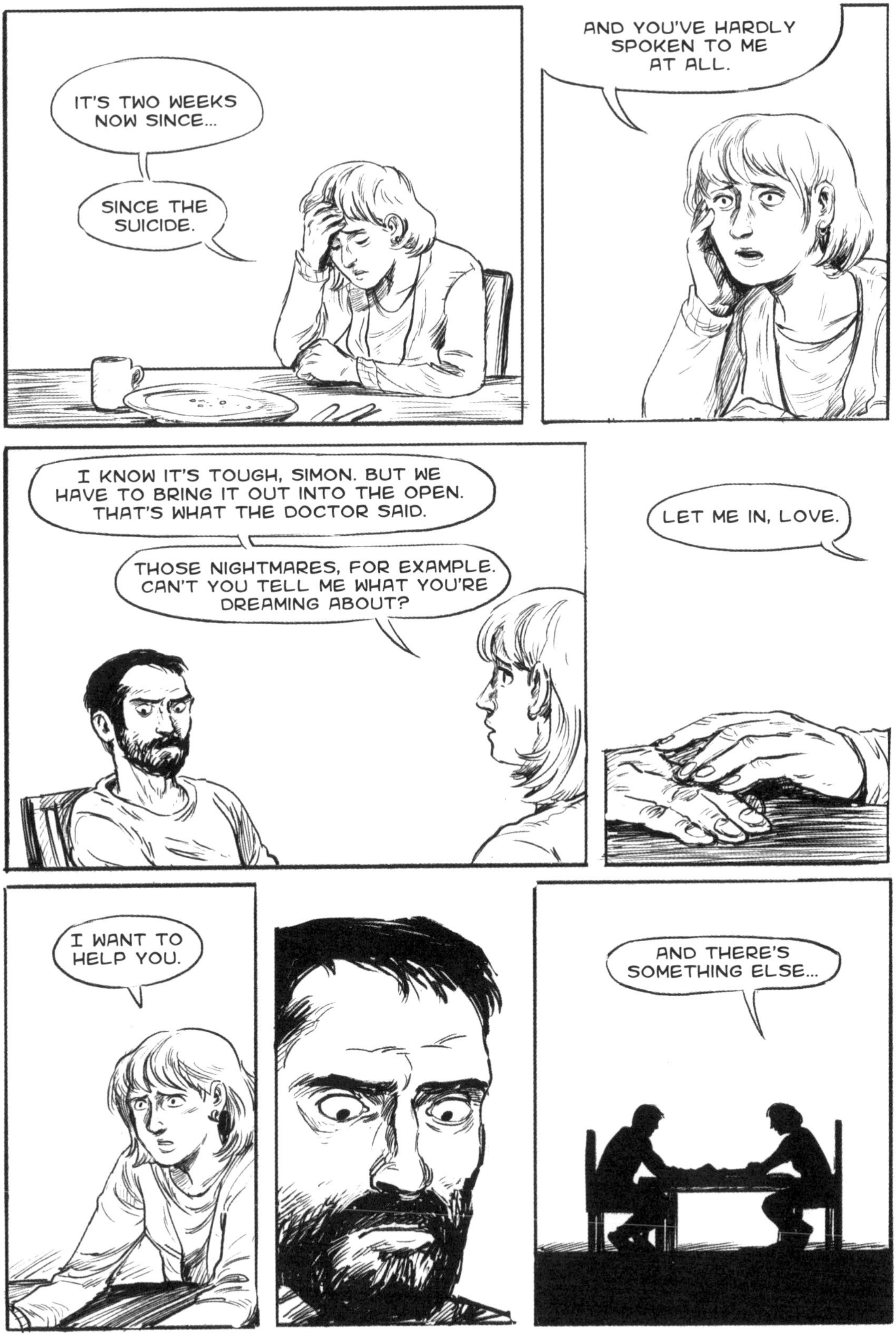
IT'S TWO WEEKS NOW SINCE...
SINCE THE SUICIDE.
AND YOU'VE HARDLY SPOKEN TO ME AT ALL.
I KNOW IT'S TOUGH, SIMON. BUT WE HAVE TO BRING IT OUT INTO THE OPEN. THAT'S WHAT THE DOCTOR SAID.
THOSE NIGHTMARES, FOR EXAMPLE. CAN'T YOU TELL ME WHAT YOU'RE DREAMING ABOUT?
LET ME IN, LOVE.
I WANT TO HELP YOU.
AND THERE'S SOMETHING ELSE...

KAREL CALLED. HE MADE A NEW OFFER FOR THE SHOP AND...

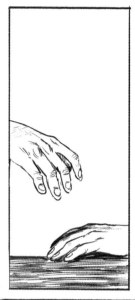

DARLING, LET ME FINISH. IT'S THE HIGHEST OFFER WE'VE HAD! THINK ABOUT IT, AT LEAST.

WHY DO I HAVE TO TELL YOU EVERYTHING A HUNDRED TIMES? *NO IS NO*.

I'M BEGINNING TO WONDER WHOSE SIDE YOU'RE ON, LAURA.

I JUST WANT THE BEST FOR US AND FOR THE SHOP. DON'T YOU SEE THAT WE WON'T HAVE JOBS FOR MUCH LONGER AT THIS RATE?

CAN'T YOU JUST DROP THIS FAMILY HONOUR THING?

SIMON!

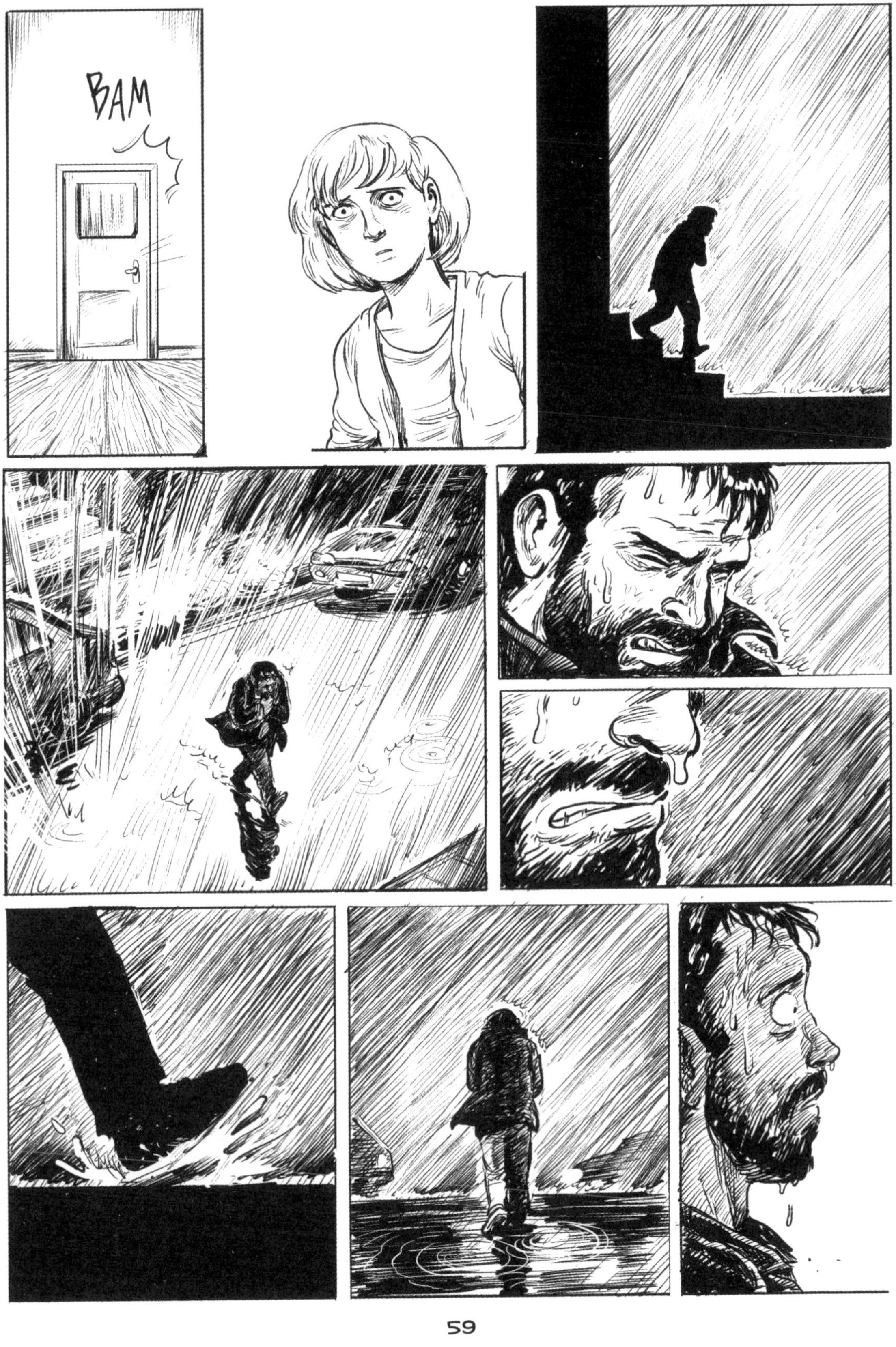
BAM

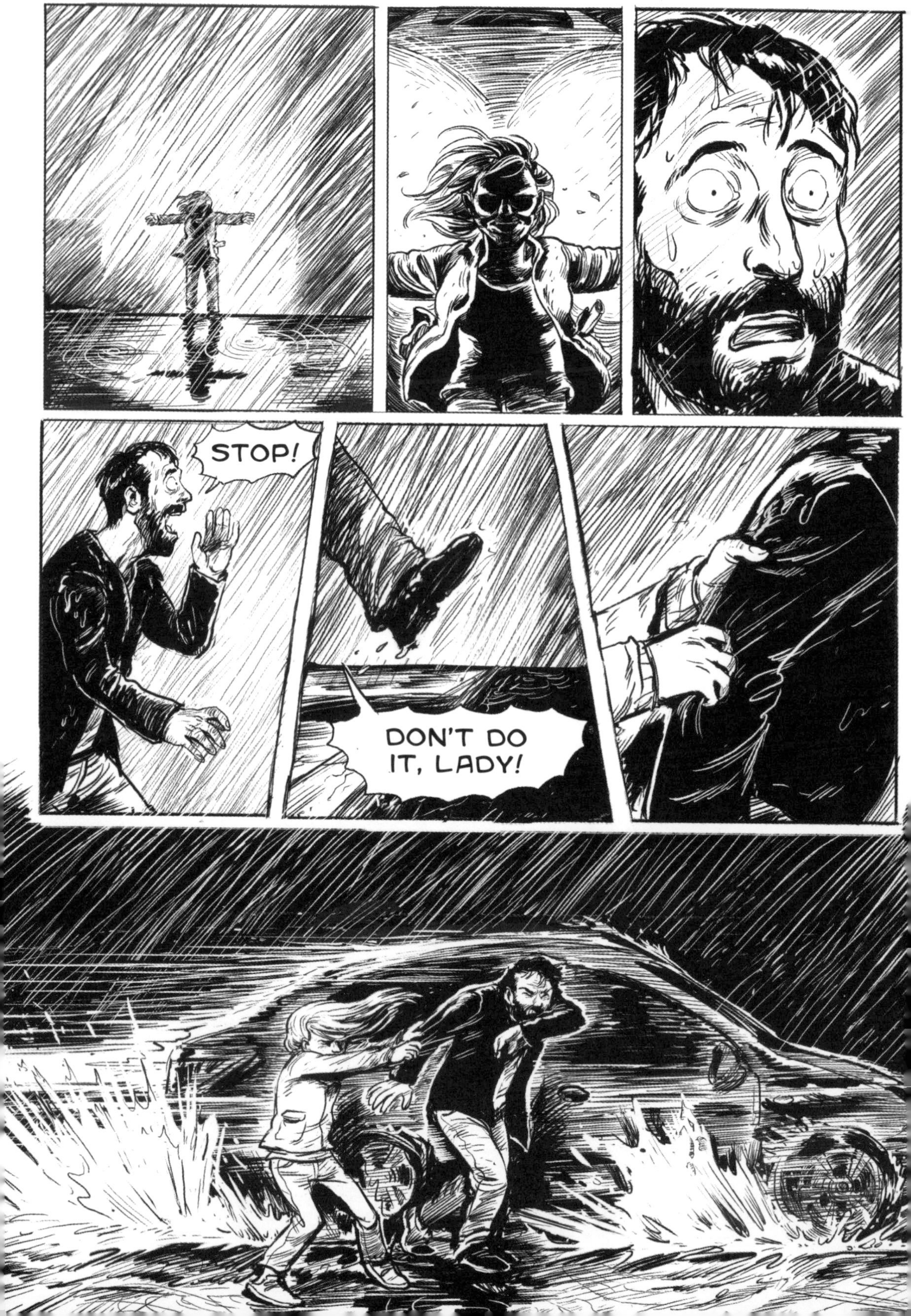
STOP!
DON'T DO IT, LADY!

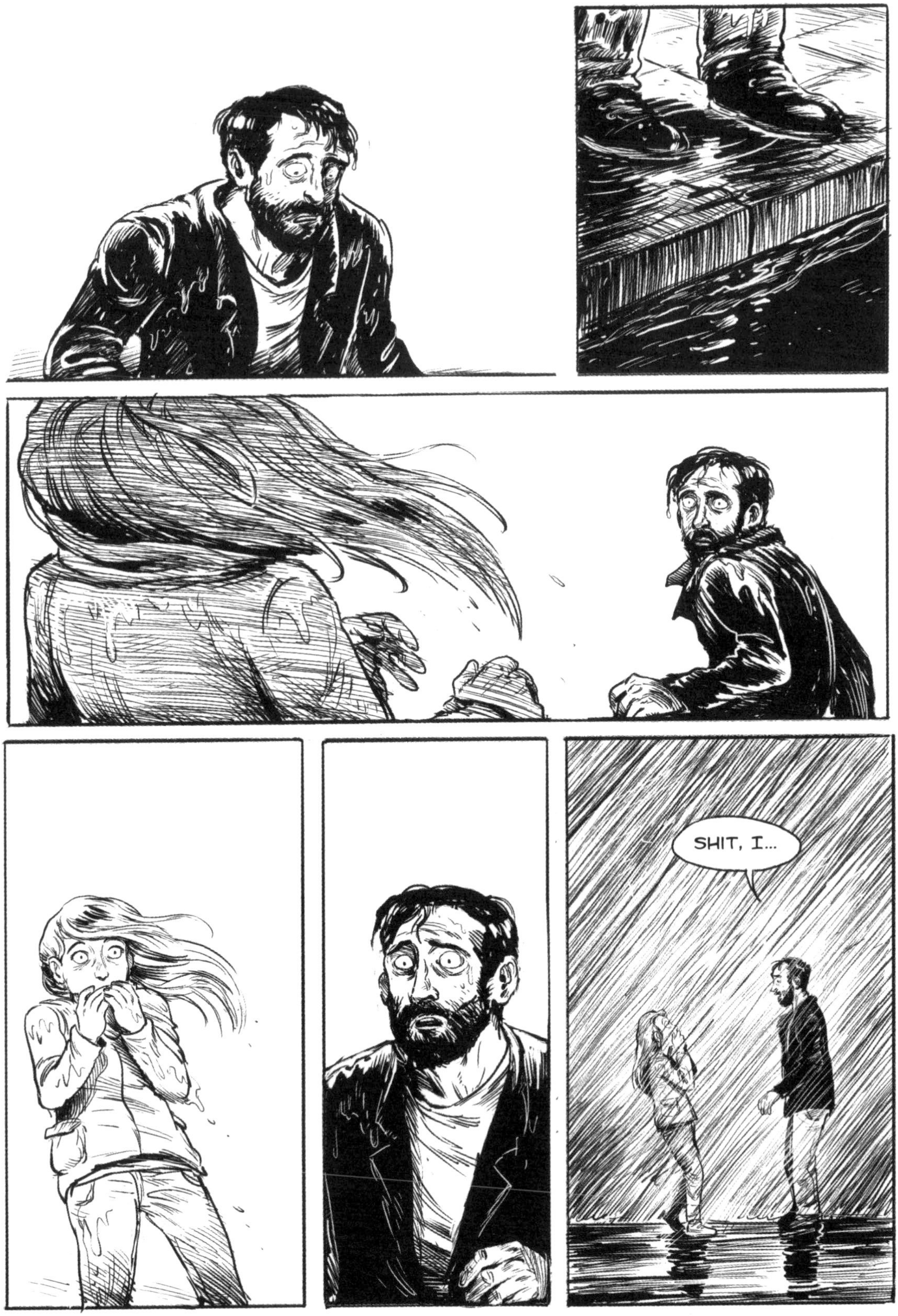
SHIT, I...

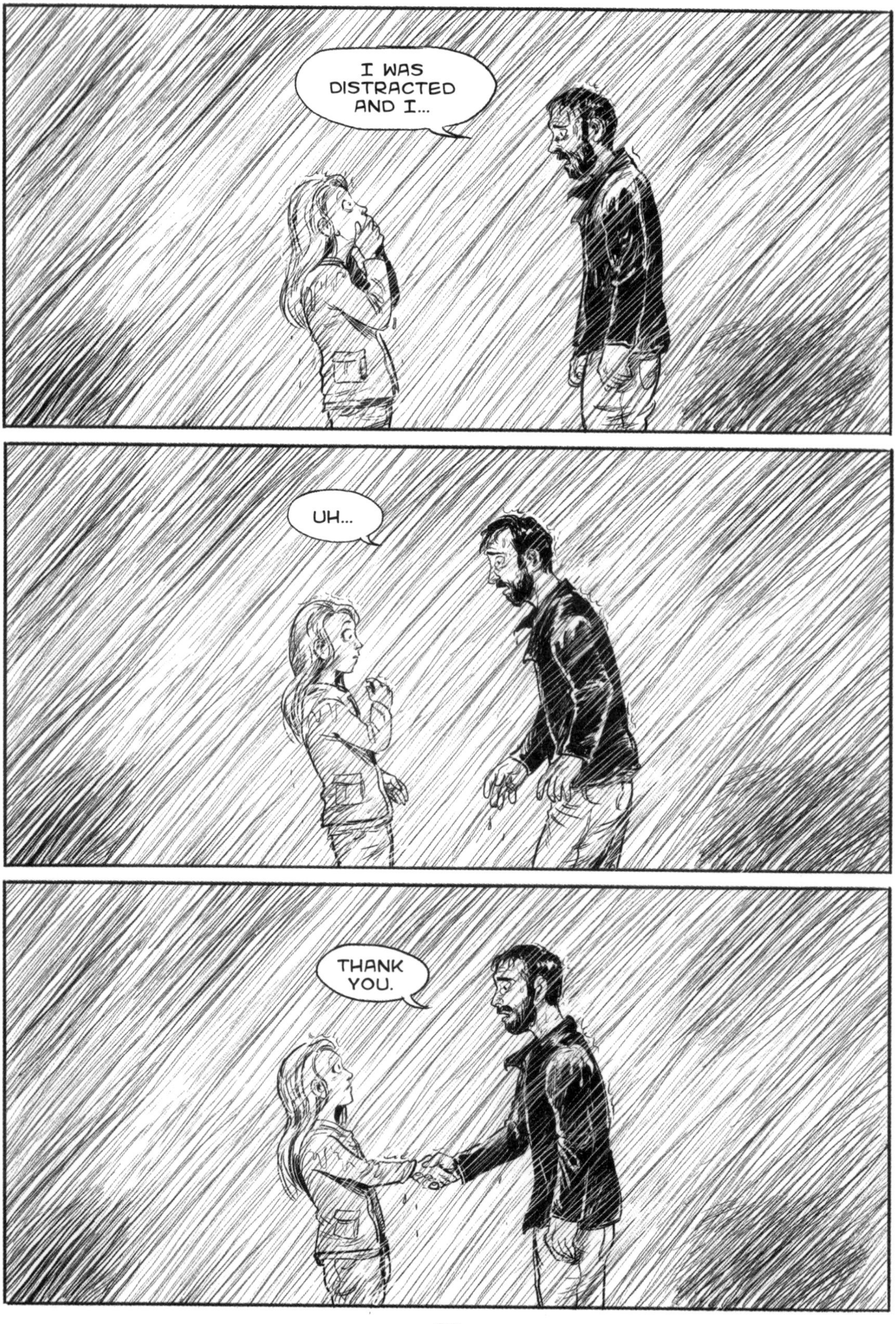
I WAS DISTRACTED AND I...
UH...
THANK YOU.

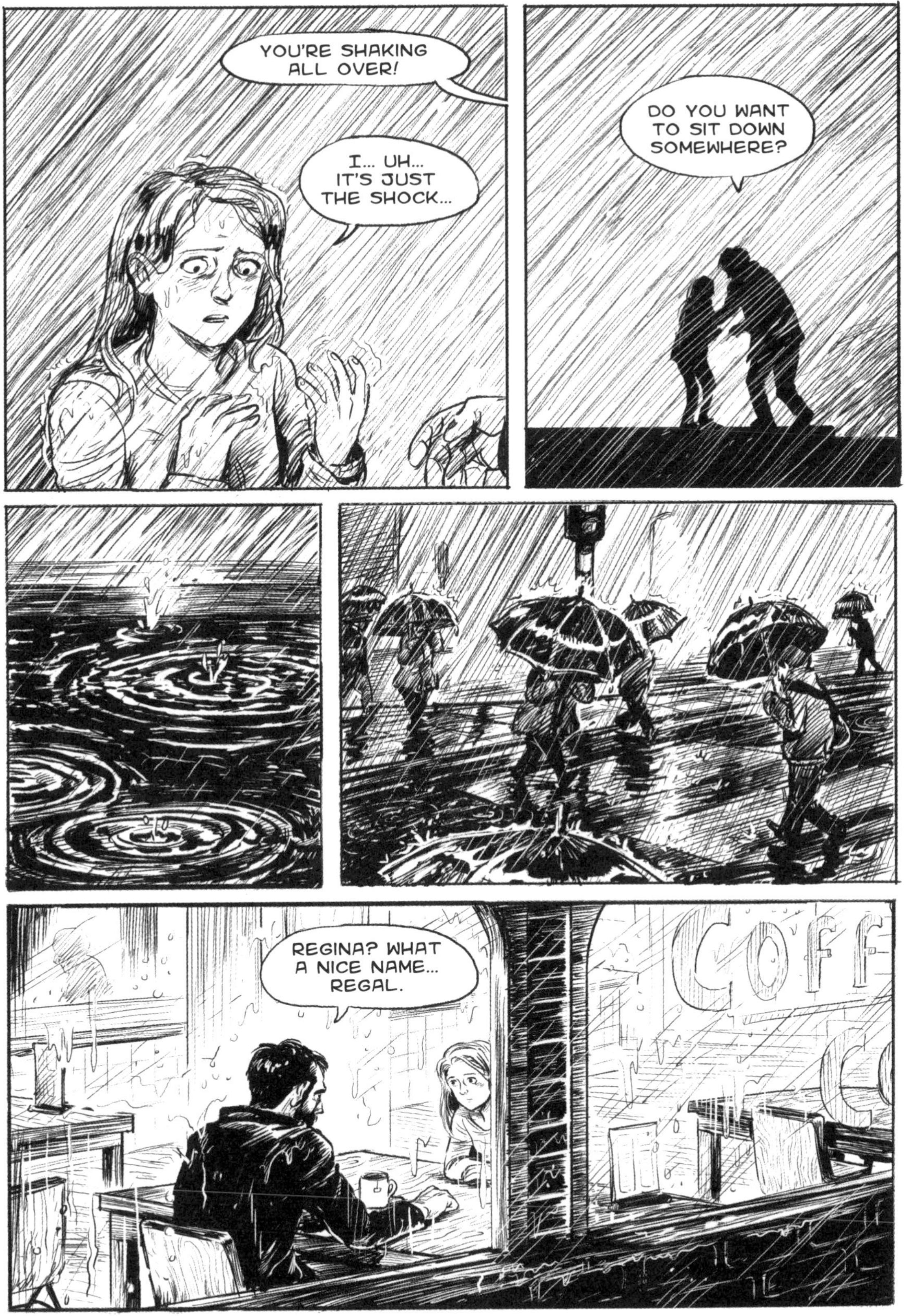
YOU'RE SHAKING ALL OVER!
I... UH... IT'S JUST THE SHOCK...
DO YOU WANT TO SIT DOWN SOMEWHERE?
REGINA? WHAT A NICE NAME... REGAL.

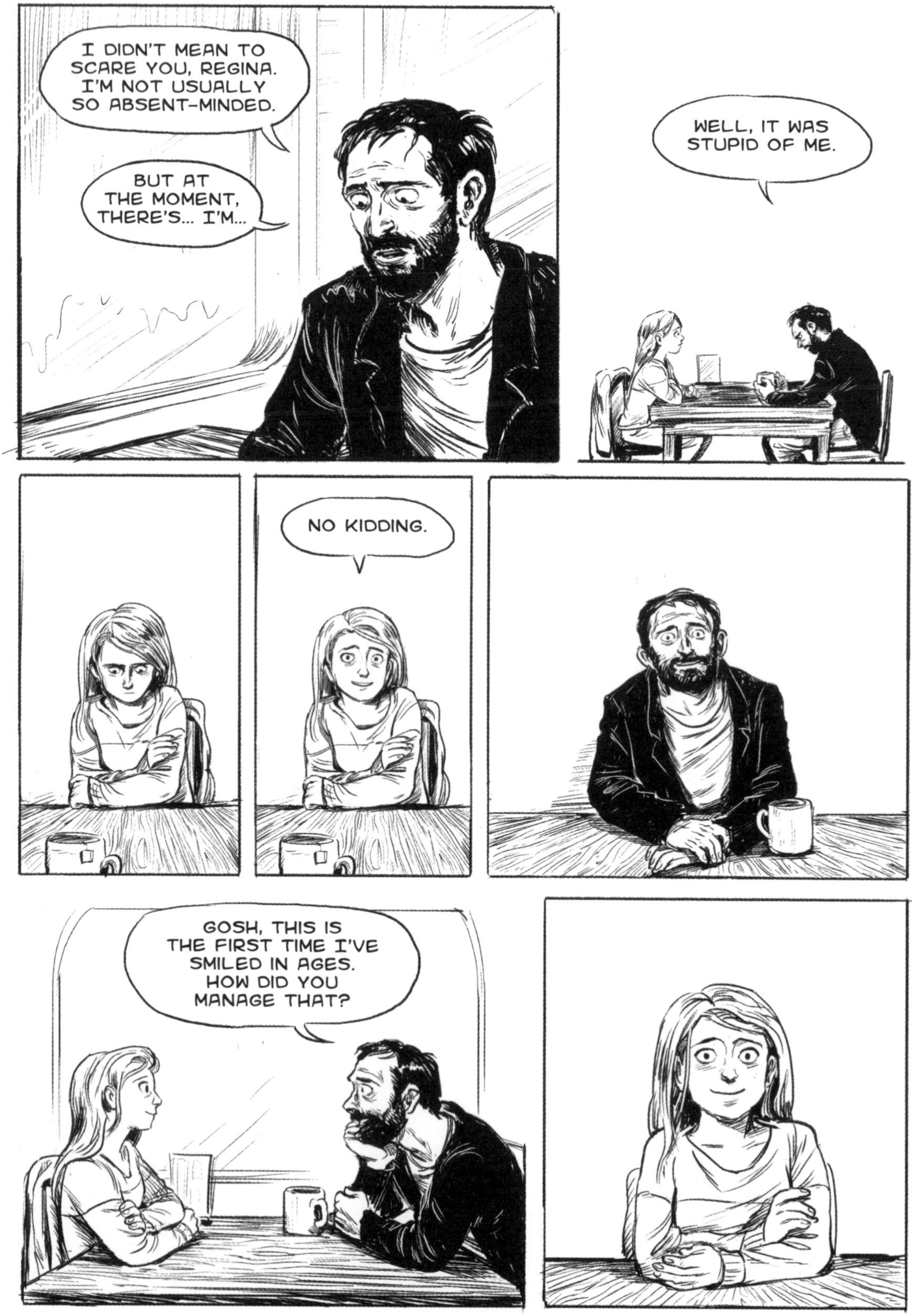
I DIDN'T MEAN TO SCARE YOU, REGINA. I'M NOT USUALLY SO ABSENT-MINDED.
BUT AT THE MOMENT, THERE'S... I'M...
WELL, IT WAS STUPID OF ME.
NO KIDDING.
GOSH, THIS IS THE FIRST TIME I'VE SMILED IN AGES. HOW DID YOU MANAGE THAT?

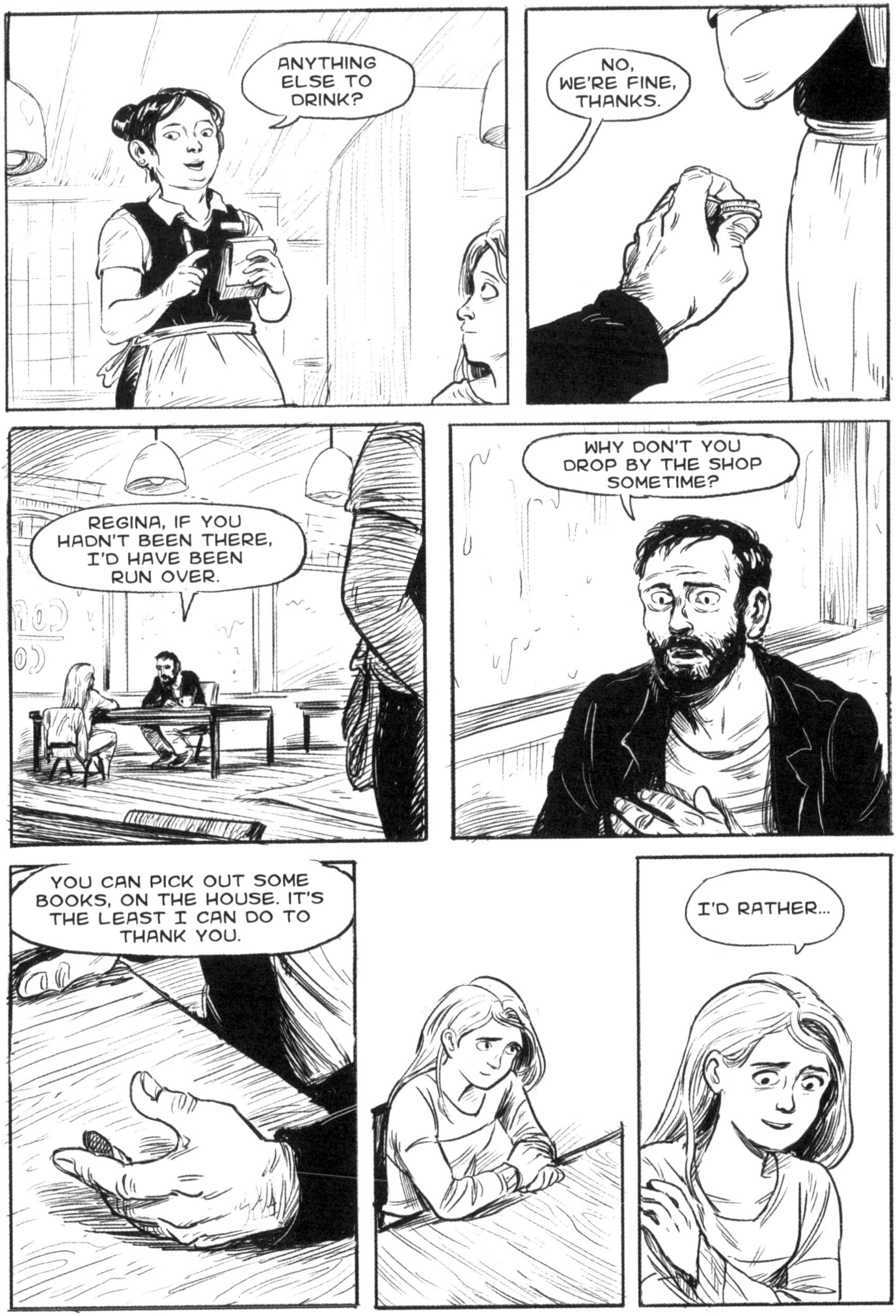
ANYTHING ELSE TO DRINK?
NO, WE'RE FINE, THANKS.
REGINA, IF YOU HADN'T BEEN THERE, I'D HAVE BEEN RUN OVER.
WHY DON'T YOU DROP BY THE SHOP SOMETIME?
YOU CAN PICK OUT SOME BOOKS, ON THE HOUSE. IT'S THE LEAST I CAN DO TO THANK YOU.
I'D RATHER...

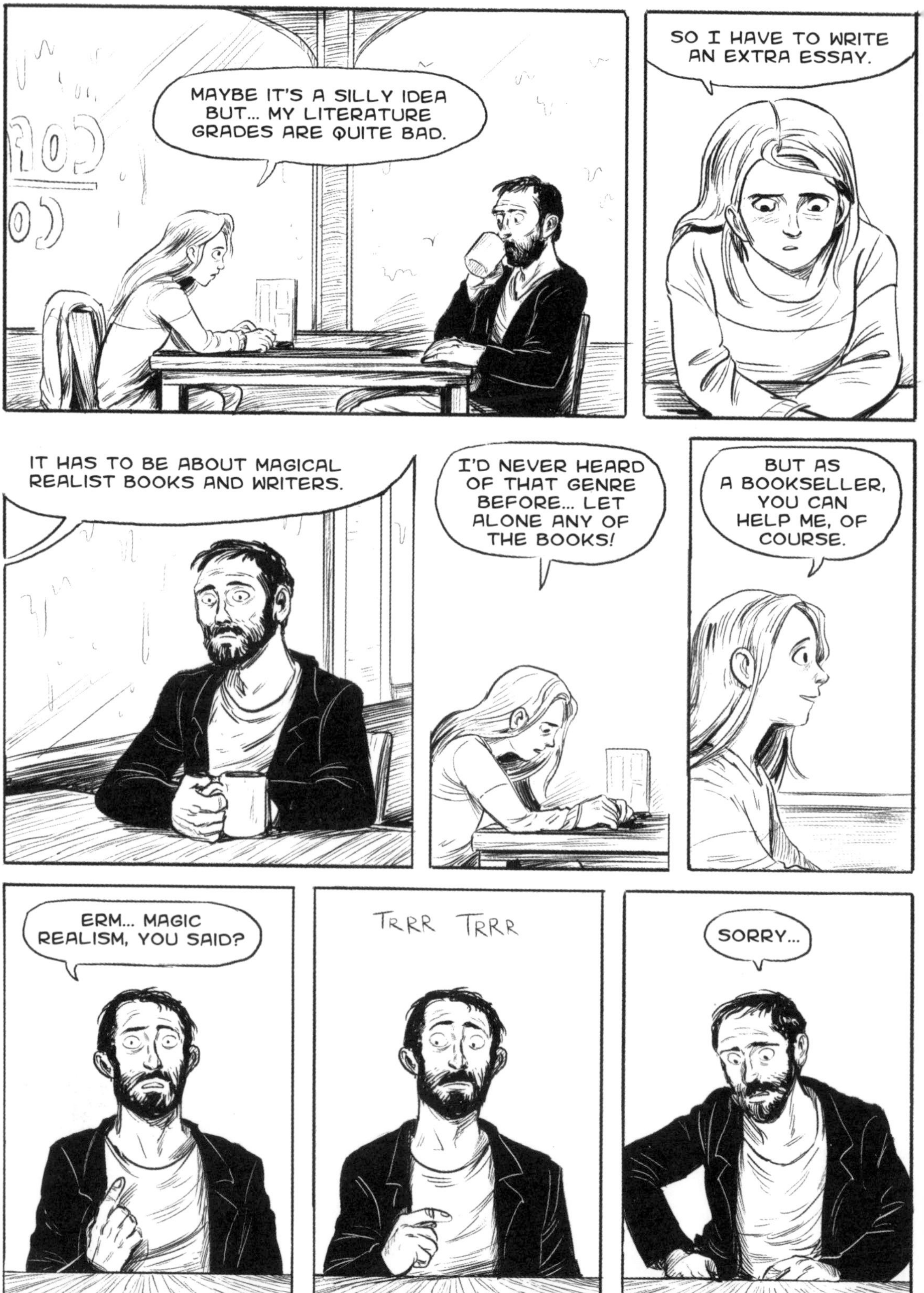
MAYBE IT'S A SILLY IDEA BUT... MY LITERATURE GRADES ARE QUITE BAD.
SO I HAVE TO WRITE AN EXTRA ESSAY.
IT HAS TO BE ABOUT MAGICAL REALIST BOOKS AND WRITERS.
I'D NEVER HEARD OF THAT GENRE BEFORE... LET ALONE ANY OF THE BOOKS!
BUT AS A BOOKSELLER, YOU CAN HELP ME, OF COURSE.
ERM... MAGIC REALISM, YOU SAID?
TRRR TRRR
SORRY...

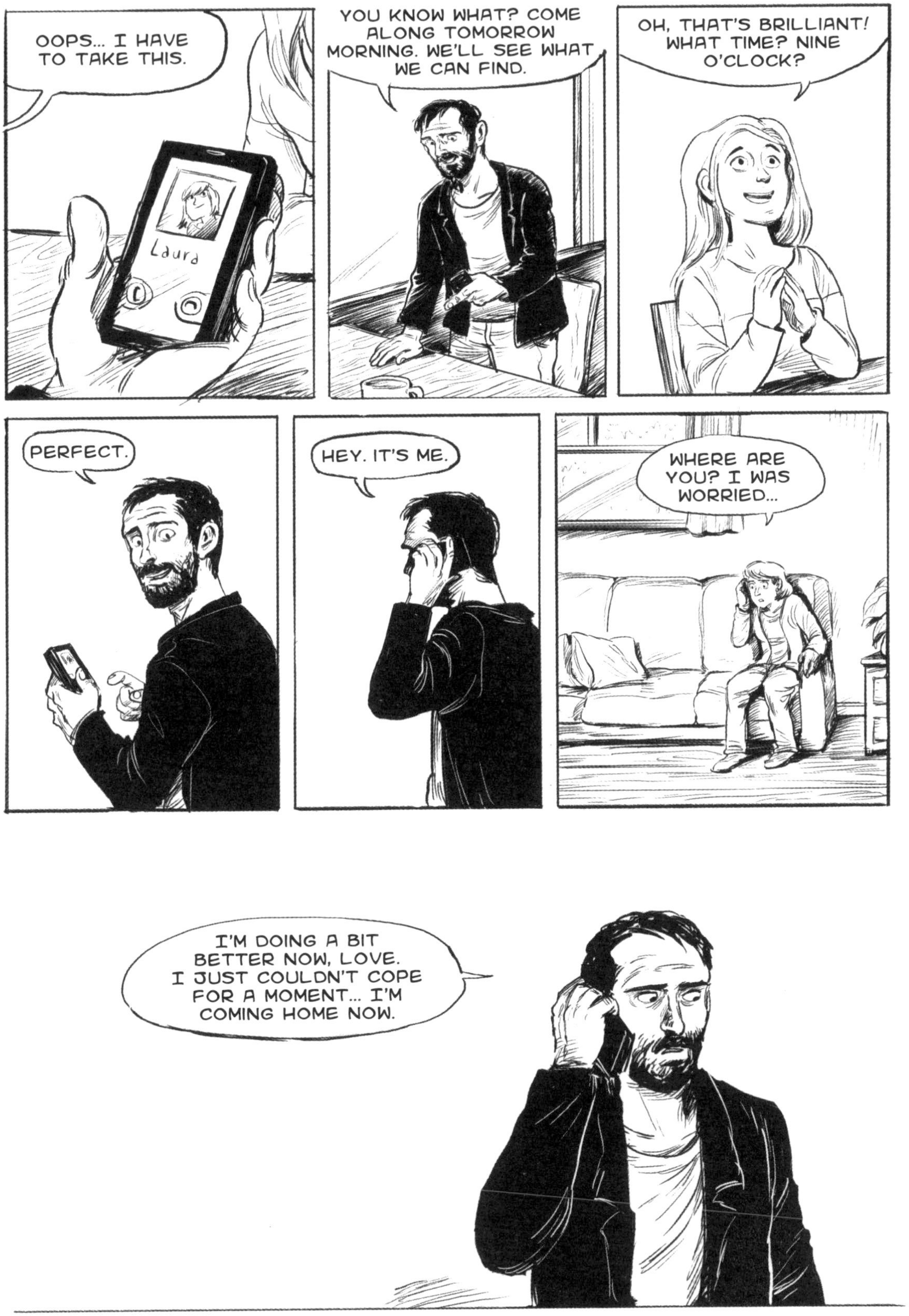
OOPS... I HAVE TO TAKE THIS.
Laura
YOU KNOW WHAT? COME ALONG TOMORROW MORNING. WE'LL SEE WHAT WE CAN FIND.
OH, THAT'S BRILLIANT! WHAT TIME? NINE O'CLOCK?
PERFECT.
HEY. IT'S ME.
WHERE ARE YOU? I WAS WORRIED...
I'M DOING A BIT BETTER NOW, LOVE. I JUST COULDN'T COPE FOR A MOMENT... I'M COMING HOME NOW.

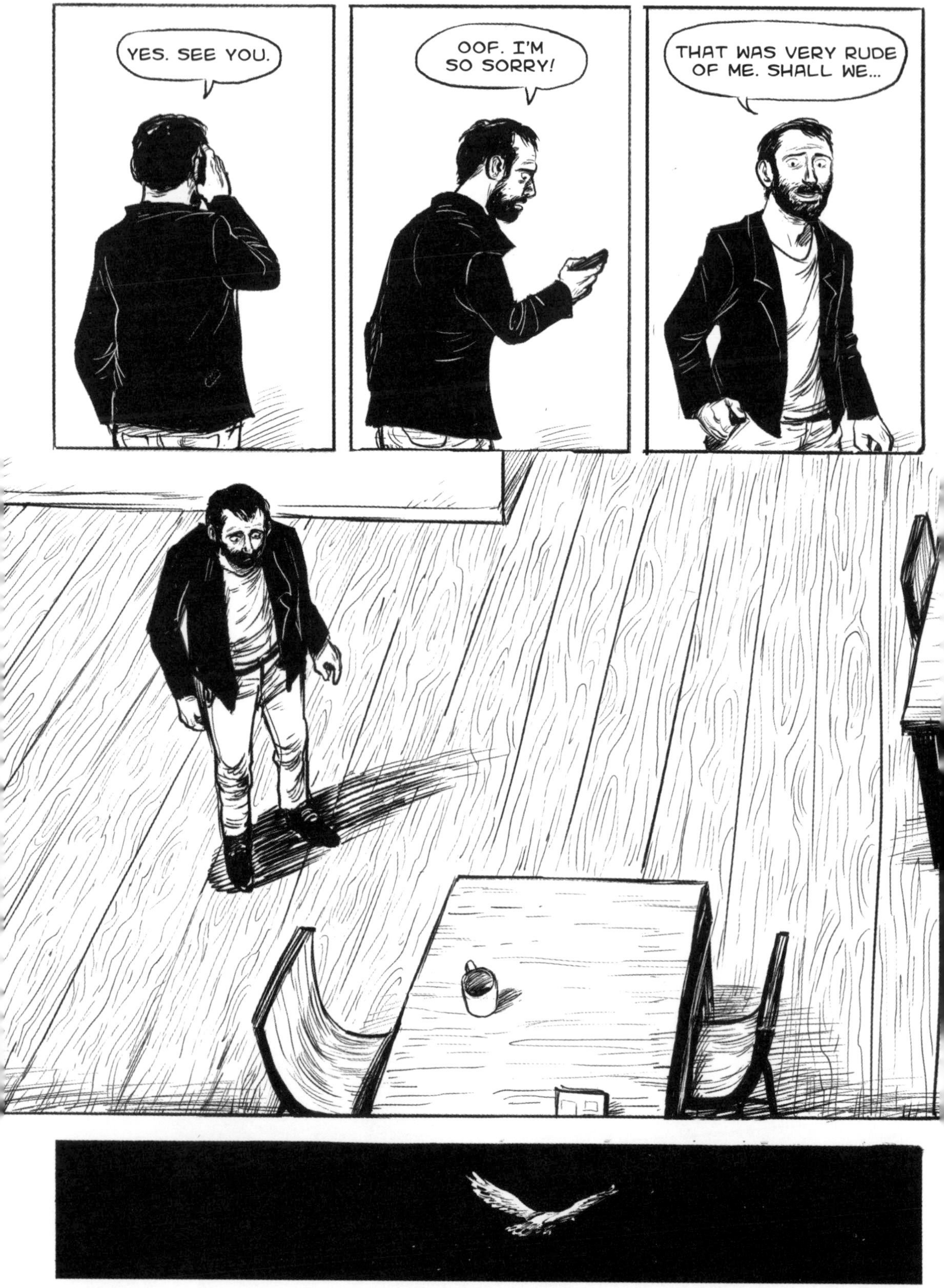
YES. SEE YOU.
OOF. I'M SO SORRY!
THAT WAS VERY RUDE OF ME. SHALL WE...

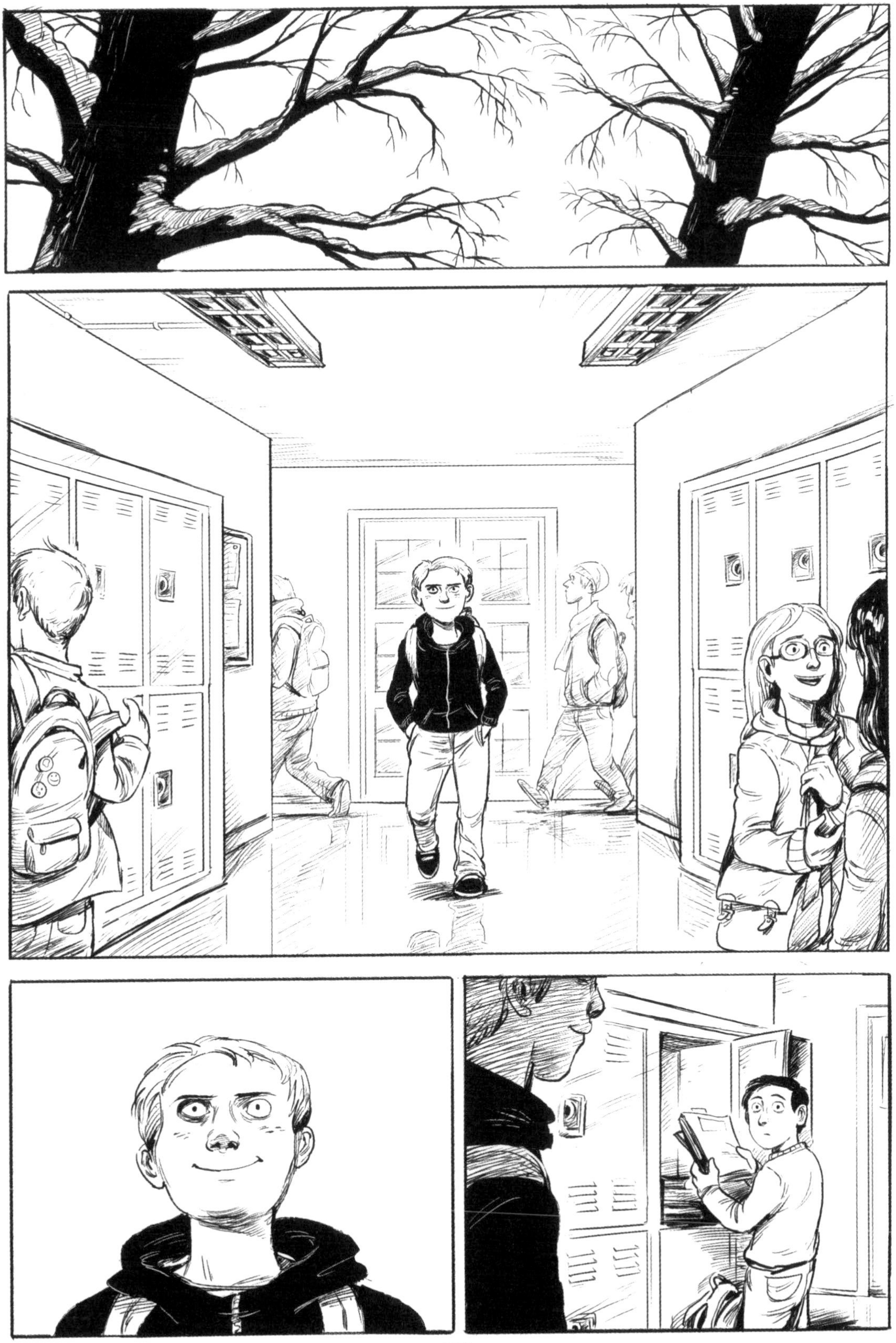

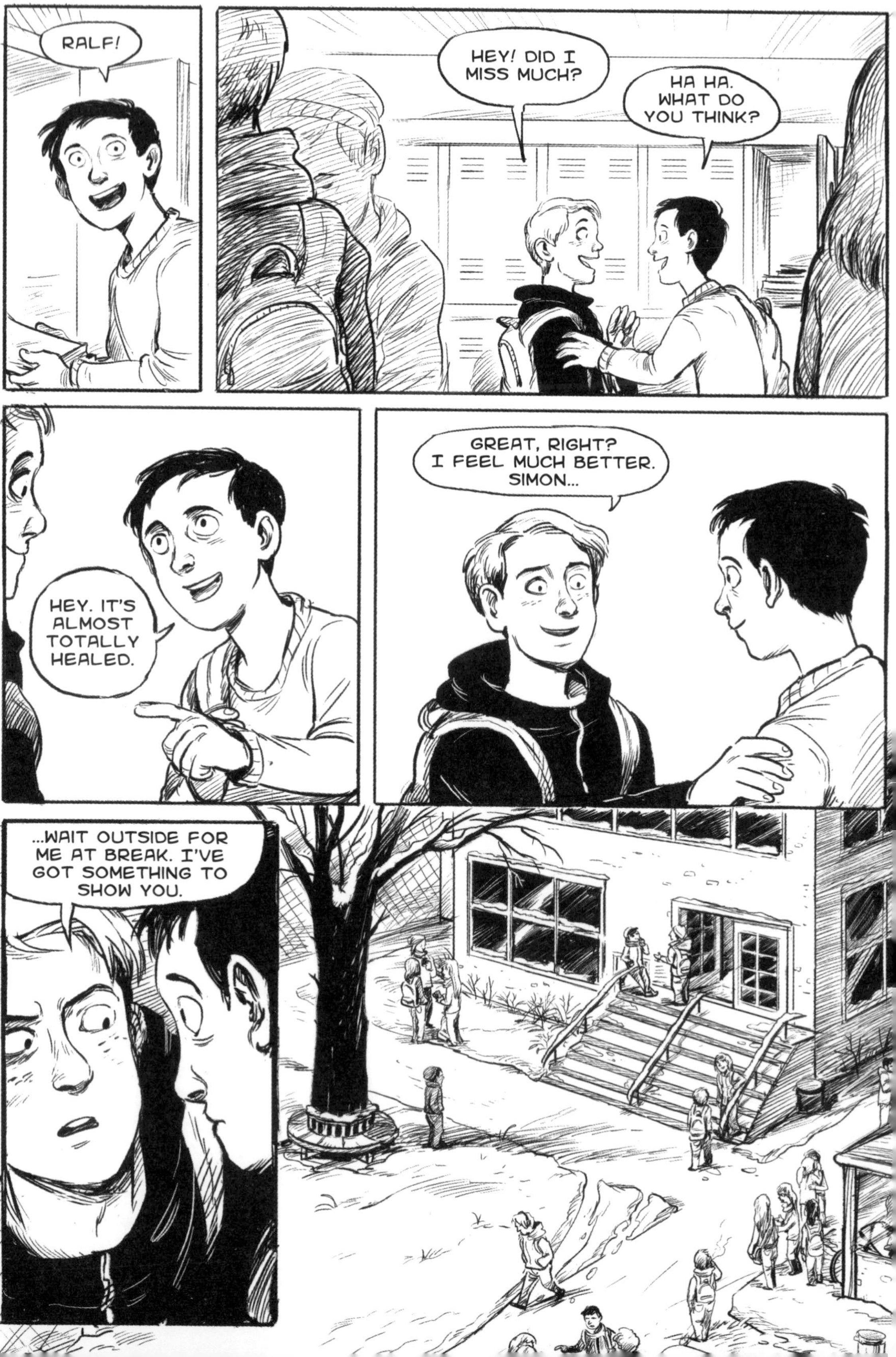
RALF!
HEY! DID I MISS MUCH?
HA HA. WHAT DO YOU THINK?
HEY. IT'S ALMOST TOTALLY HEALED.
GREAT, RIGHT? I FEEL MUCH BETTER. SIMON...
...WAIT OUTSIDE FOR ME AT BREAK. I'VE GOT SOMETHING TO SHOW YOU.

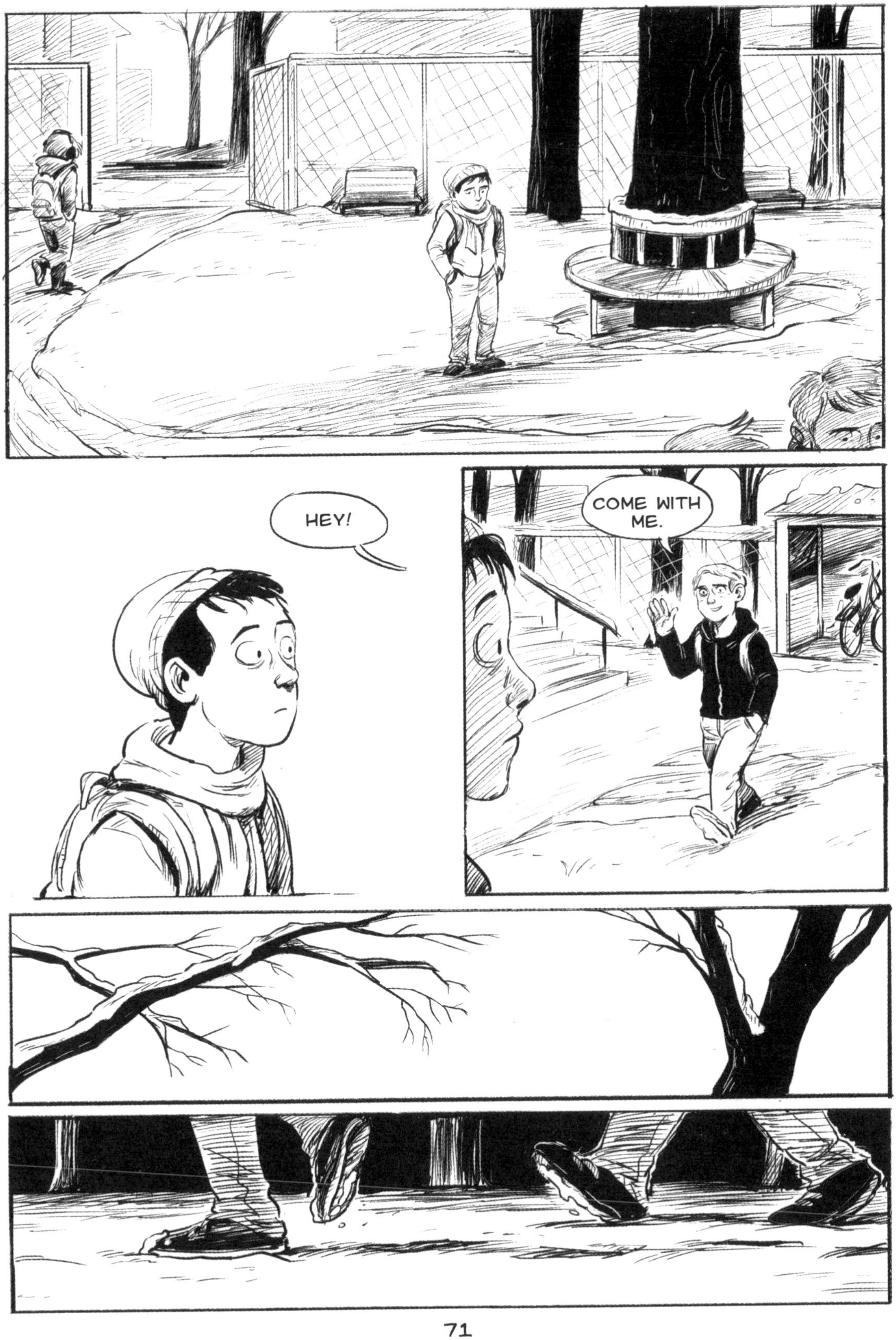
HEY!
COME WITH ME.

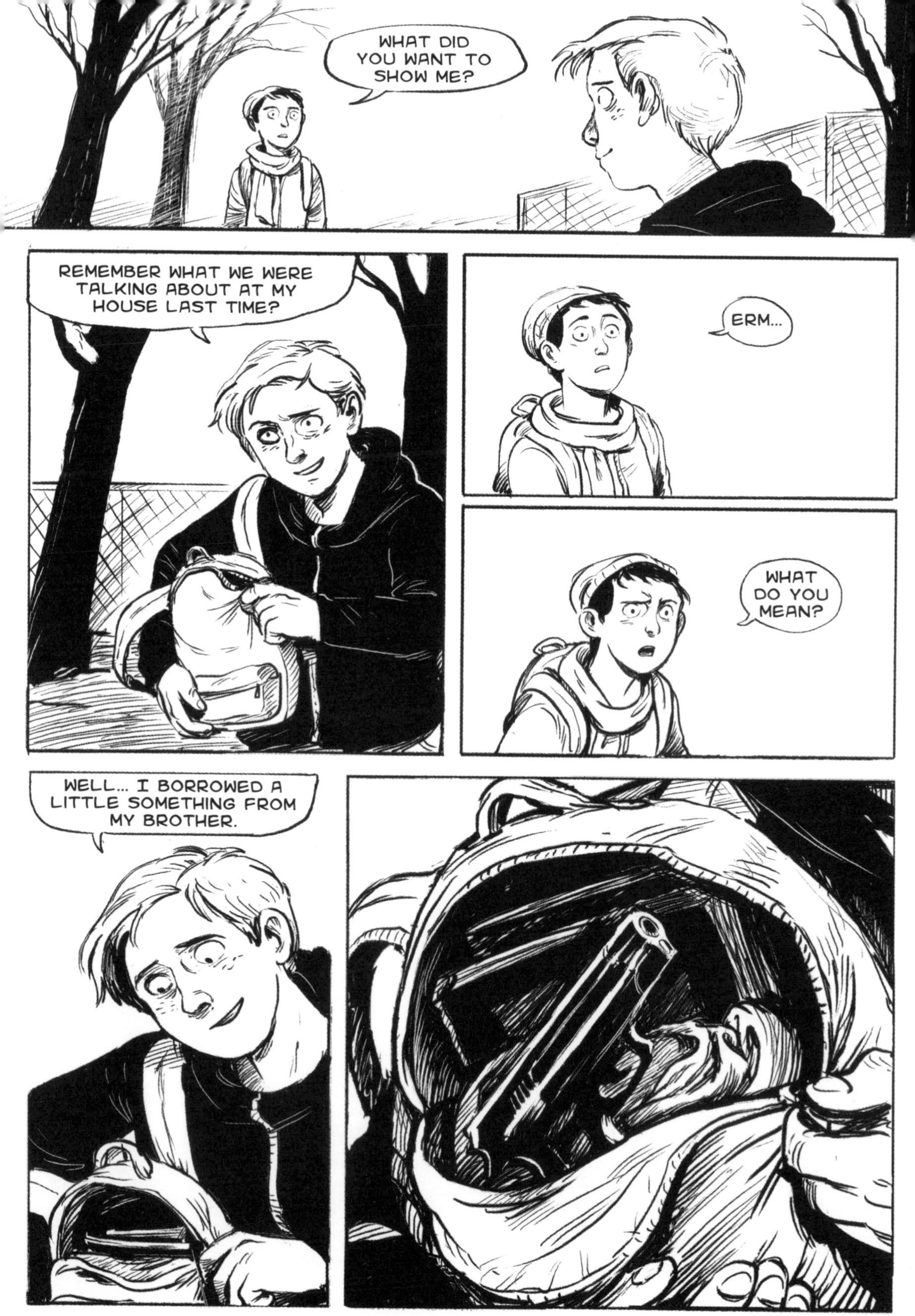
WHAT DID YOU WANT TO SHOW ME?
REMEMBER WHAT WE WERE TALKING ABOUT AT MY HOUSE LAST TIME?
ERM...
WHAT DO YOU MEAN?
WELL... I BORROWED A LITTLE SOMETHING FROM MY BROTHER.

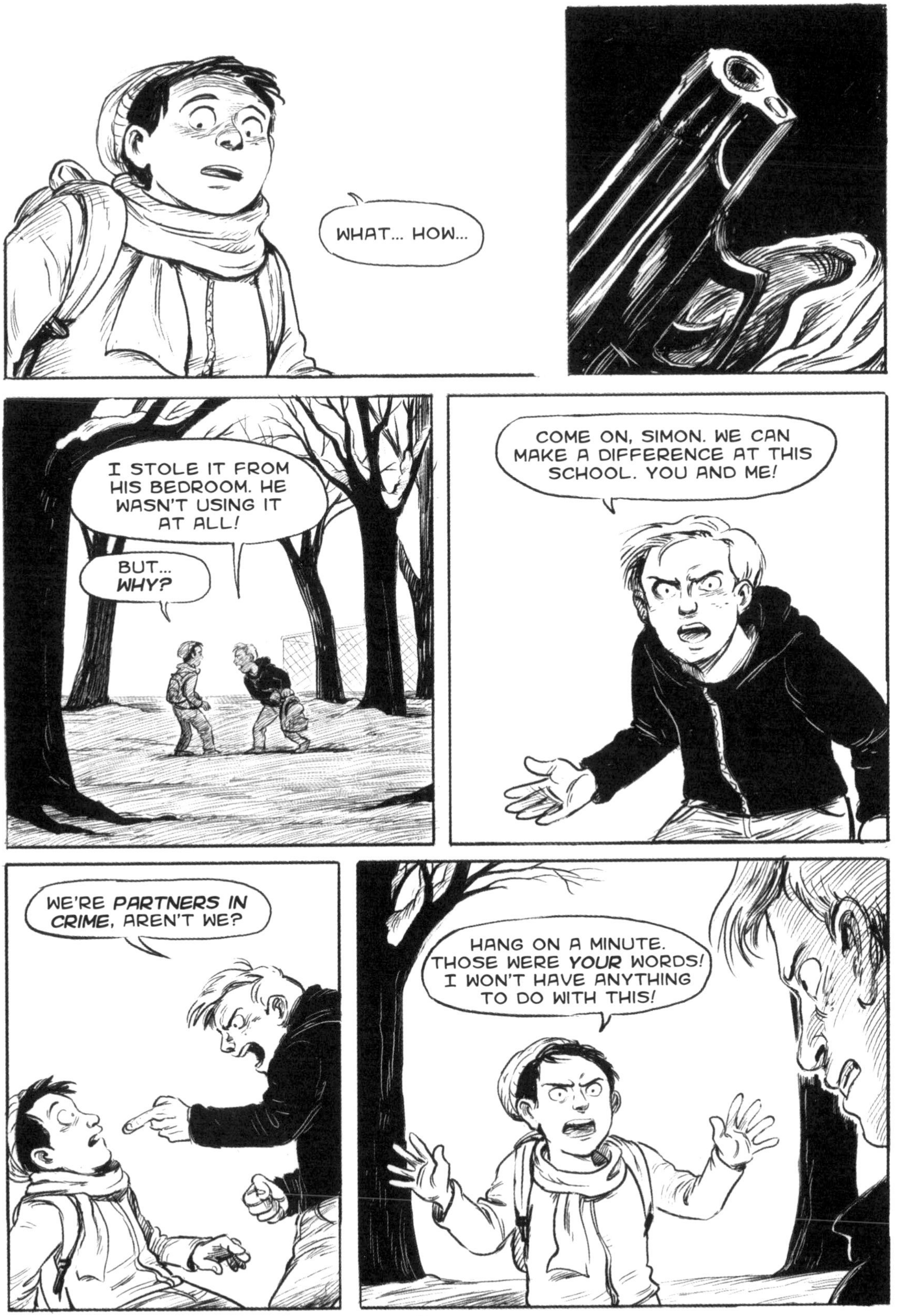
WHAT... HOW...
I STOLE IT FROM HIS BEDROOM. HE WASN'T USING IT AT ALL!
BUT... WHY?
COME ON, SIMON. WE CAN MAKE A DIFFERENCE AT THIS SCHOOL. YOU AND ME!
WE'RE PARTNERS IN CRIME, AREN'T WE?
HANG ON A MINUTE. THOSE WERE YOUR WORDS! I WON'T HAVE ANYTHING TO DO WITH THIS!

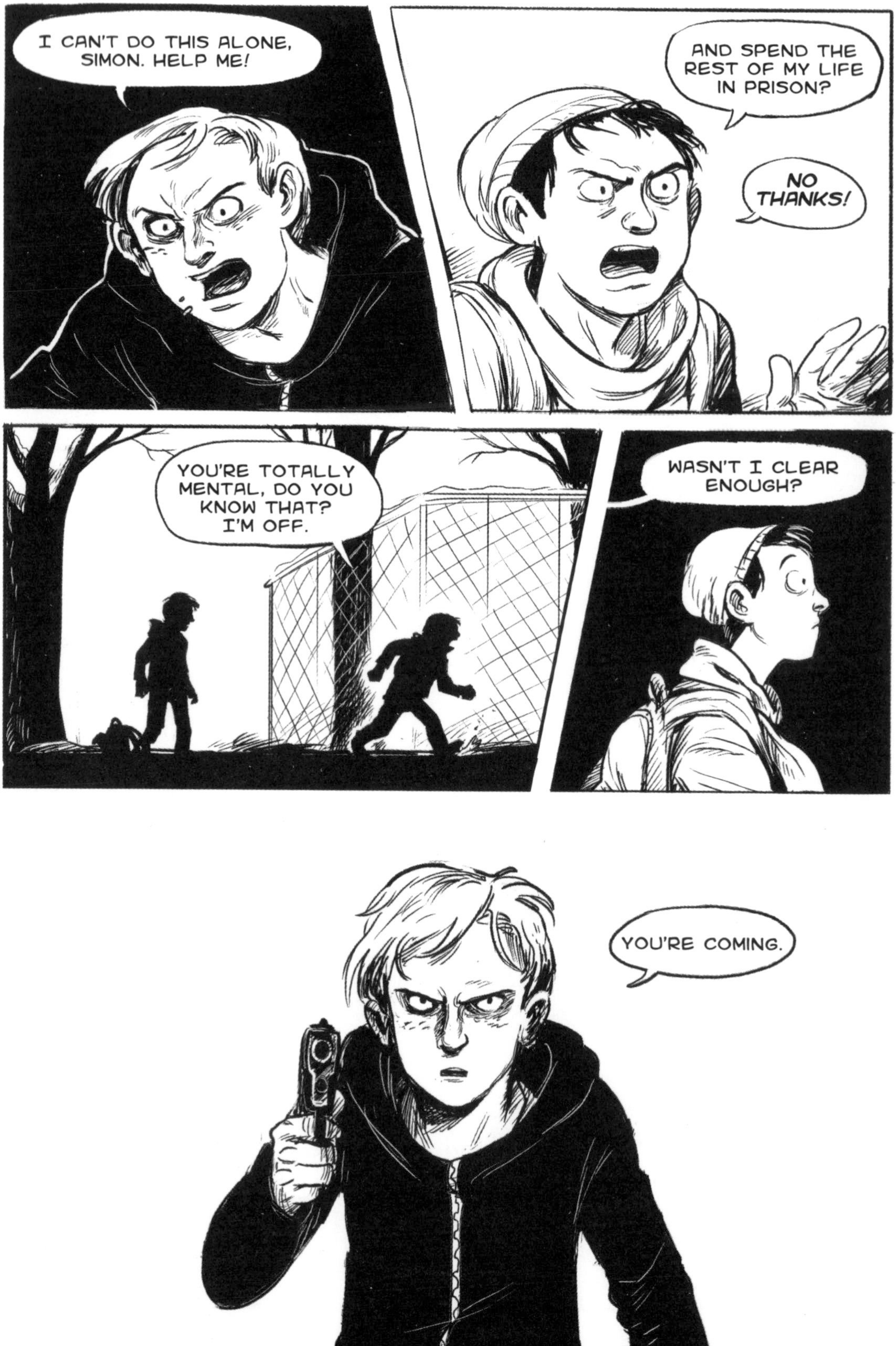
I CAN'T DO THIS ALONE, SIMON. HELP ME!
AND SPEND THE REST OF MY LIFE IN PRISON?
NO THANKS!
YOU'RE TOTALLY MENTAL, DO YOU KNOW THAT? I'M OFF.
WASN'T I CLEAR ENOUGH?
YOU'RE COMING.

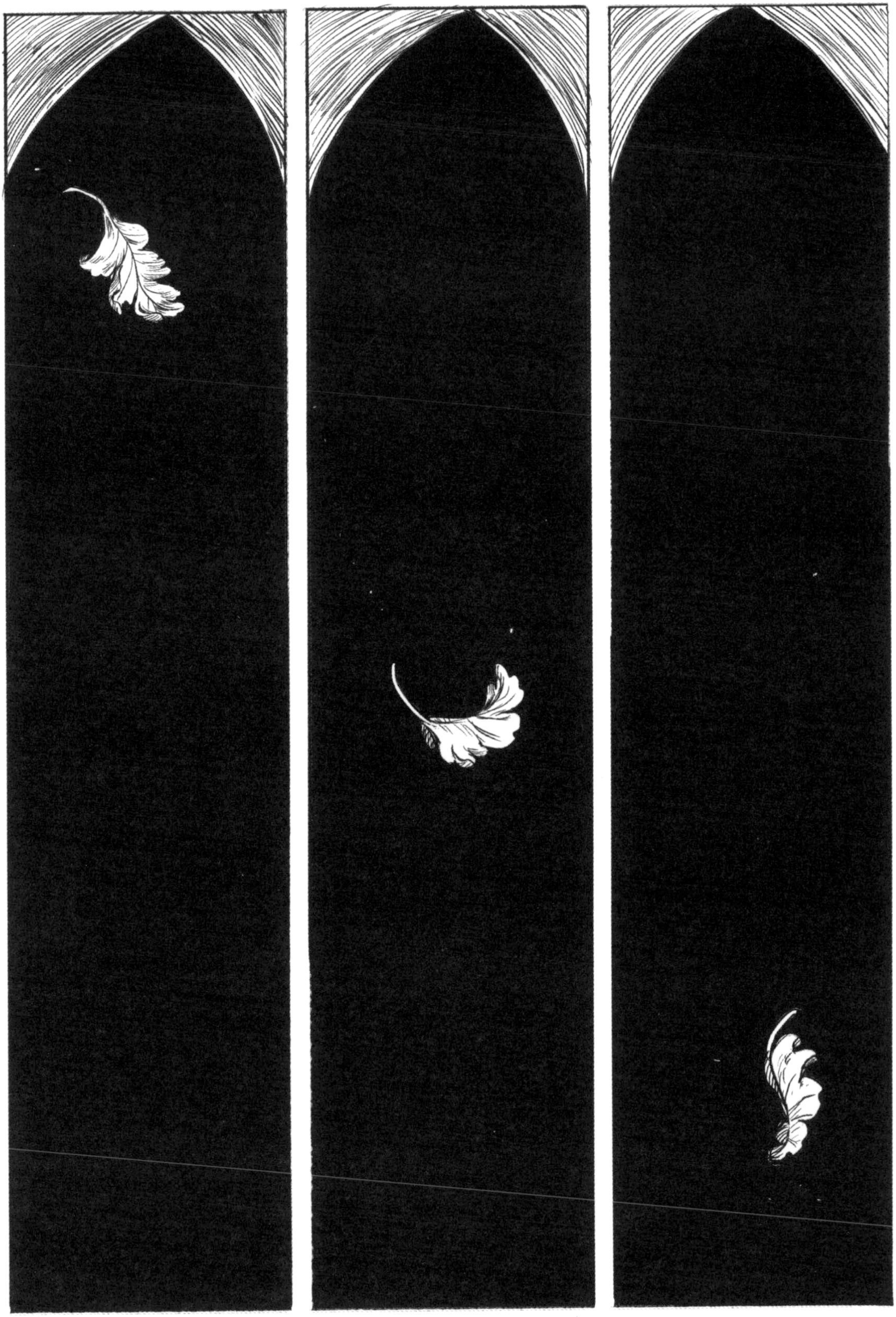

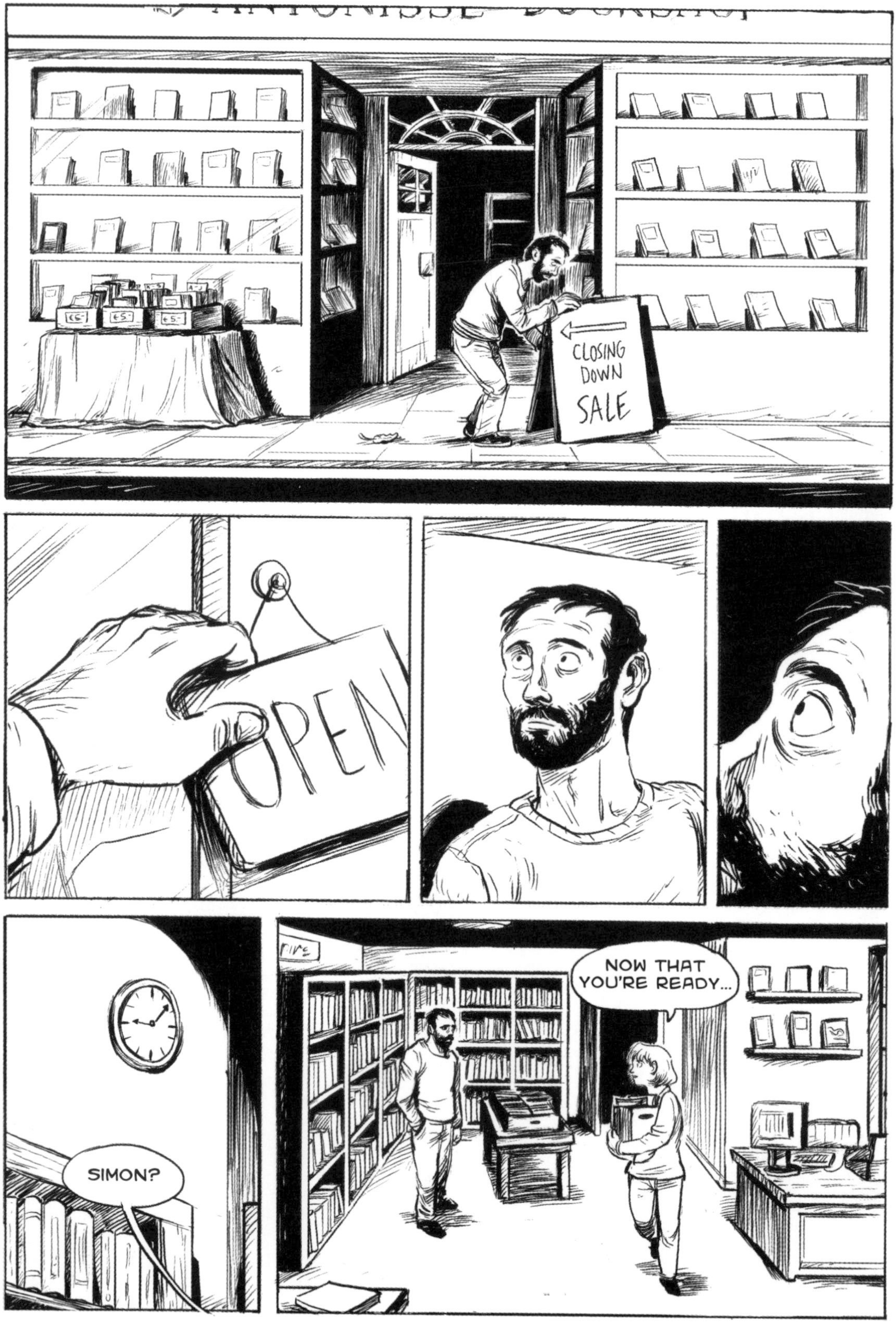
CLOSING DOWN SALE
OPEN
SIMON?
NOW THAT YOU'RE READY...

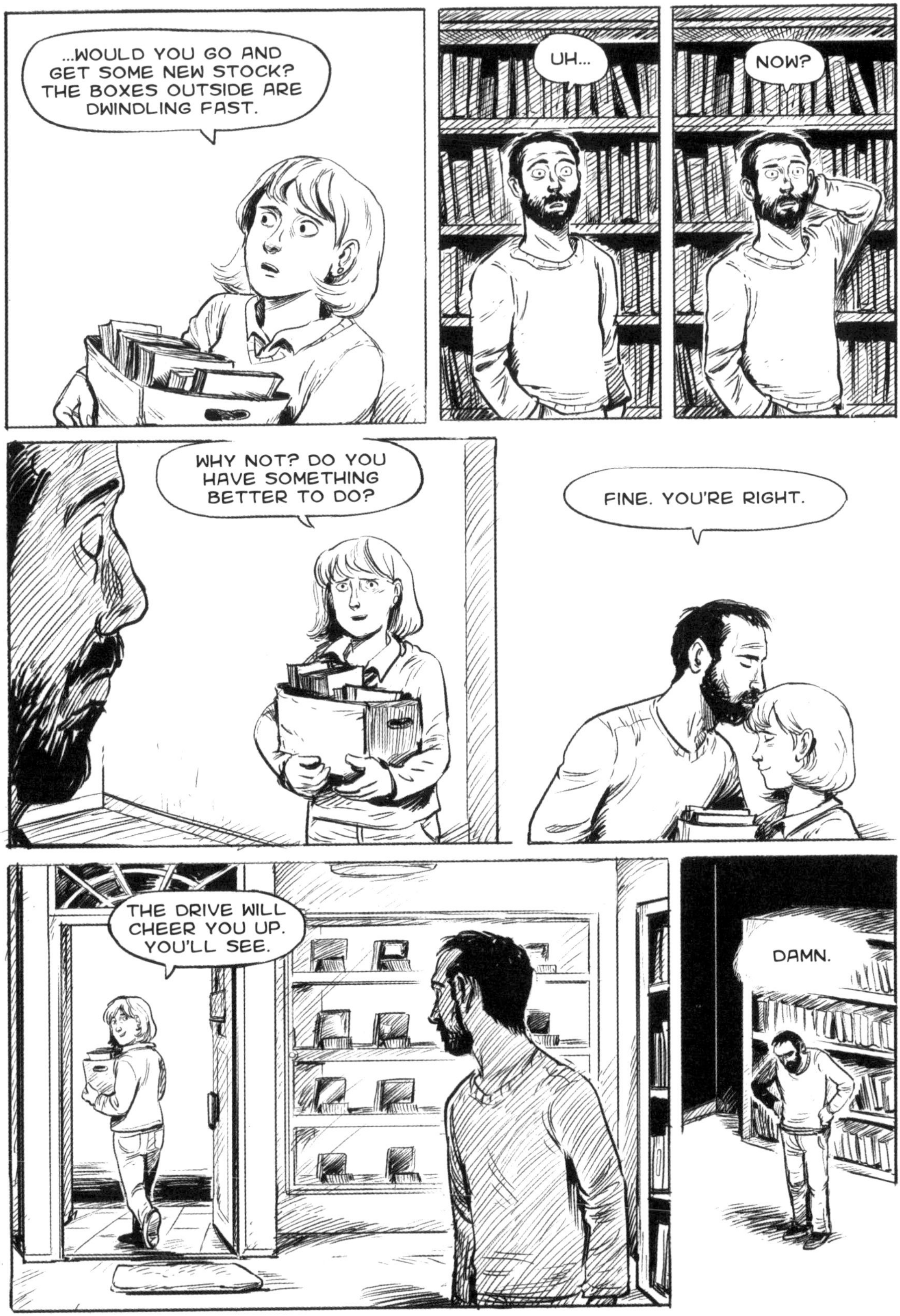
...WOULD YOU GO AND GET SOME NEW STOCK? THE BOXES OUTSIDE ARE DWINDLING FAST.
UH...
NOW?
WHY NOT? DO YOU HAVE SOMETHING BETTER TO DO?
FINE. YOU'RE RIGHT.
THE DRIVE WILL CHEER YOU UP. YOU'LL SEE.
DAMN.

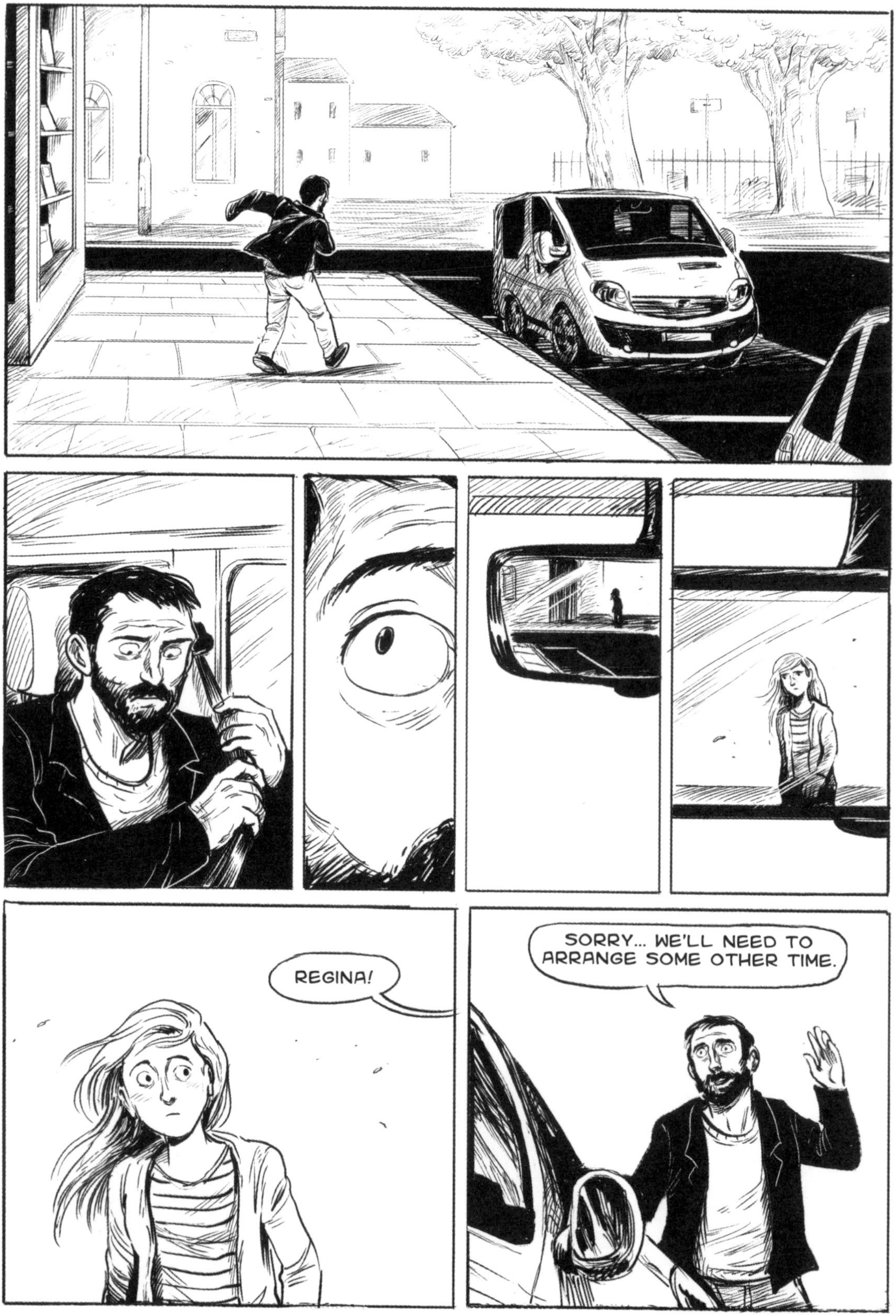
REGINA!
SORRY... WE'LL NEED TO ARRANGE SOME OTHER TIME.

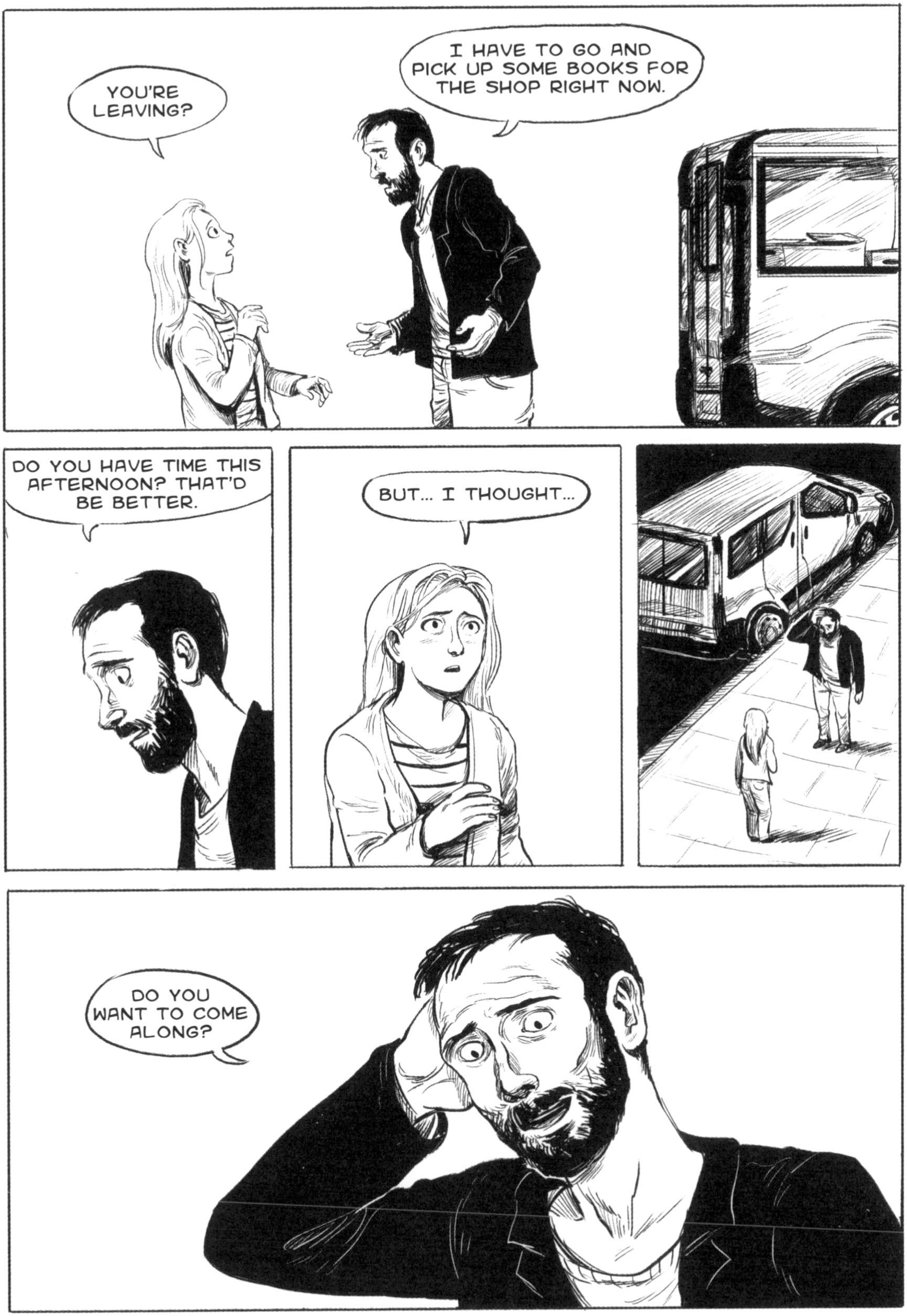
YOU'RE LEAVING?
I HAVE TO GO AND PICK UP SOME BOOKS FOR THE SHOP RIGHT NOW.
DO YOU HAVE TIME THIS AFTERNOON? THAT'D BE BETTER.
BUT... I THOUGHT...
DO YOU WANT TO COME ALONG?

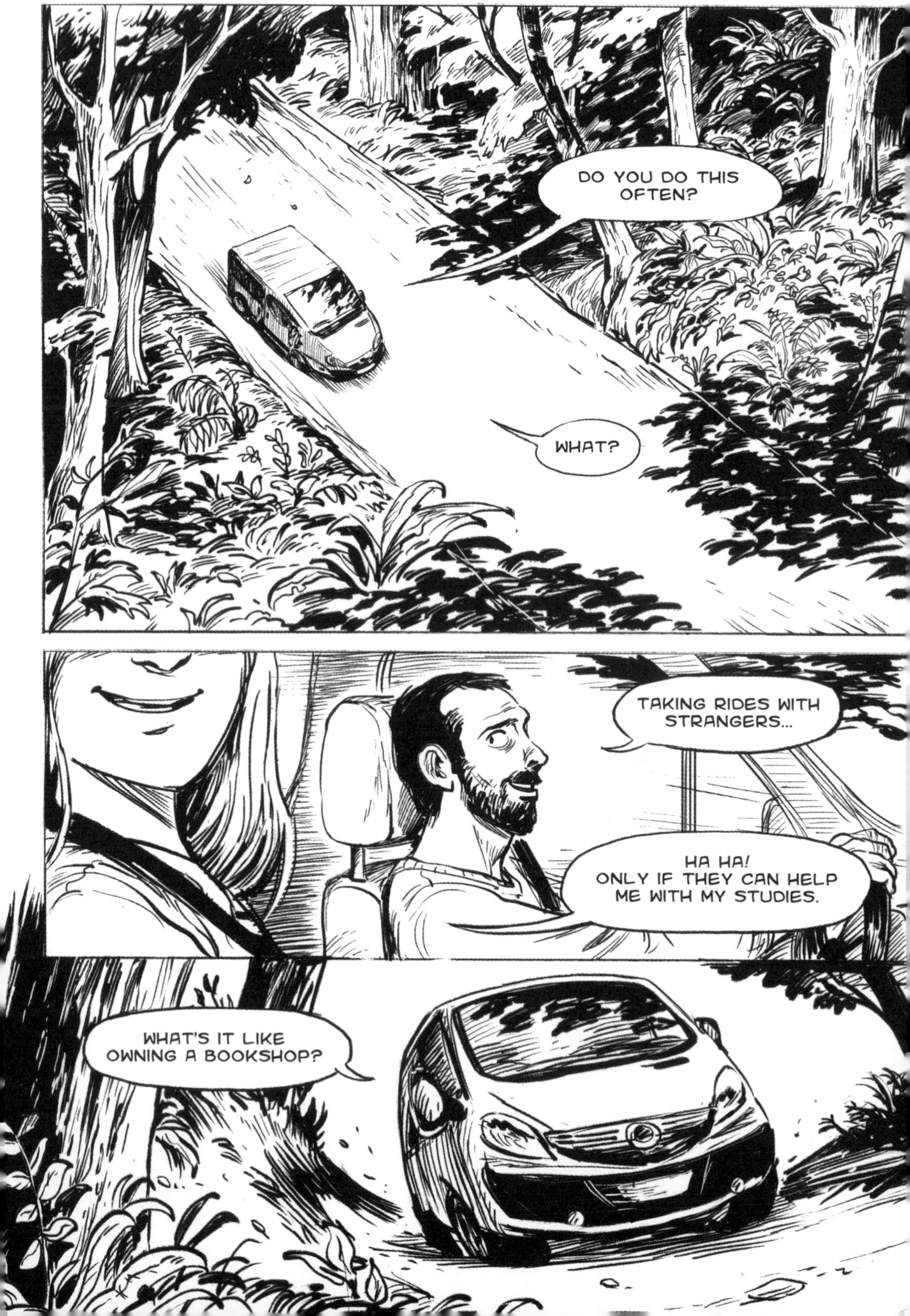
DO YOU DO THIS OFTEN?
WHAT?
TAKING RIDES WITH STRANGERS...
HA HA! ONLY IF THEY CAN HELP ME WITH MY STUDIES.
WHAT'S IT LIKE OWNING A BOOKSHOP?

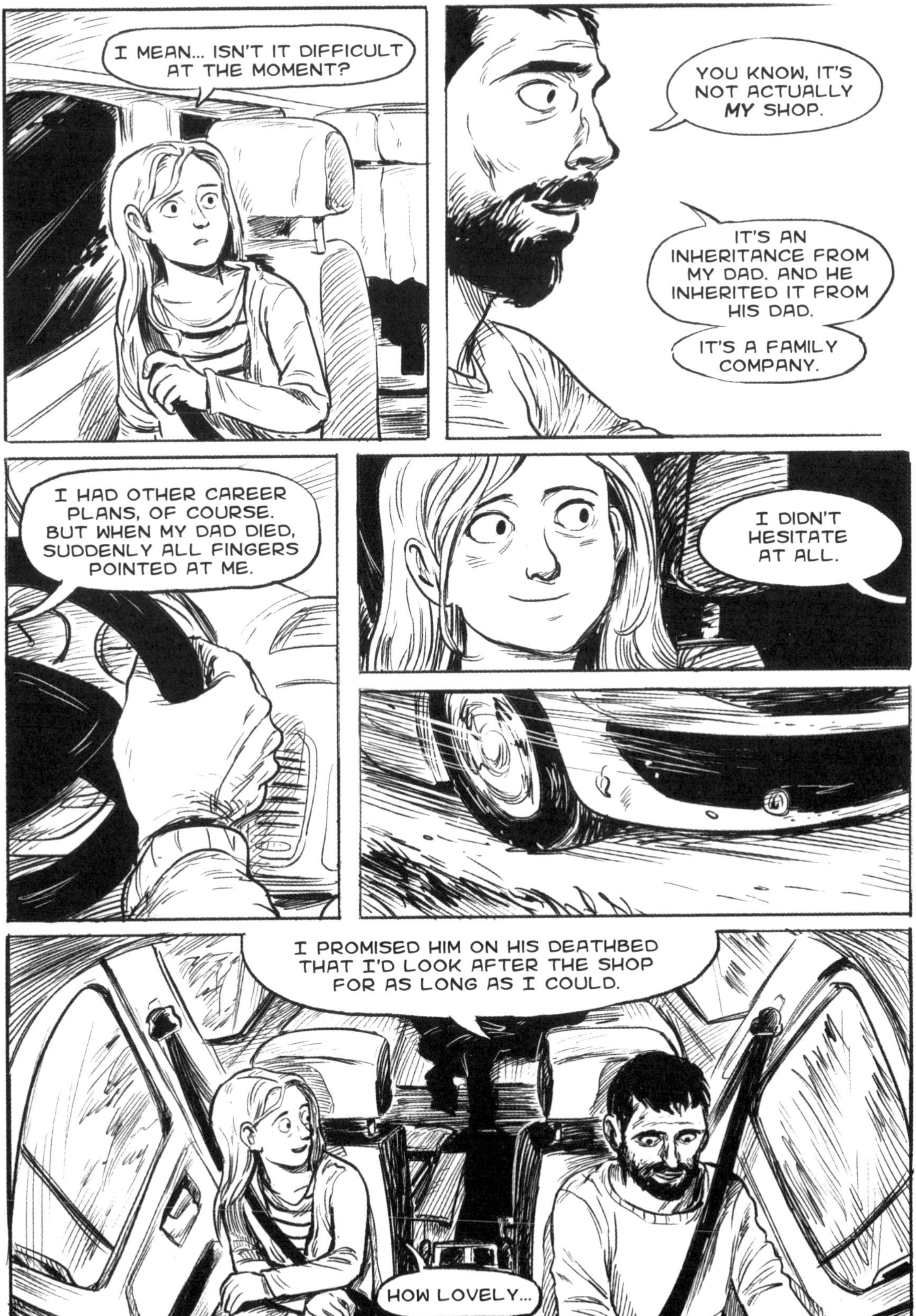
I MEAN... ISN'T IT DIFFICULT AT THE MOMENT?
YOU KNOW, IT'S NOT ACTUALLY MY SHOP.
IT'S AN INHERITANCE FROM MY DAD. AND HE INHERITED IT FROM HIS DAD.
IT'S A FAMILY COMPANY.
I HAD OTHER CAREER PLANS, OF COURSE. BUT WHEN MY DAD DIED, SUDDENLY ALL FINGERS POINTED AT ME.
I DIDN'T HESITATE AT ALL.
I PROMISED HIM ON HIS DEATHBED THAT I'D LOOK AFTER THE SHOP FOR AS LONG AS I COULD.
HOW LOVELY...

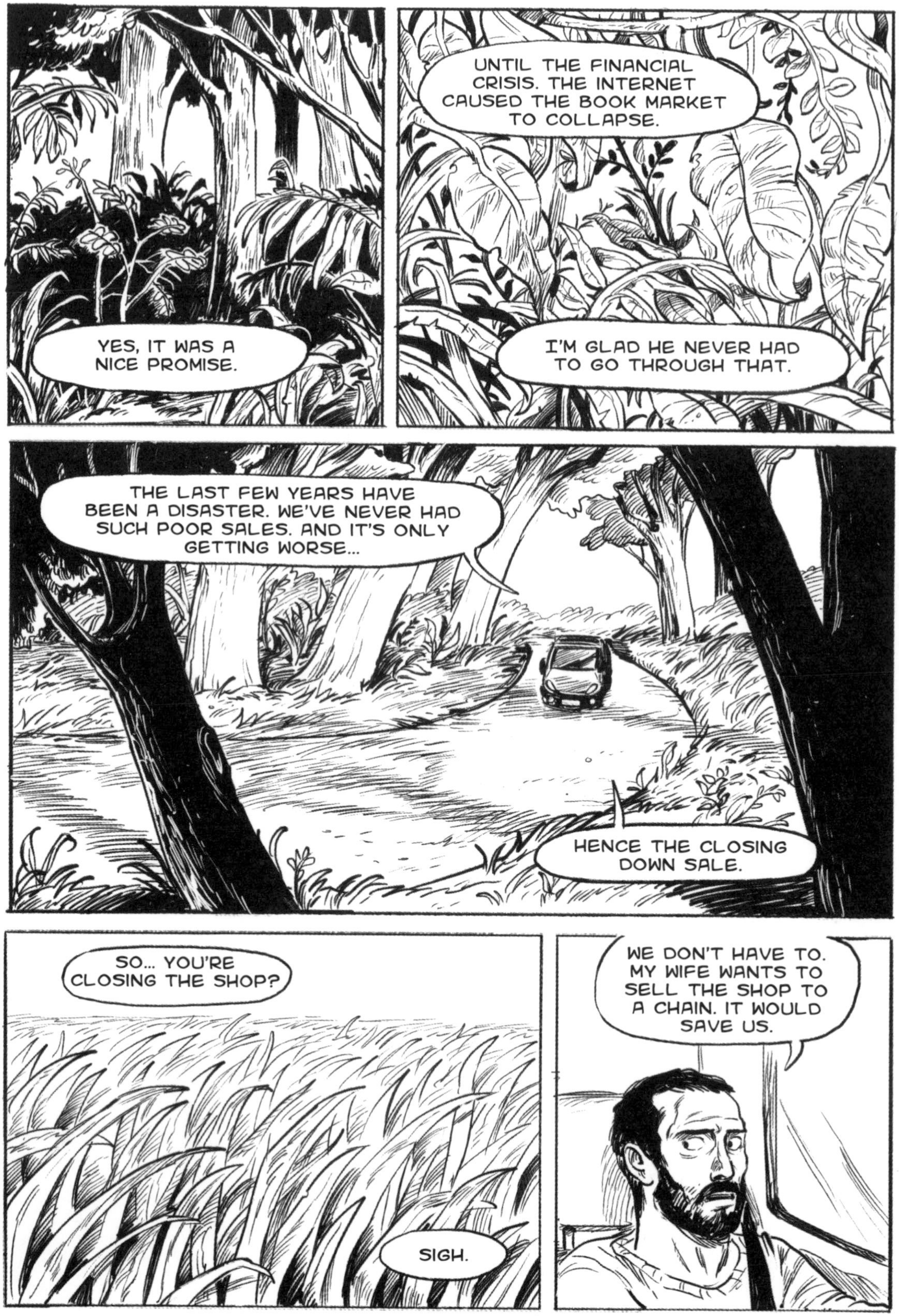
YES, IT WAS A NICE PROMISE.
UNTIL THE FINANCIAL CRISIS. THE INTERNET CAUSED THE BOOK MARKET TO COLLAPSE.
I'M GLAD HE NEVER HAD TO GO THROUGH THAT.
THE LAST FEW YEARS HAVE BEEN A DISASTER. WE'VE NEVER HAD SUCH POOR SALES. AND IT'S ONLY GETTING WORSE...
HENCE THE CLOSING DOWN SALE.
SO... YOU'RE CLOSING THE SHOP?
SIGH.
WE DON'T HAVE TO. MY WIFE WANTS TO SELL THE SHOP TO A CHAIN. IT WOULD SAVE US.

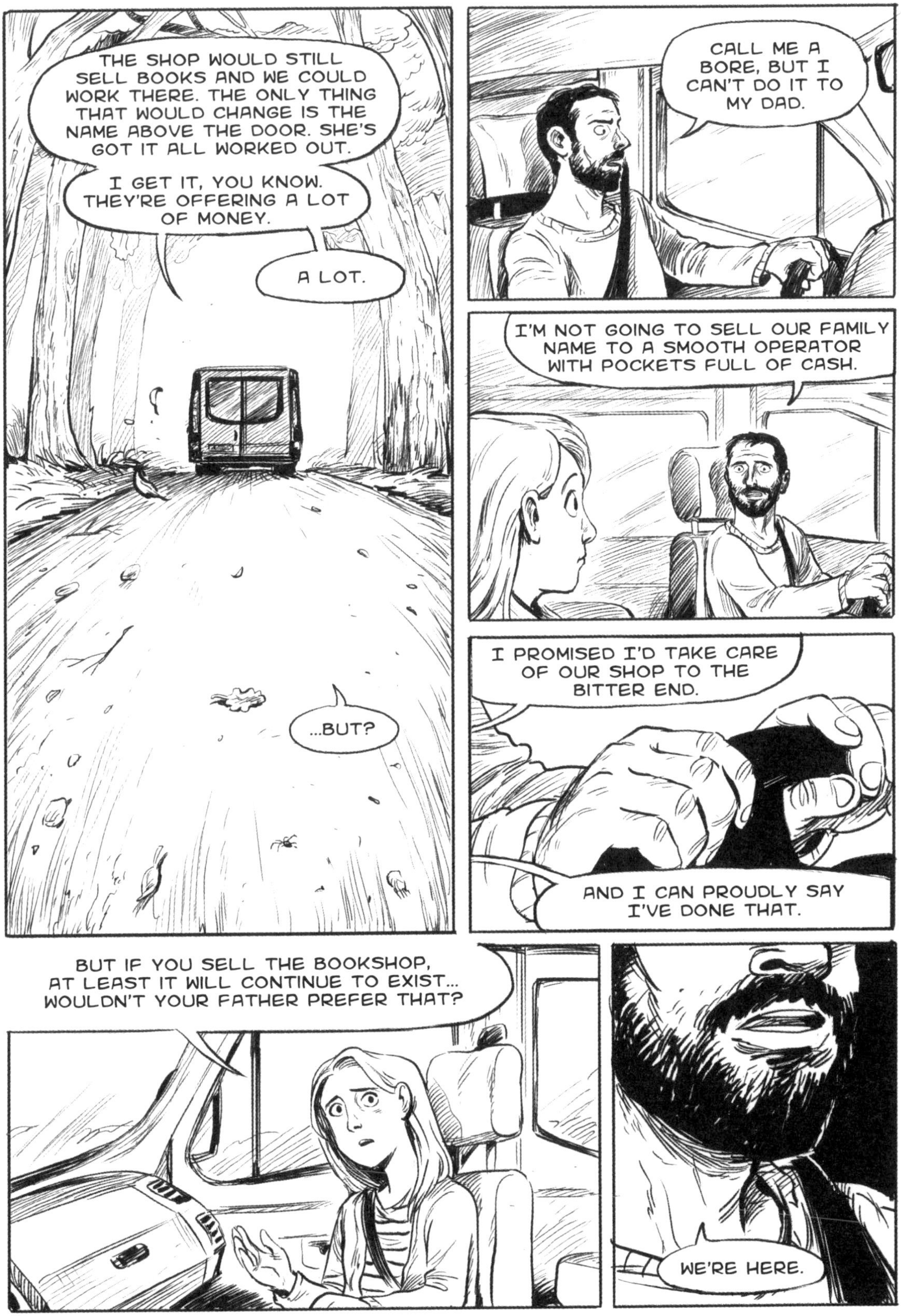
THE SHOP WOULD STILL SELL BOOKS AND WE COULD WORK THERE. THE ONLY THING THAT WOULD CHANGE IS THE NAME ABOVE THE DOOR. SHE'S GOT IT ALL WORKED OUT.
I GET IT, YOU KNOW. THEY'RE OFFERING A LOT OF MONEY.
A LOT.
...BUT?
CALL ME A BORE, BUT I CAN'T DO IT TO MY DAD.
I'M NOT GOING TO SELL OUR FAMILY NAME TO A SMOOTH OPERATOR WITH POCKETS FULL OF CASH.
I PROMISED I'D TAKE CARE OF OUR SHOP TO THE BITTER END.
AND I CAN PROUDLY SAY I'VE DONE THAT.
BUT IF YOU SELL THE BOOKSHOP, AT LEAST IT WILL CONTINUE TO EXIST... WOULDN'T YOUR FATHER PREFER THAT?
WE'RE HERE.

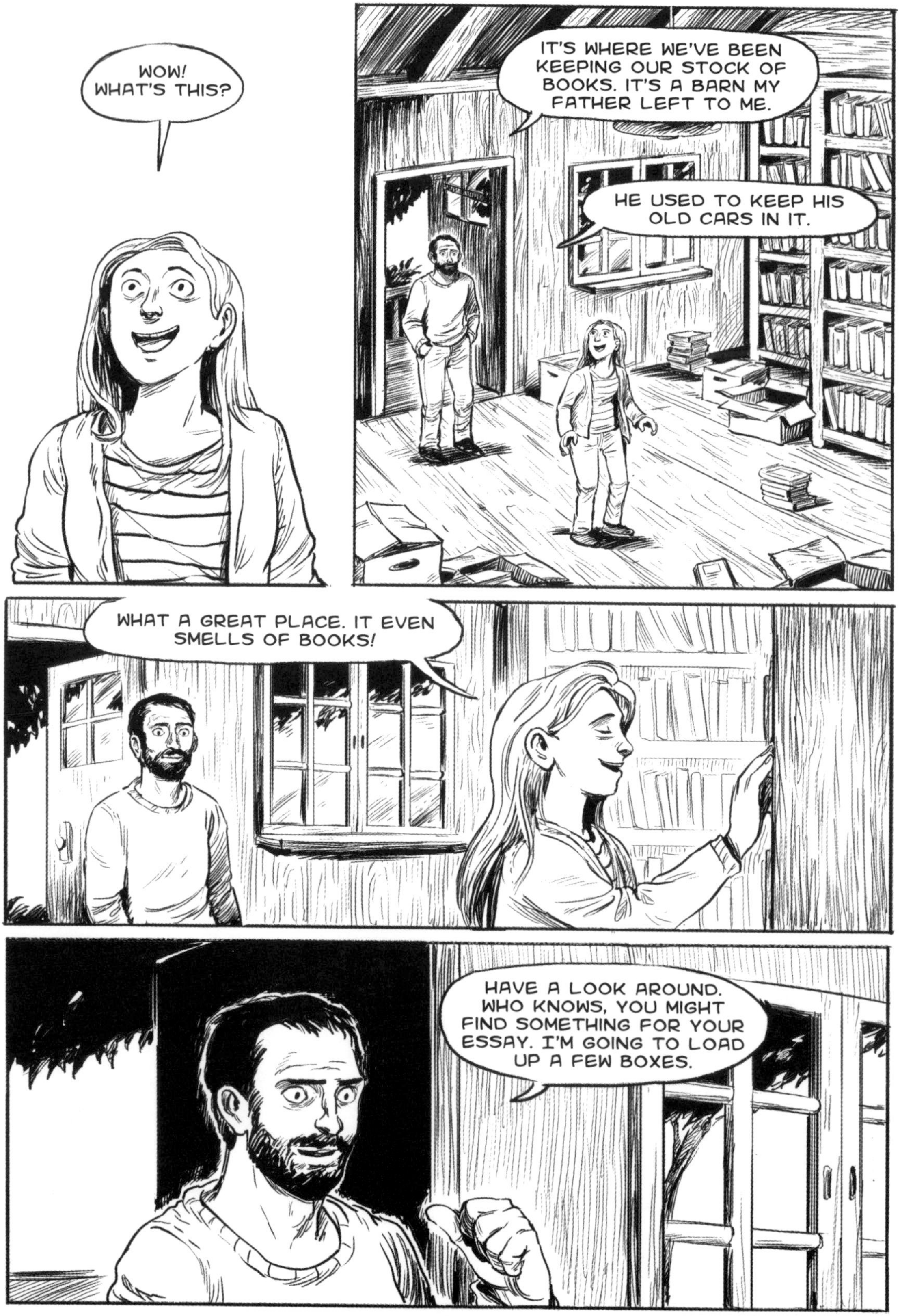
WOW! WHAT'S THIS?
IT'S WHERE WE'VE BEEN KEEPING OUR STOCK OF BOOKS. IT'S A BARN MY FATHER LEFT TO ME.
HE USED TO KEEP HIS OLD CARS IN IT.
WHAT A GREAT PLACE. IT EVEN SMELLS OF BOOKS!
HAVE A LOOK AROUND. WHO KNOWS, YOU MIGHT FIND SOMETHING FOR YOUR ESSAY. I'M GOING TO LOAD UP A FEW BOXES.

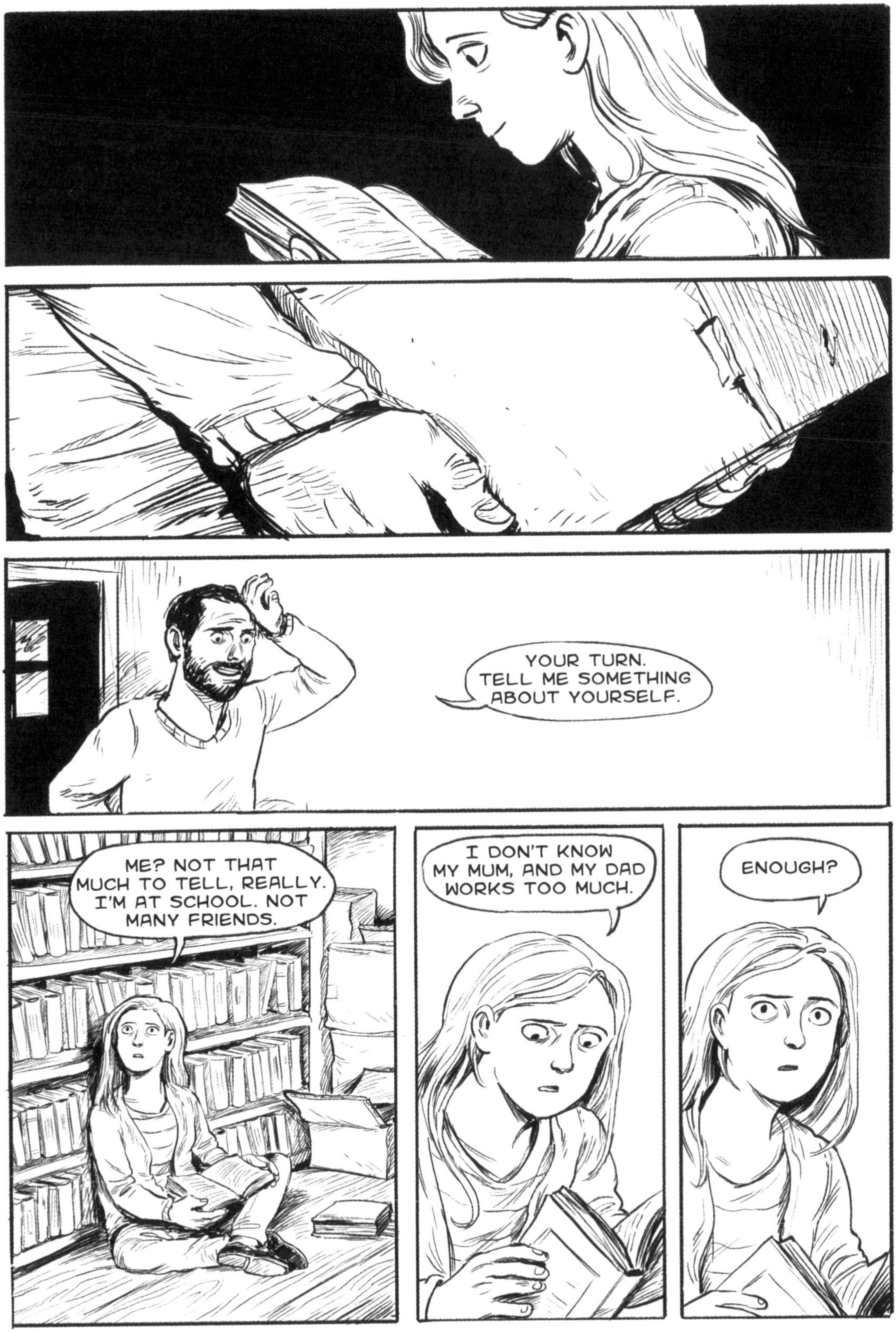
YOUR TURN. TELL ME SOMETHING ABOUT YOURSELF.
ME? NOT THAT MUCH TO TELL, REALLY. I'M AT SCHOOL. NOT MANY FRIENDS.
I DON'T KNOW MY MUM, AND MY DAD WORKS TOO MUCH.
ENOUGH?

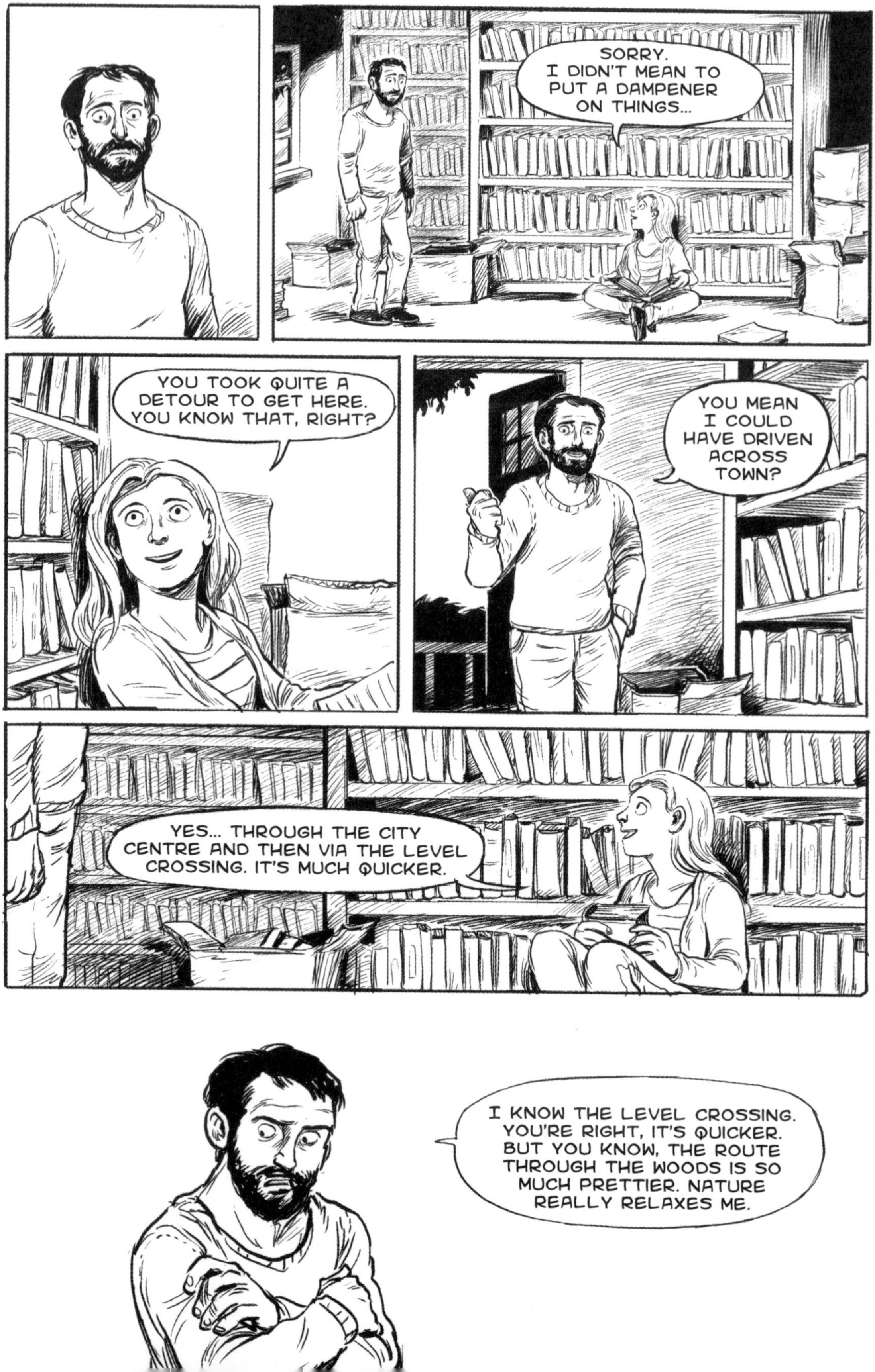
SORRY. I DIDN'T MEAN TO PUT A DAMPENER ON THINGS...
YOU TOOK QUITE A DETOUR TO GET HERE. YOU KNOW THAT, RIGHT?
YOU MEAN I COULD HAVE DRIVEN ACROSS TOWN?
YES... THROUGH THE CITY CENTRE AND THEN VIA THE LEVEL CROSSING. IT'S MUCH QUICKER.
I KNOW THE LEVEL CROSSING. YOU'RE RIGHT, IT'S QUICKER. BUT YOU KNOW, THE ROUTE THROUGH THE WOODS IS SO MUCH PRETTIER. NATURE REALLY RELAXES ME.

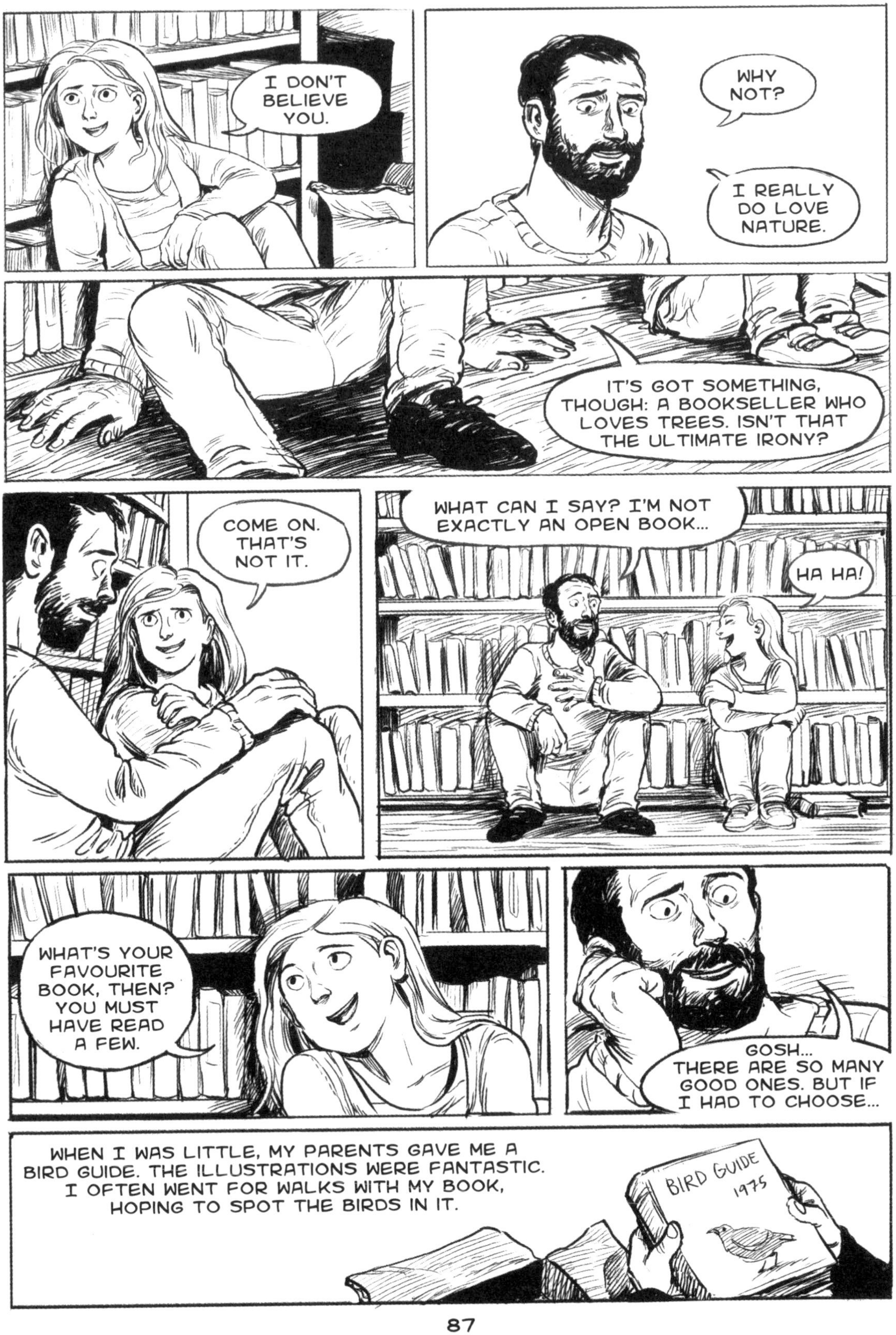
I DON'T BELIEVE YOU.
WHY NOT?
I REALLY DO LOVE NATURE.
IT'S GOT SOMETHING, THOUGH: A BOOKSELLER WHO LOVES TREES. ISN'T THAT THE ULTIMATE IRONY?
COME ON. THAT'S NOT IT.
WHAT CAN I SAY? I'M NOT EXACTLY AN OPEN BOOK...
HA HA!
WHAT'S YOUR FAVOURITE BOOK, THEN? YOU MUST HAVE READ A FEW.
GOSH... THERE ARE SO MANY GOOD ONES. BUT IF I HAD TO CHOOSE...
WHEN I WAS LITTLE, MY PARENTS GAVE ME A BIRD GUIDE. THE ILLUSTRATIONS WERE FANTASTIC. I OFTEN WENT FOR WALKS WITH MY BOOK, HOPING TO SPOT THE BIRDS IN IT.
BIRD GUIDE 1975

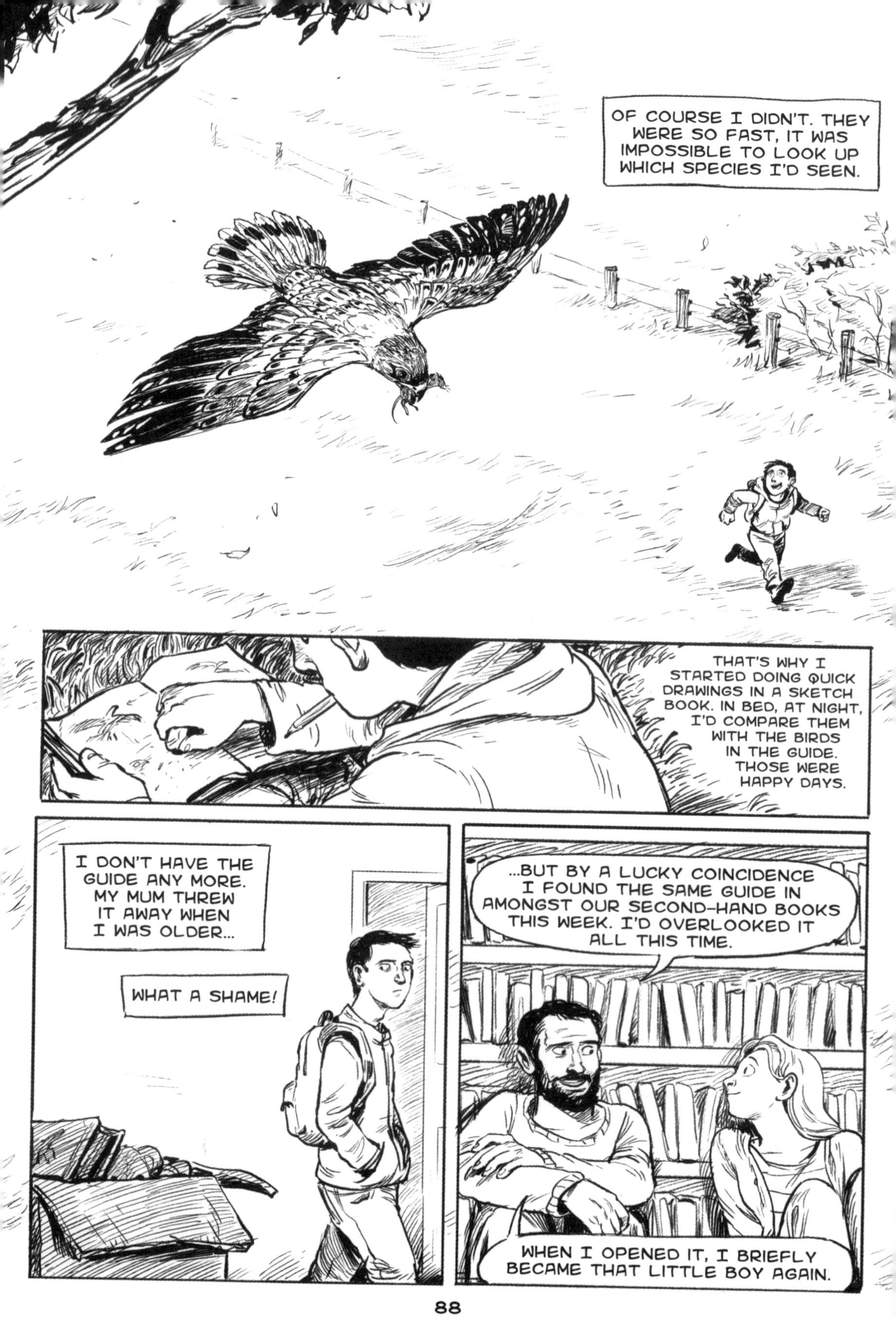
OF COURSE I DIDN'T. THEY WERE SO FAST, IT WAS IMPOSSIBLE TO LOOK UP WHICH SPECIES I'D SEEN.
THAT'S WHY I STARTED DOING QUICK DRAWINGS IN A SKETCH BOOK. IN BED, AT NIGHT, I'D COMPARE THEM WITH THE BIRDS IN THE GUIDE. THOSE WERE HAPPY DAYS.
I DON'T HAVE THE GUIDE ANY MORE. MY MUM THREW IT AWAY WHEN I WAS OLDER...
WHAT A SHAME!
...BUT BY A LUCKY COINCIDENCE I FOUND THE SAME GUIDE IN AMONGST OUR SECOND-HAND BOOKS THIS WEEK. I'D OVERLOOKED IT ALL THIS TIME.
WHEN I OPENED IT, I BRIEFLY BECAME THAT LITTLE BOY AGAIN.

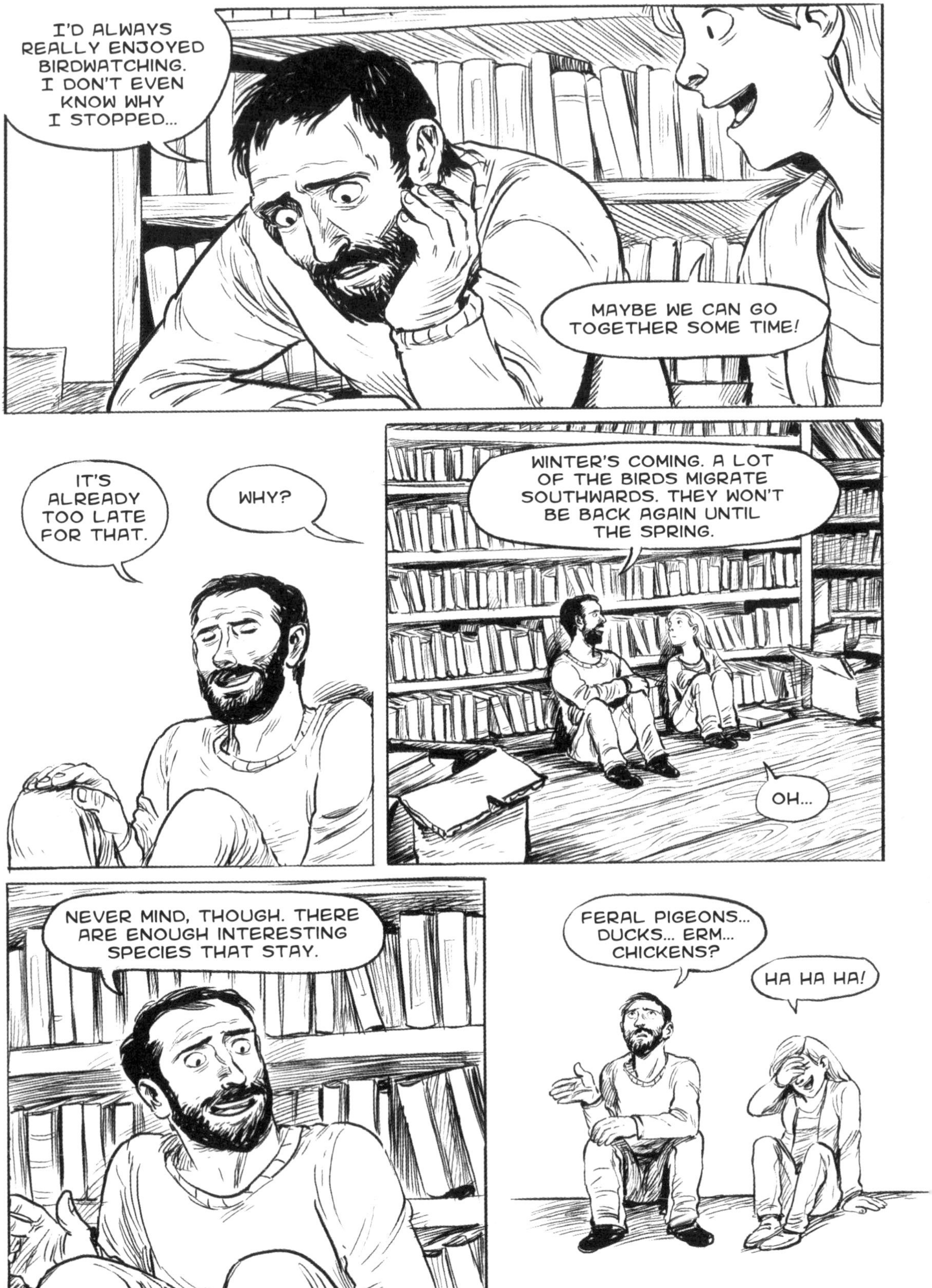
I'D ALWAYS REALLY ENJOYED BIRDWATCHING. I DON'T EVEN KNOW WHY I STOPPED...
MAYBE WE CAN GO TOGETHER SOME TIME!
WHY?
IT'S ALREADY TOO LATE FOR THAT.
WINTER'S COMING. A LOT OF THE BIRDS MIGRATE SOUTHWARDS. THEY WON'T BE BACK AGAIN UNTIL THE SPRING.
OH...
NEVER MIND, THOUGH. THERE ARE ENOUGH INTERESTING SPECIES THAT STAY.
FERAL PIGEONS... DUCKS... ERM... CHICKENS?
HA HA HA!

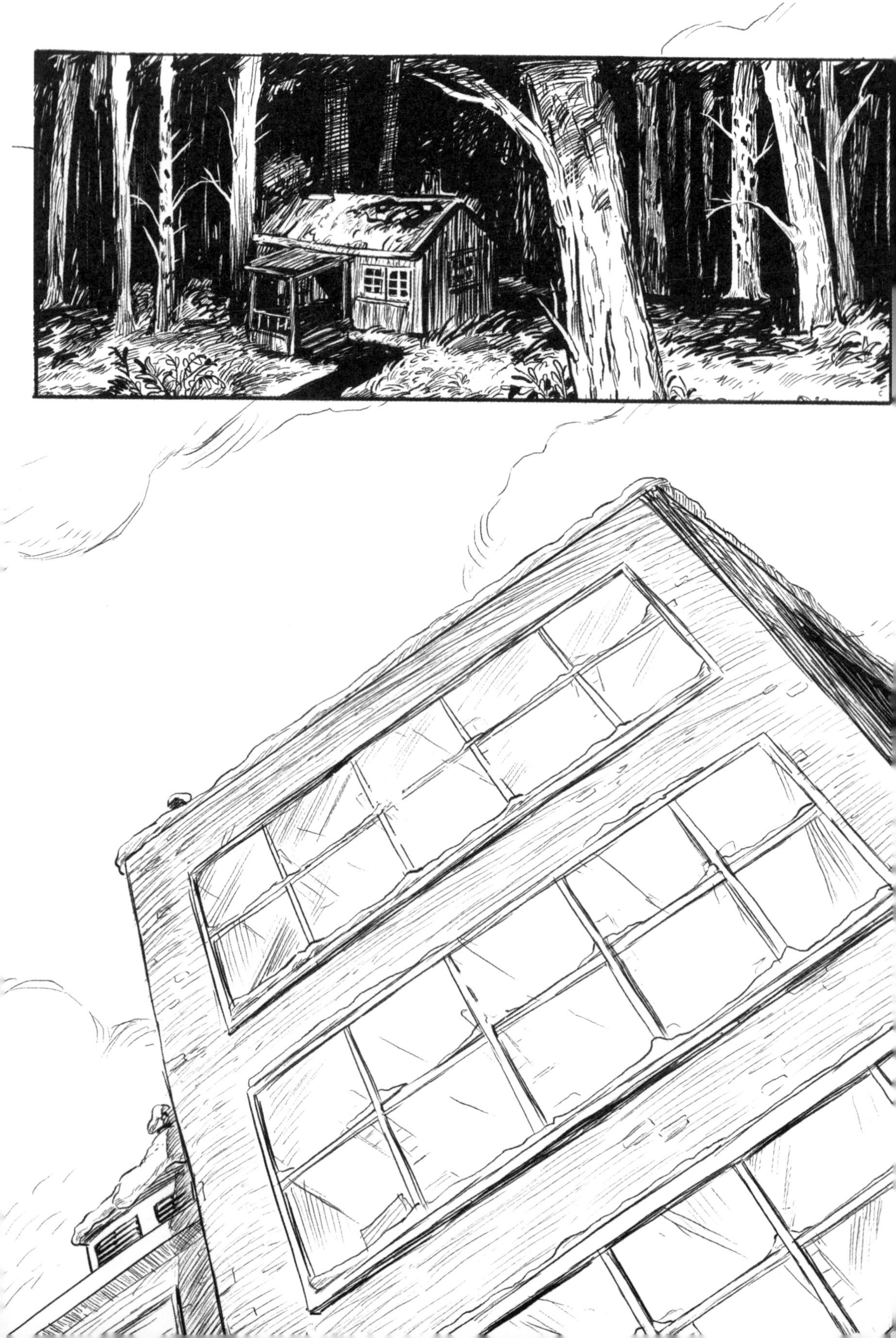

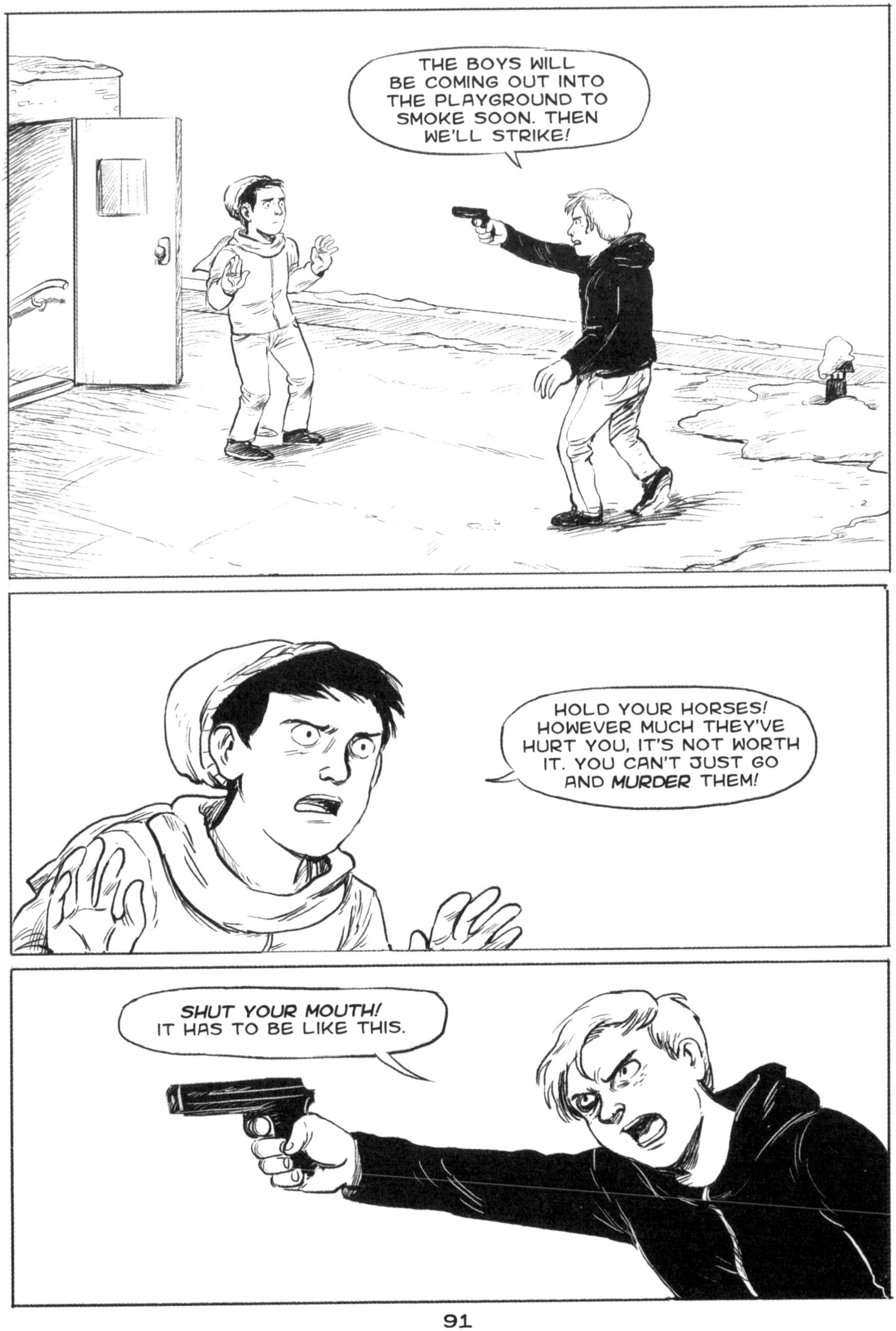
THE BOYS WILL BE COMING OUT INTO THE PLAYGROUND TO SMOKE SOON. THEN WE'LL STRIKE!
HOLD YOUR HORSES! HOWEVER MUCH THEY'VE HURT YOU, IT'S NOT WORTH IT. YOU CAN'T JUST GO AND *MURDER* THEM!
SHUT YOUR MOUTH! IT HAS TO BE LIKE THIS.

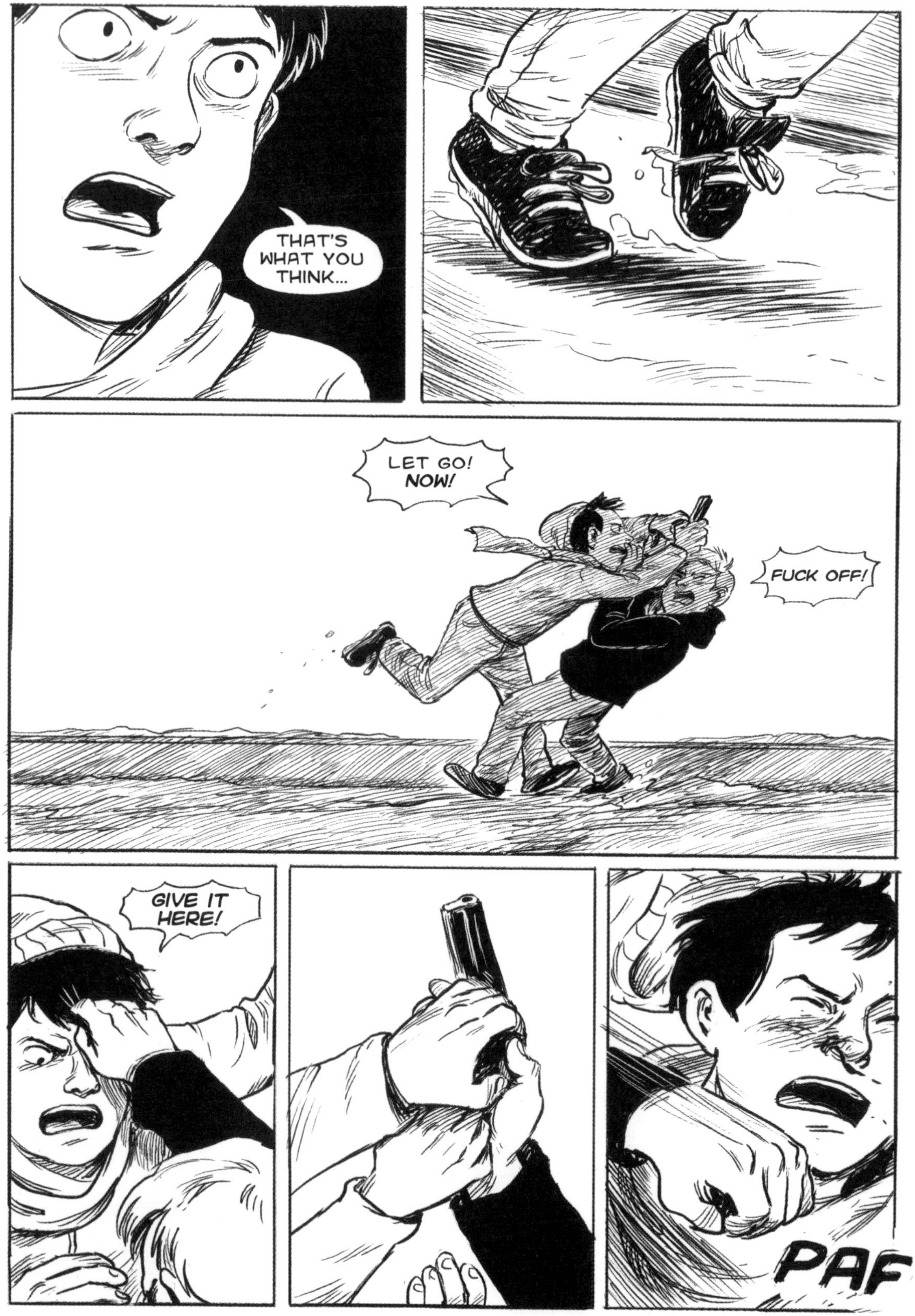
THAT'S WHAT YOU THINK...
LET GO! NOW!
FUCK OFF!
GIVE IT HERE!
PAF

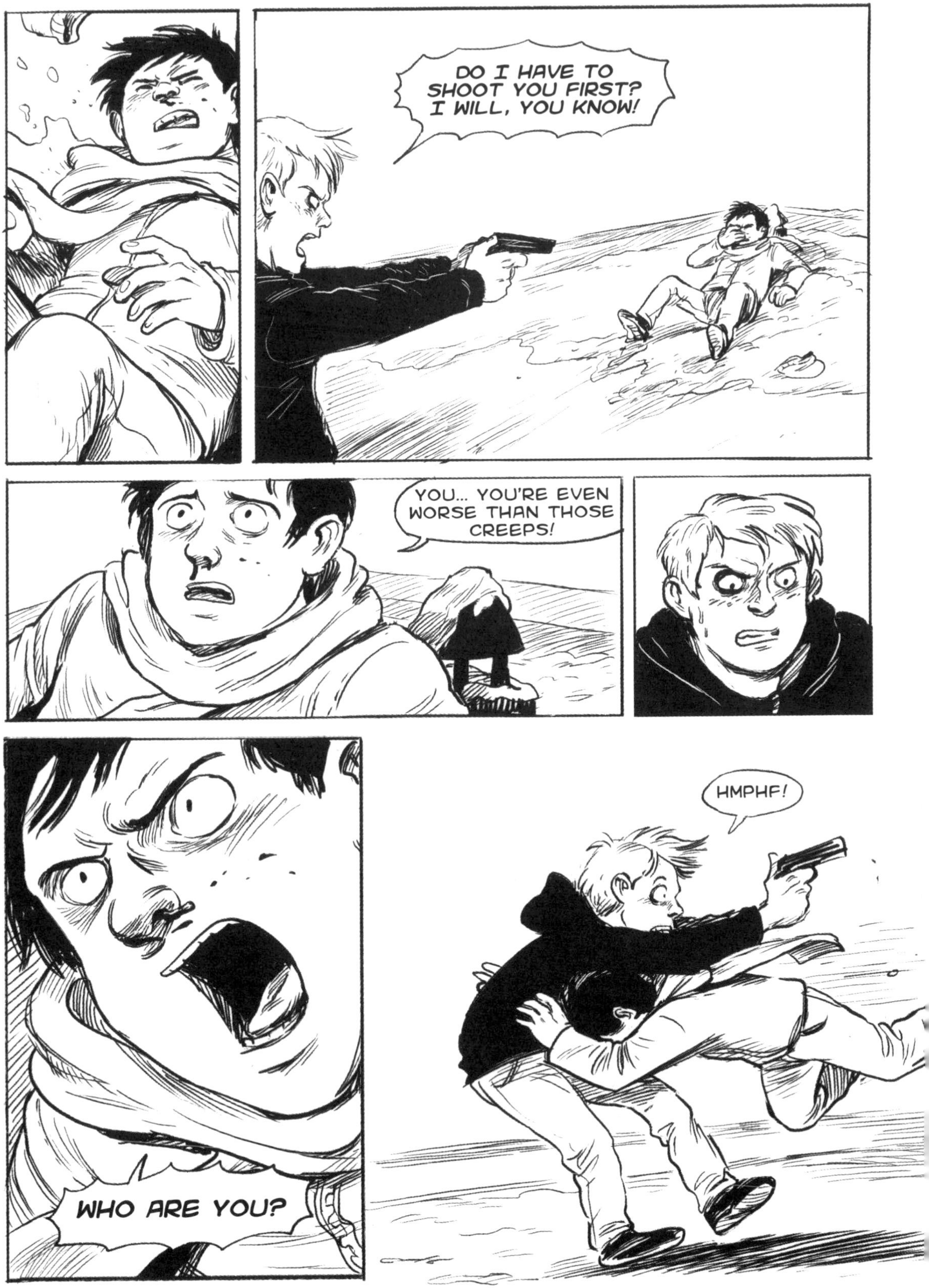
DO I HAVE TO SHOOT YOU FIRST? I WILL, YOU KNOW!
YOU... YOU'RE EVEN WORSE THAN THOSE CREEPS!
WHO ARE YOU?
HMPHF!

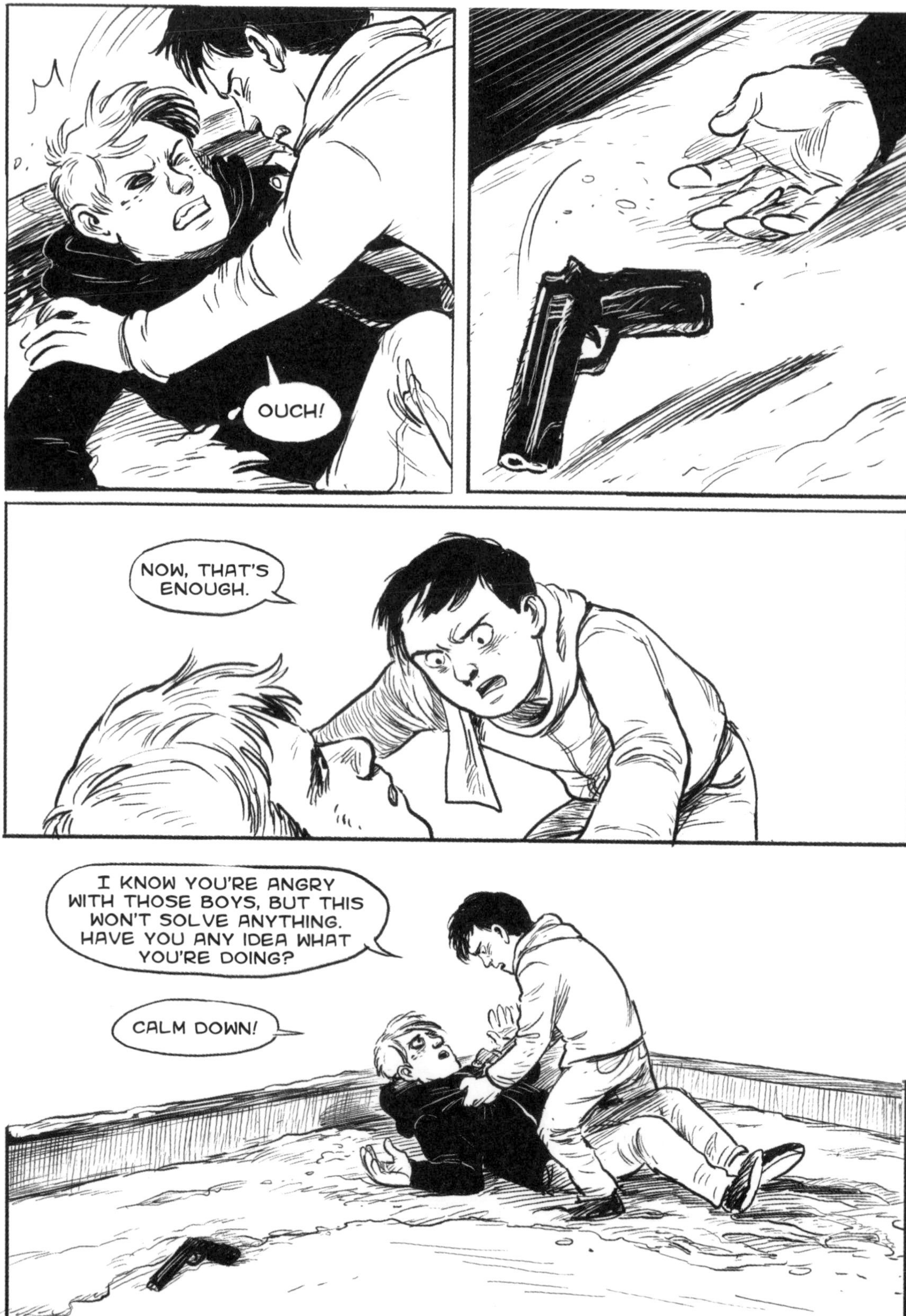

OUCH!
NOW, THAT'S ENOUGH.
I KNOW YOU'RE ANGRY WITH THOSE BOYS, BUT THIS WON'T SOLVE ANYTHING. HAVE YOU ANY IDEA WHAT YOU'RE DOING?
CALM DOWN!

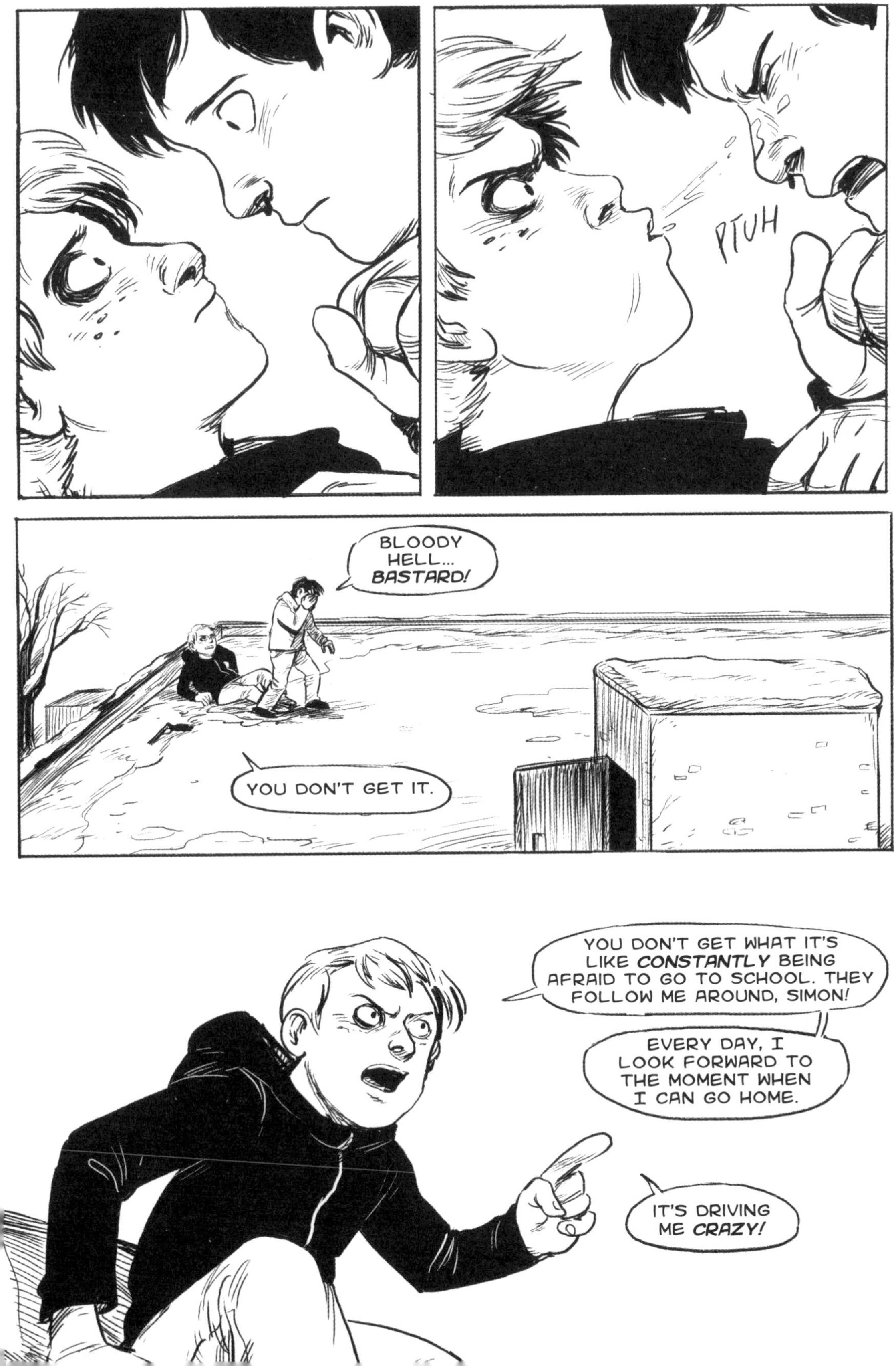
PTUH
BLOODY HELL... BASTARD!
YOU DON'T GET IT.
YOU DON'T GET WHAT IT'S LIKE CONSTANTLY BEING AFRAID TO GO TO SCHOOL. THEY FOLLOW ME AROUND, SIMON!
EVERY DAY, I LOOK FORWARD TO THE MOMENT WHEN I CAN GO HOME.
IT'S DRIVING ME CRAZY!

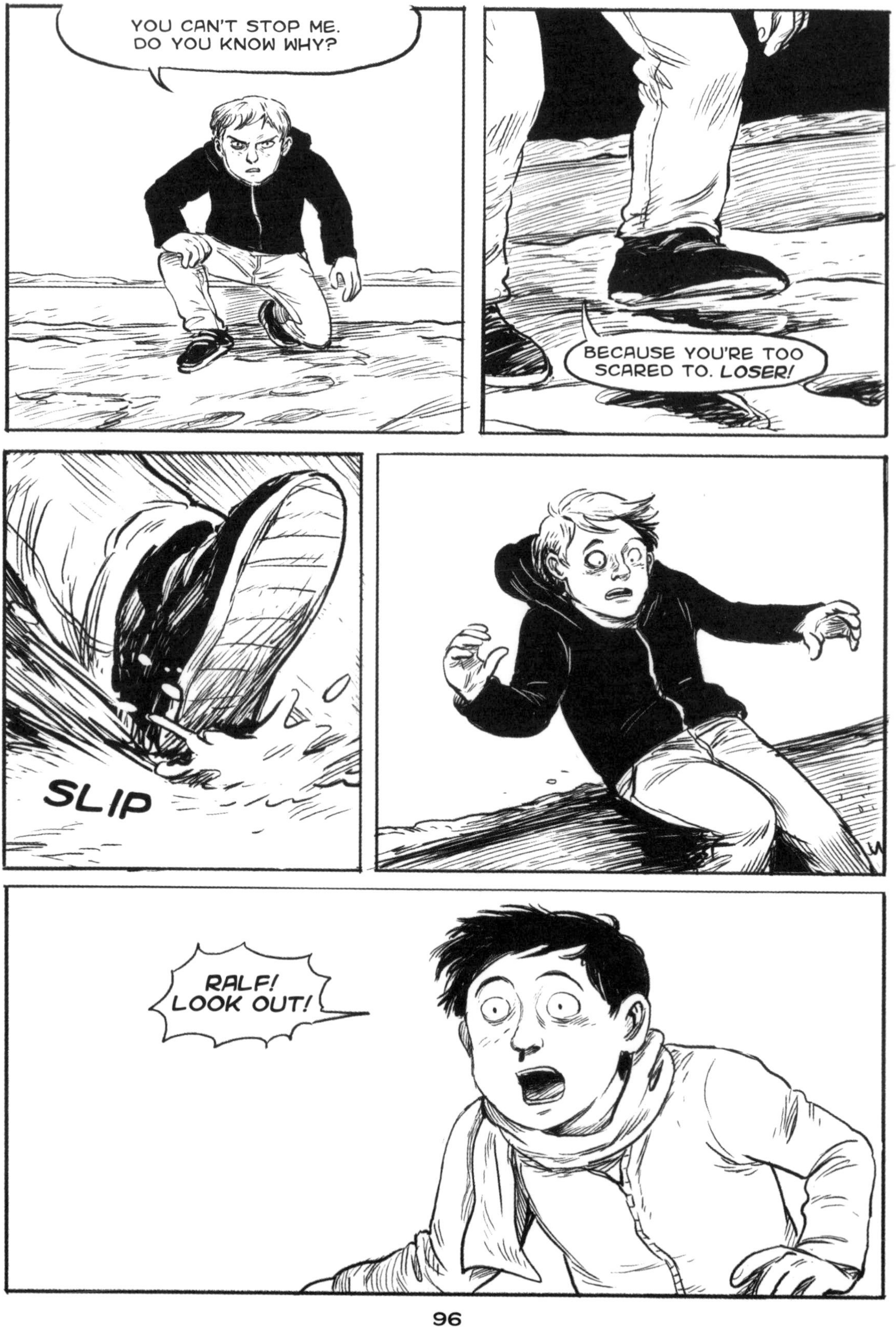
YOU CAN'T STOP ME. DO YOU KNOW WHY?
BECAUSE YOU'RE TOO SCARED TO. *LOSER!*
SLIP
RALF! LOOK OUT!

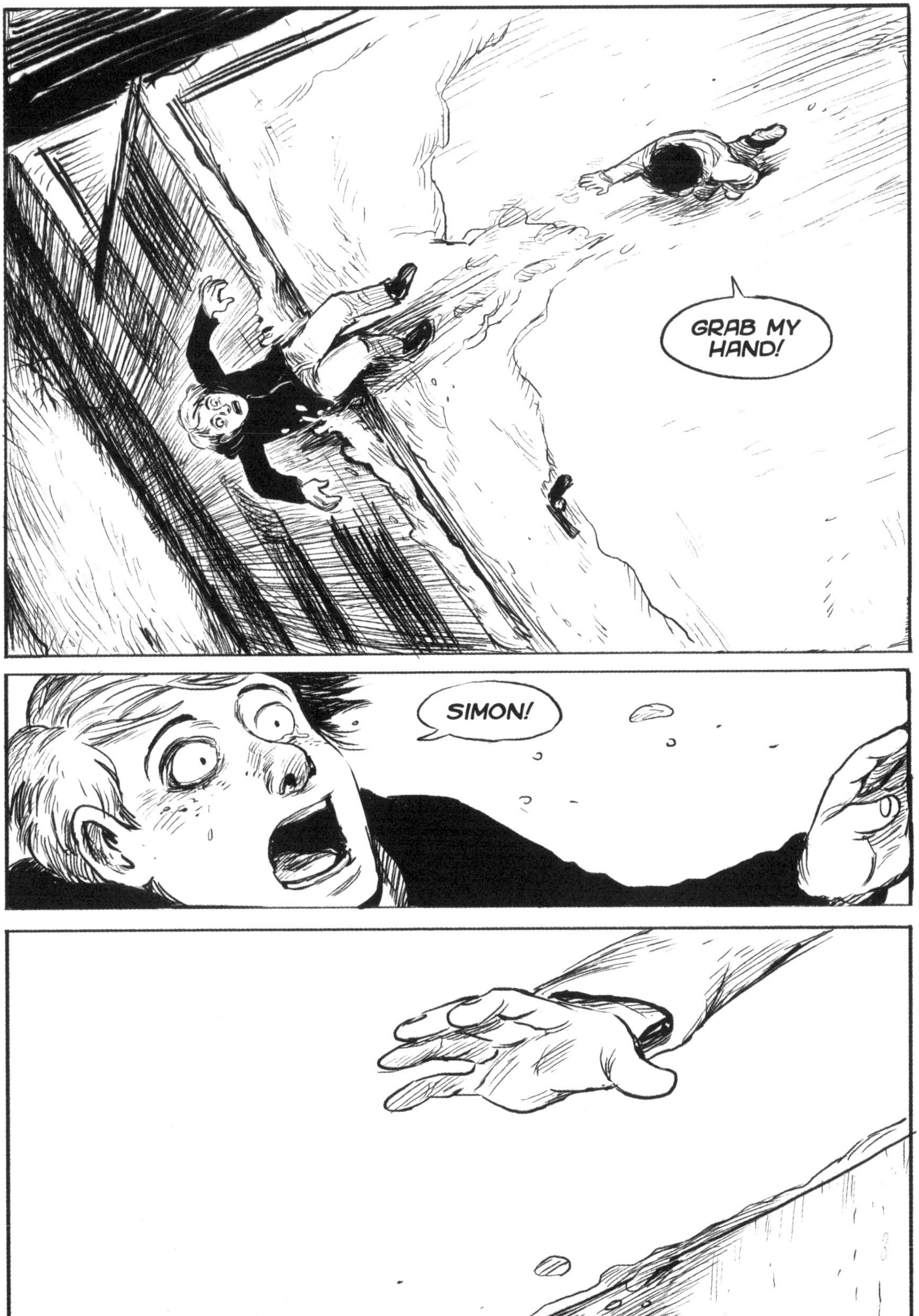
GRAB MY HAND!
SIMON!

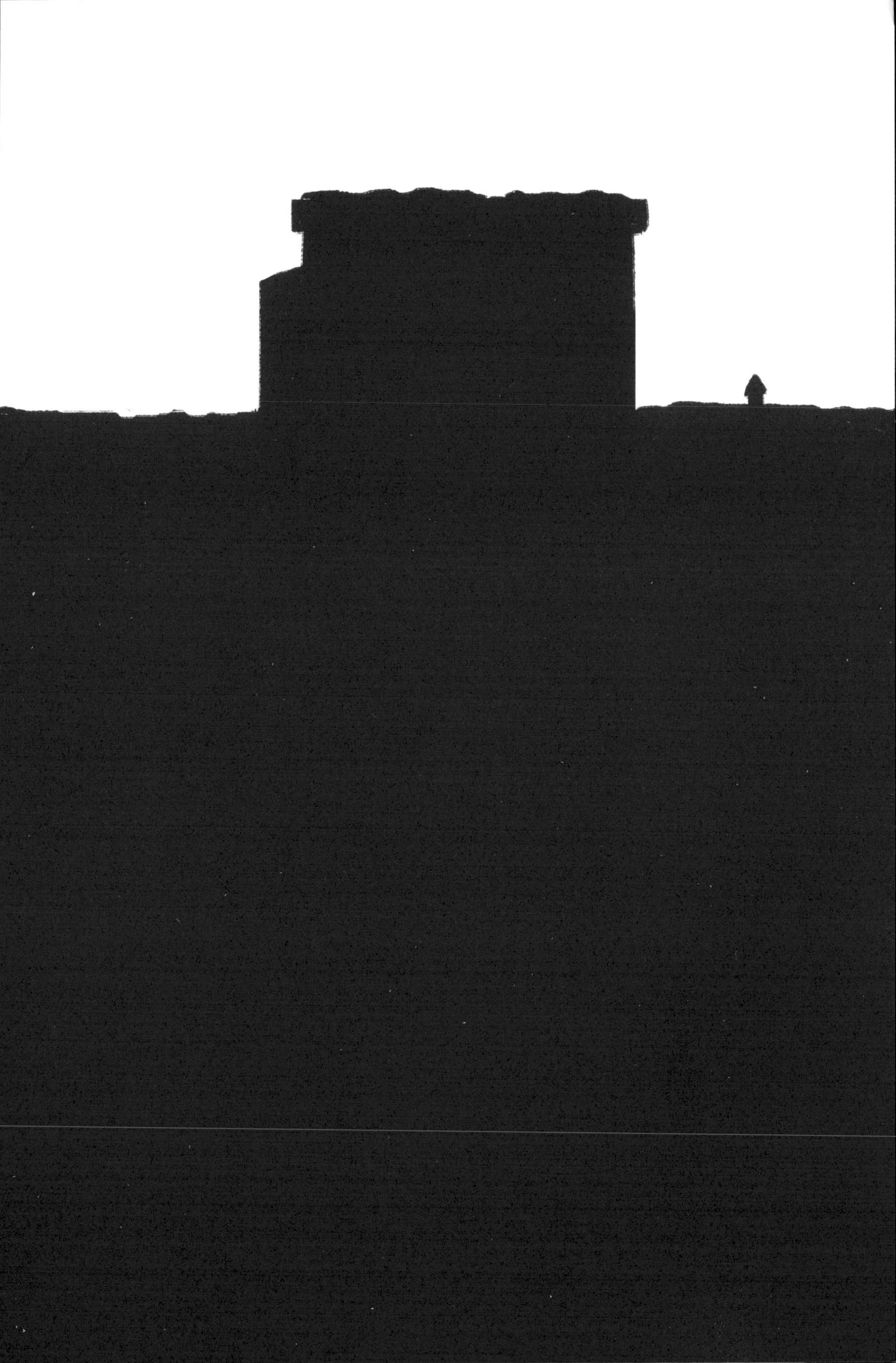

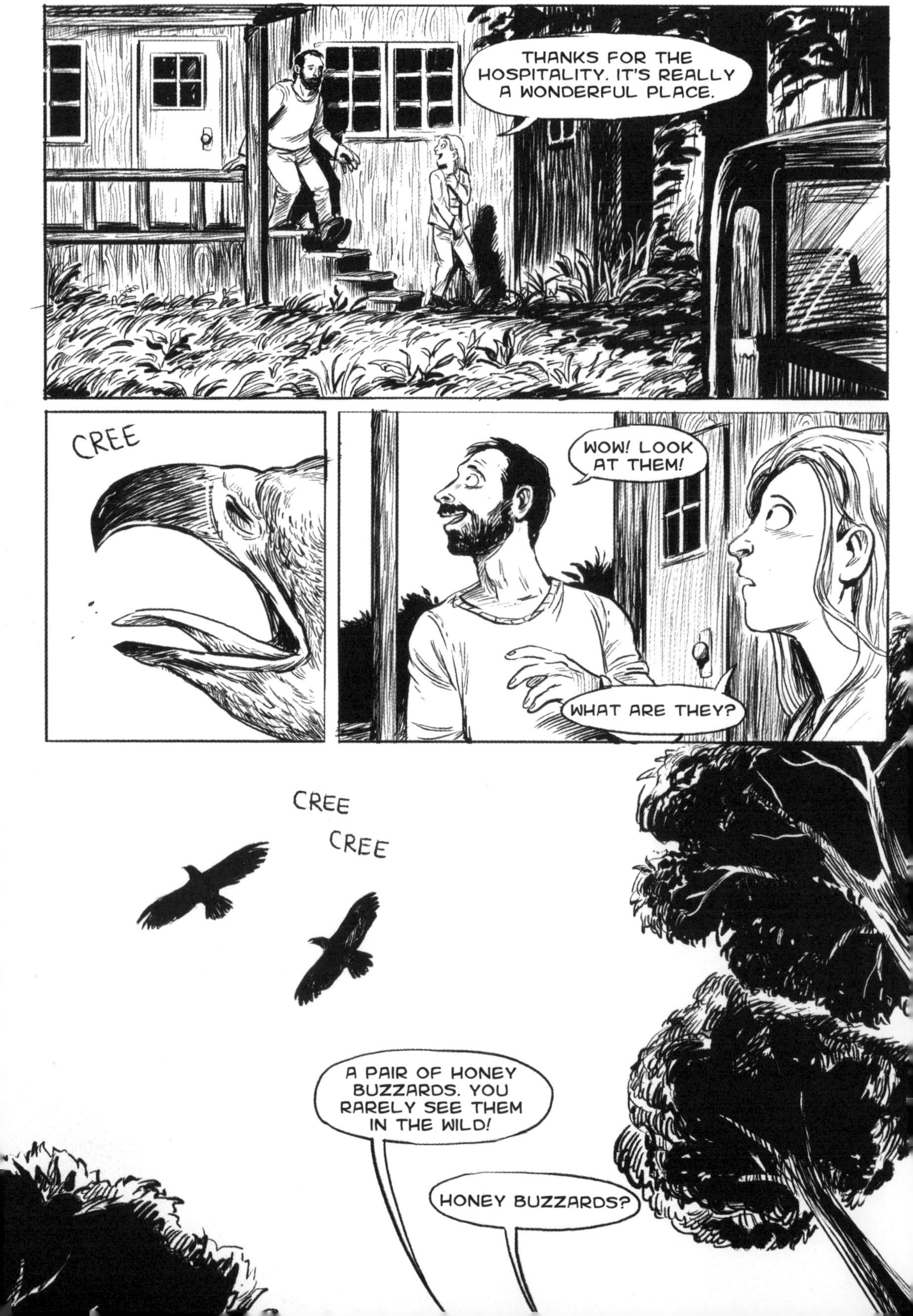
THANKS FOR THE HOSPITALITY. IT'S REALLY A WONDERFUL PLACE.
CREE
WOW! LOOK AT THEM!
WHAT ARE THEY?
CREE
CREE
A PAIR OF HONEY BUZZARDS. YOU RARELY SEE THEM IN THE WILD!
HONEY BUZZARDS?

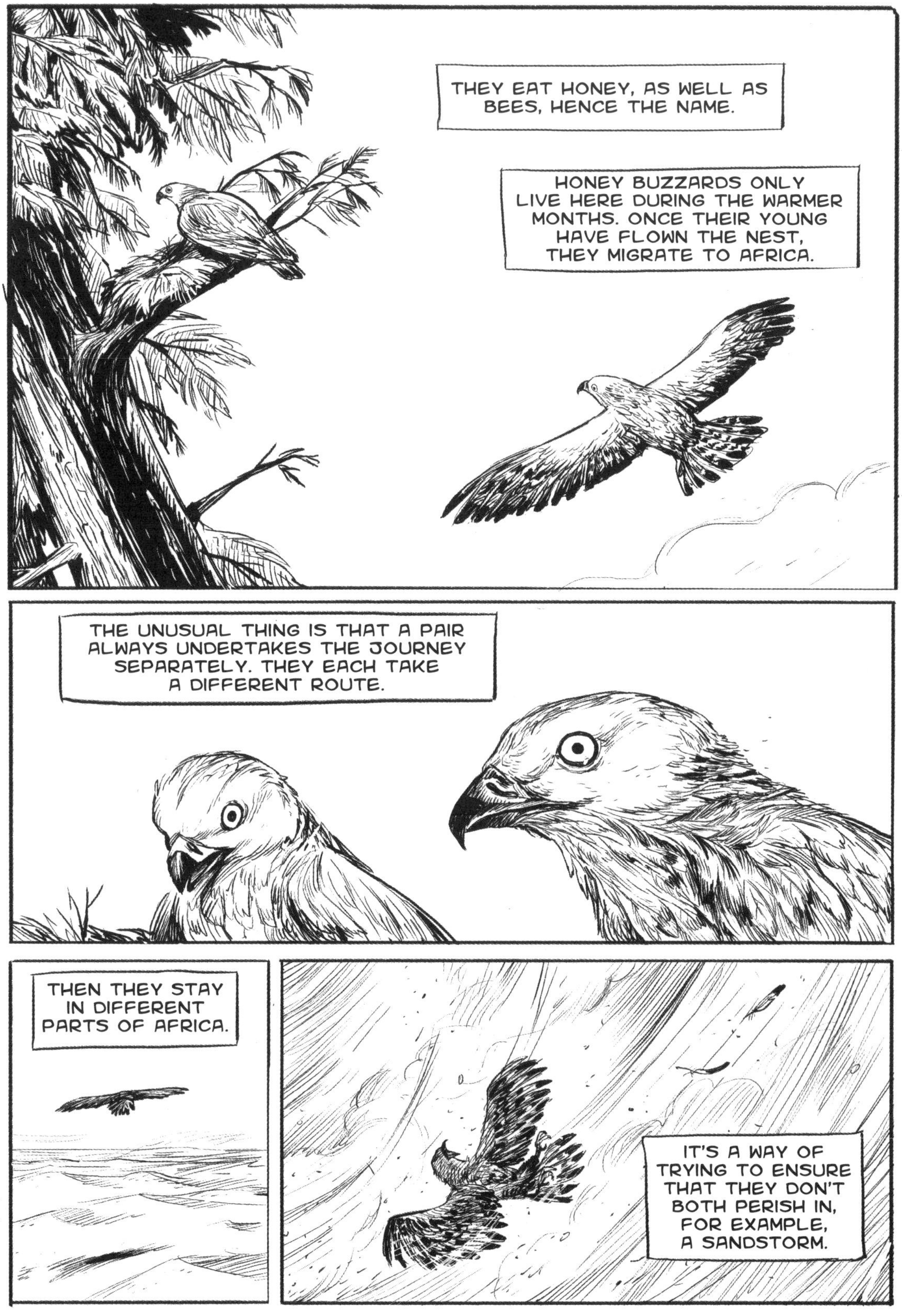
THEY EAT HONEY, AS WELL AS BEES, HENCE THE NAME.
HONEY BUZZARDS ONLY LIVE HERE DURING THE WARMER MONTHS. ONCE THEIR YOUNG HAVE FLOWN THE NEST, THEY MIGRATE TO AFRICA.
THE UNUSUAL THING IS THAT A PAIR ALWAYS UNDERTAKES THE JOURNEY SEPARATELY. THEY EACH TAKE A DIFFERENT ROUTE.
THEN THEY STAY IN DIFFERENT PARTS OF AFRICA.
IT'S A WAY OF TRYING TO ENSURE THAT THEY DON'T BOTH PERISH IN, FOR EXAMPLE, A SANDSTORM.

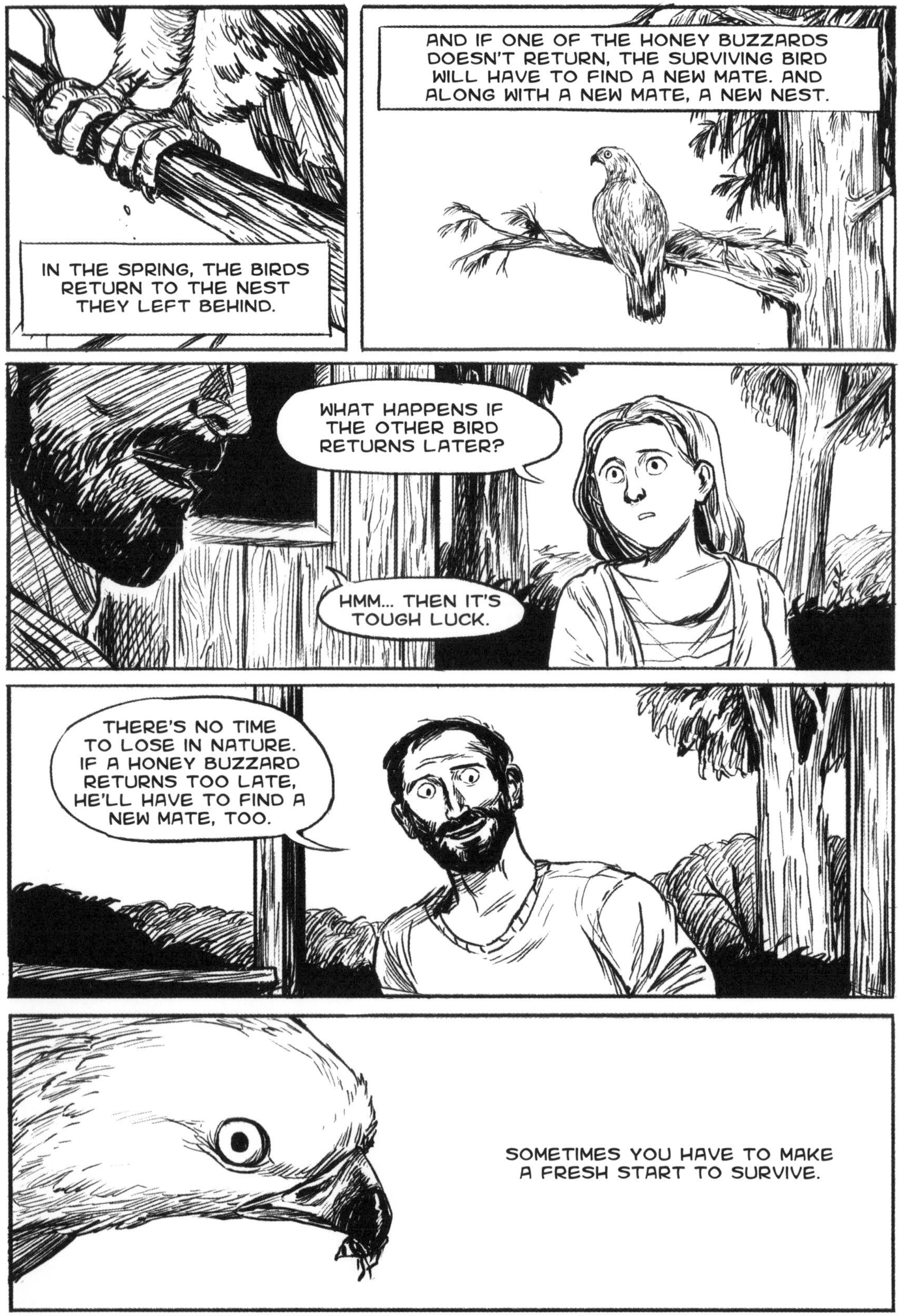
IN THE SPRING, THE BIRDS RETURN TO THE NEST THEY LEFT BEHIND.
AND IF ONE OF THE HONEY BUZZARDS DOESN'T RETURN, THE SURVIVING BIRD WILL HAVE TO FIND A NEW MATE. AND ALONG WITH A NEW MATE, A NEW NEST.
WHAT HAPPENS IF THE OTHER BIRD RETURNS LATER?
HMM... THEN IT'S TOUGH LUCK.
THERE'S NO TIME TO LOSE IN NATURE. IF A HONEY BUZZARD RETURNS TOO LATE, HE'LL HAVE TO FIND A NEW MATE, TOO.
SOMETIMES YOU HAVE TO MAKE A FRESH START TO SURVIVE.

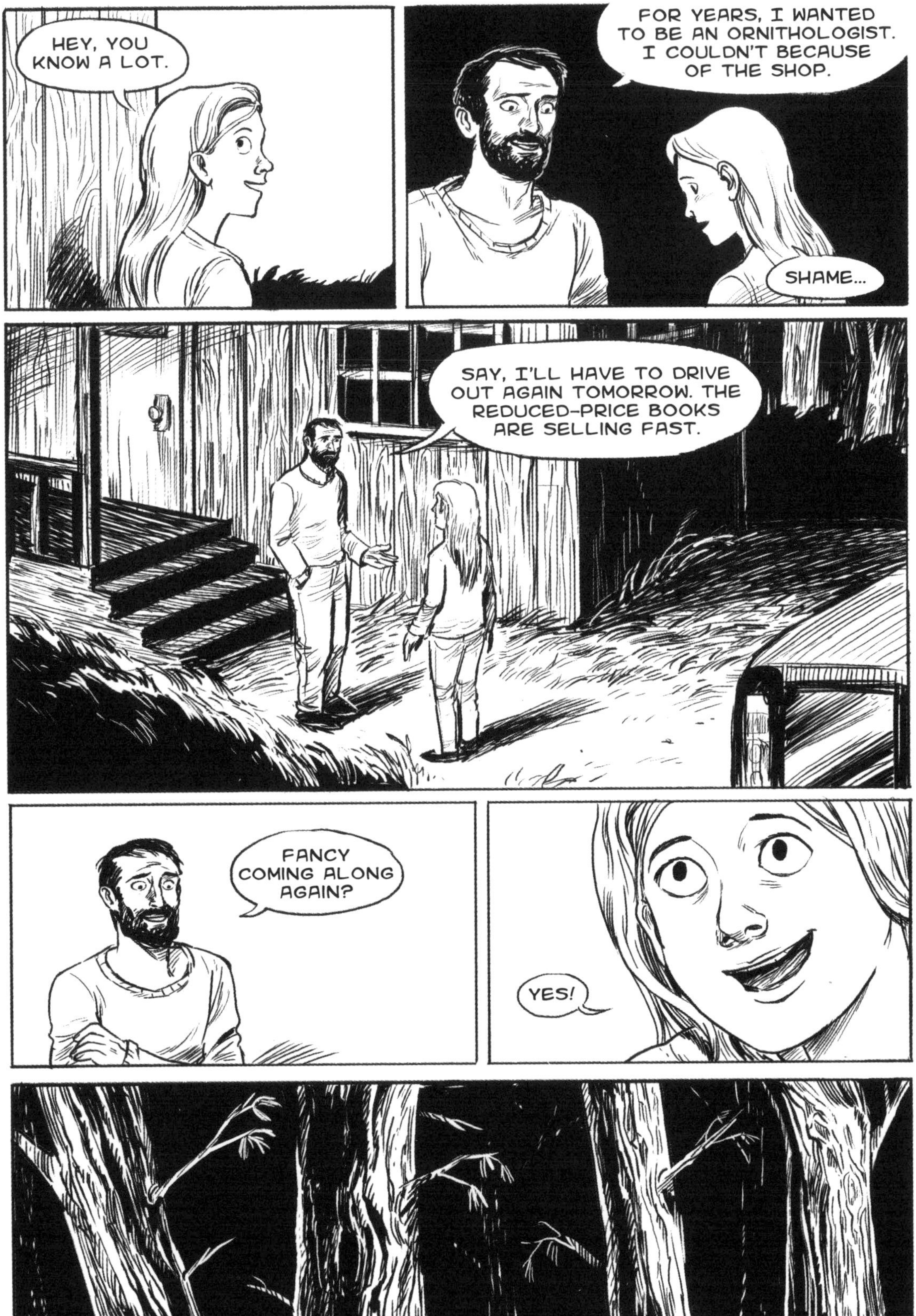
HEY, YOU KNOW A LOT.
FOR YEARS, I WANTED TO BE AN ORNITHOLOGIST. I COULDN'T BECAUSE OF THE SHOP.
SHAME...
SAY, I'LL HAVE TO DRIVE OUT AGAIN TOMORROW. THE REDUCED-PRICE BOOKS ARE SELLING FAST.
FANCY COMING ALONG AGAIN?
YES!

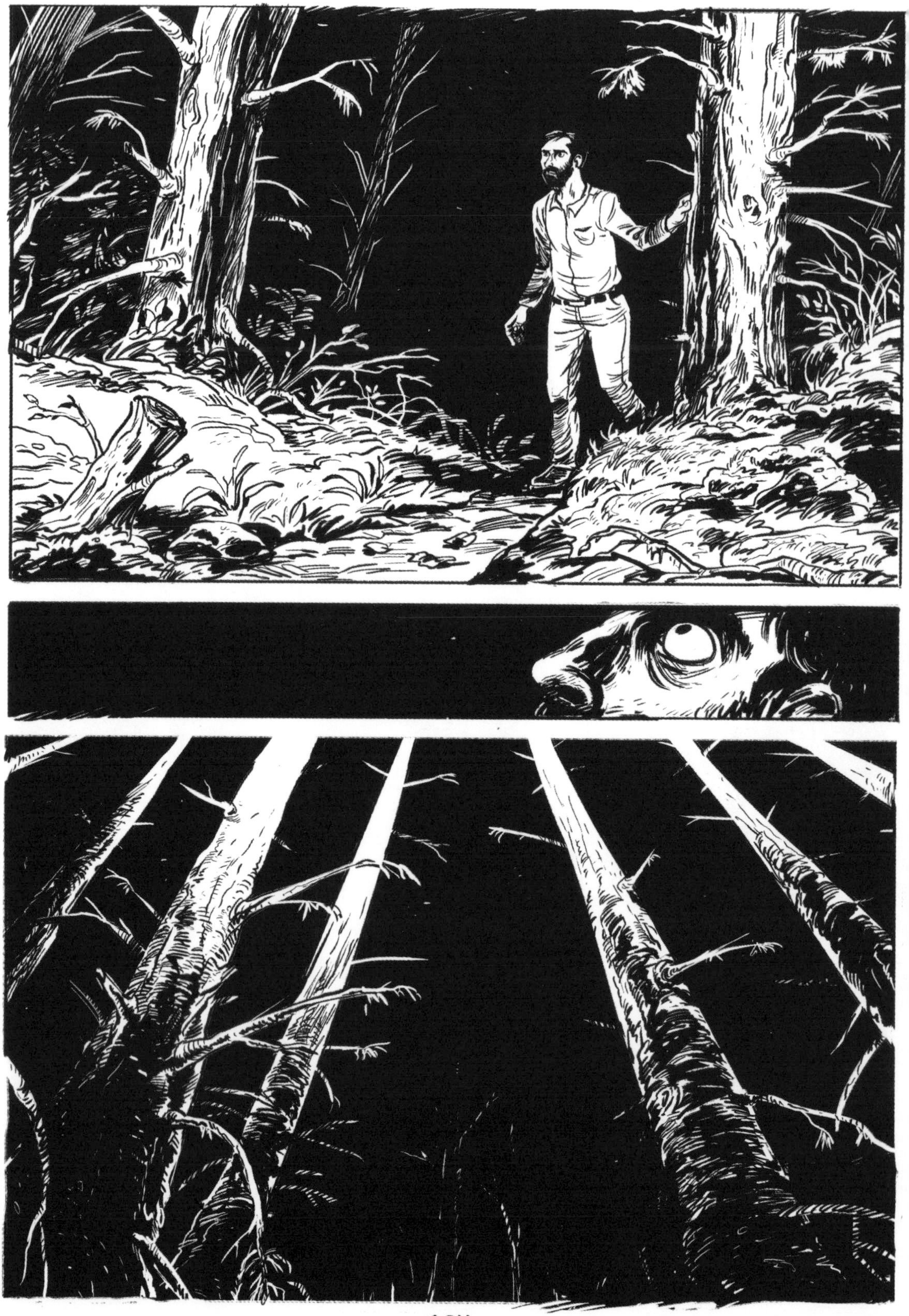

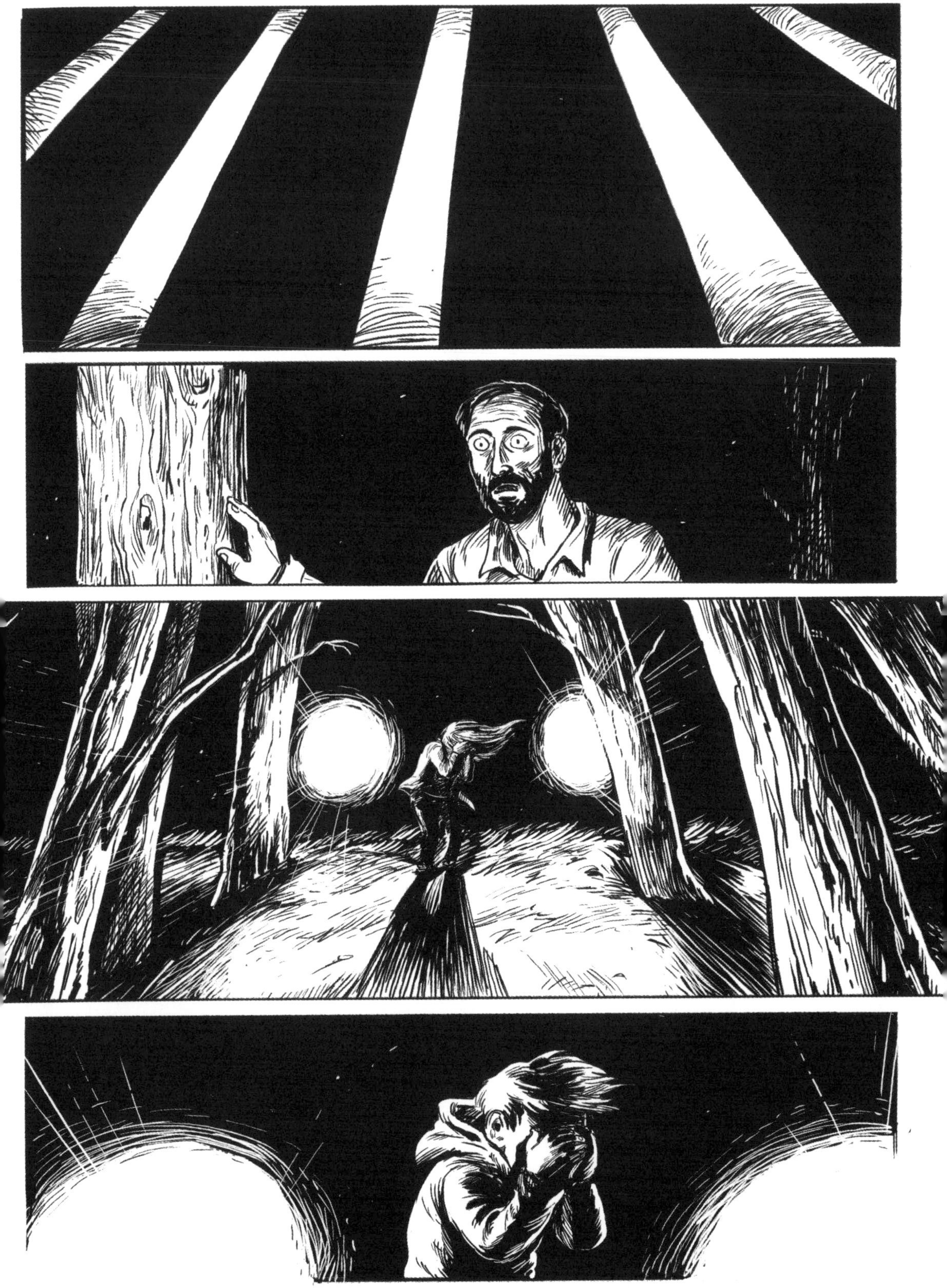

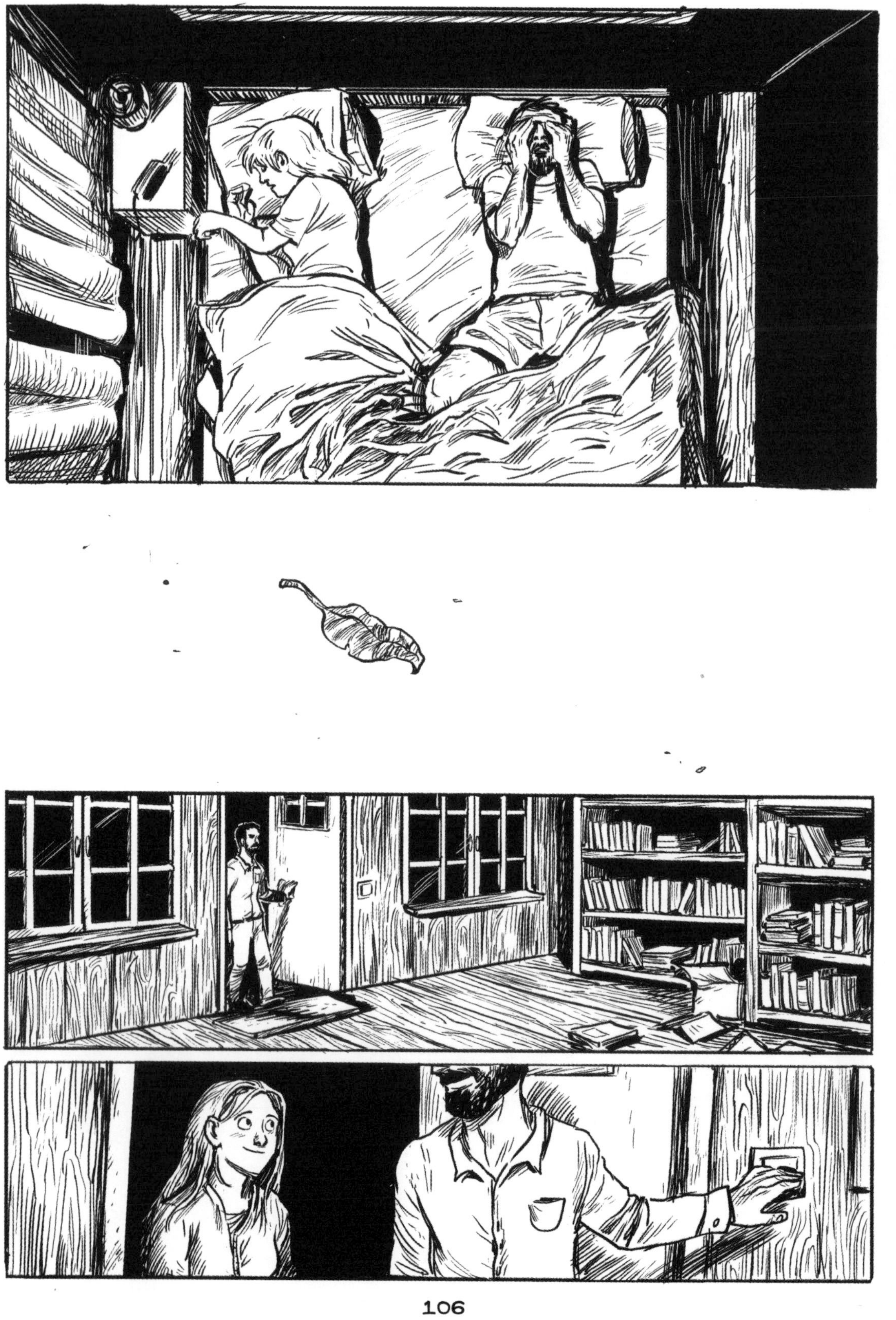

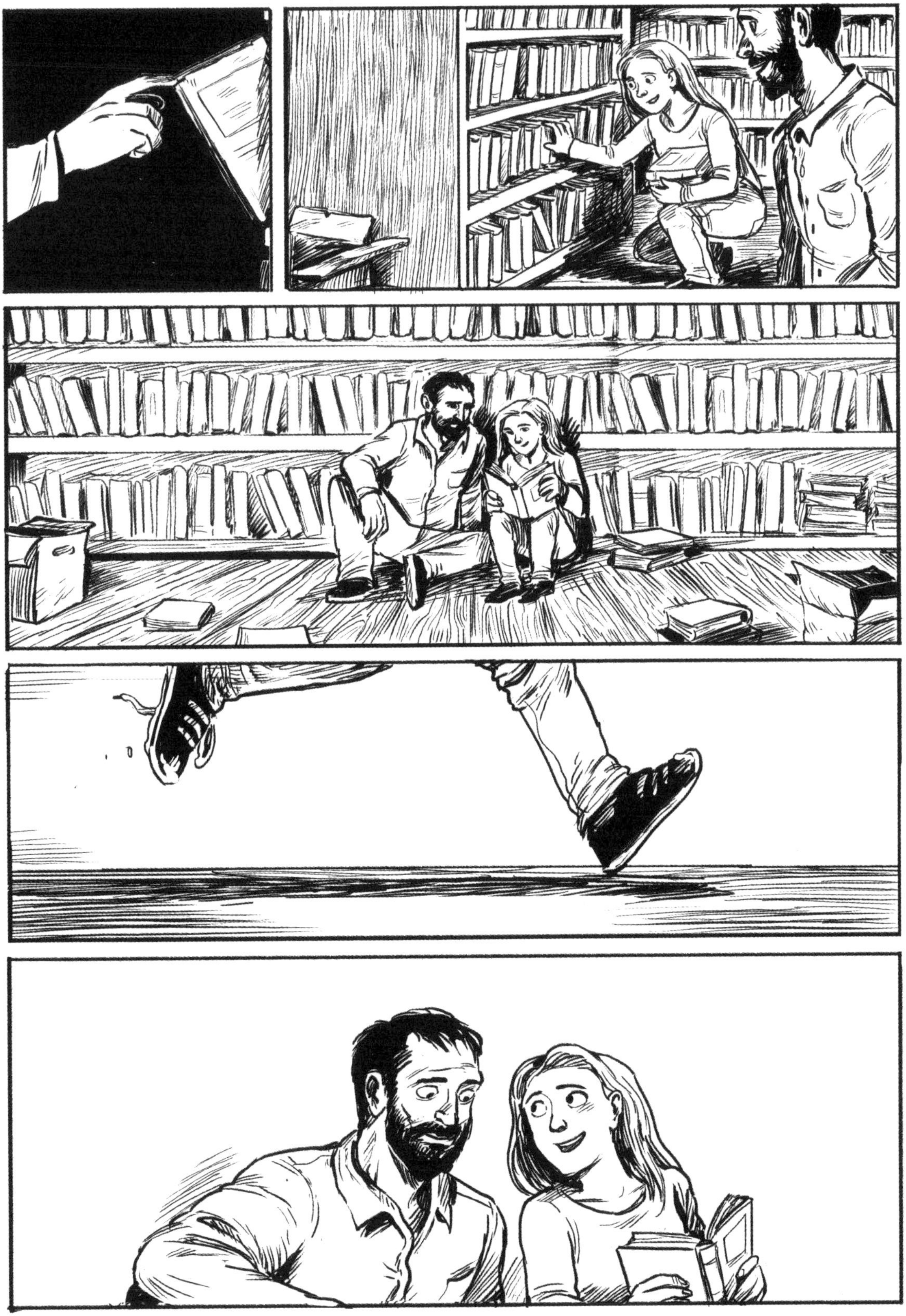

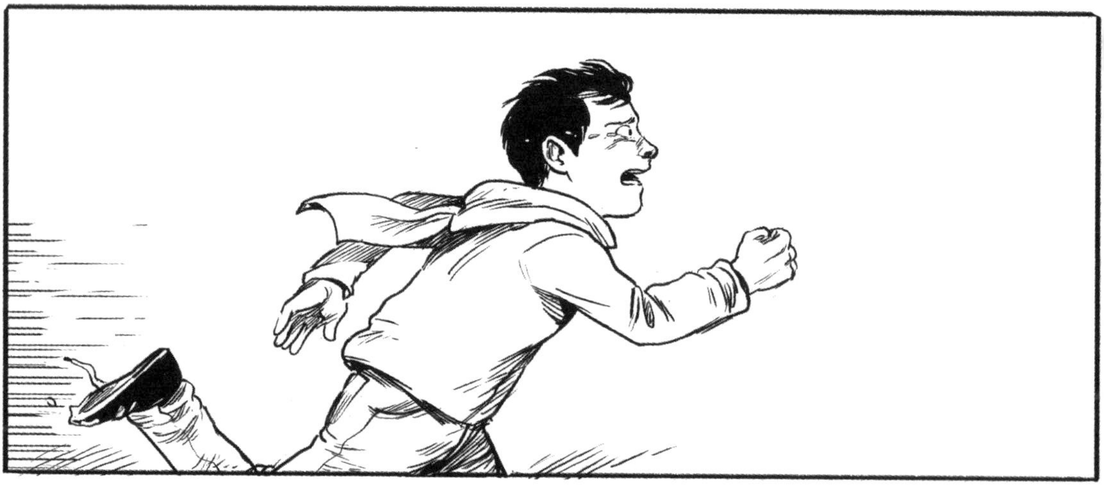

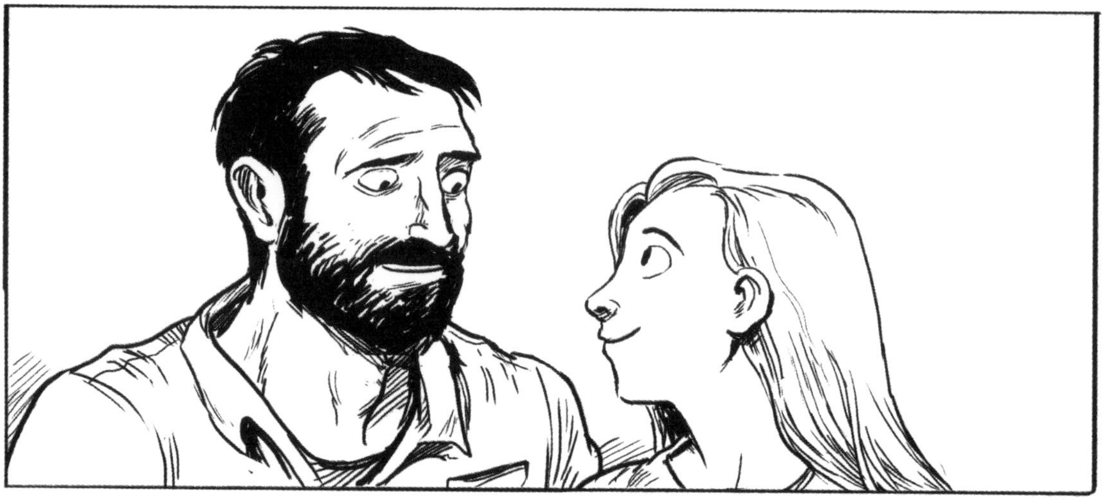

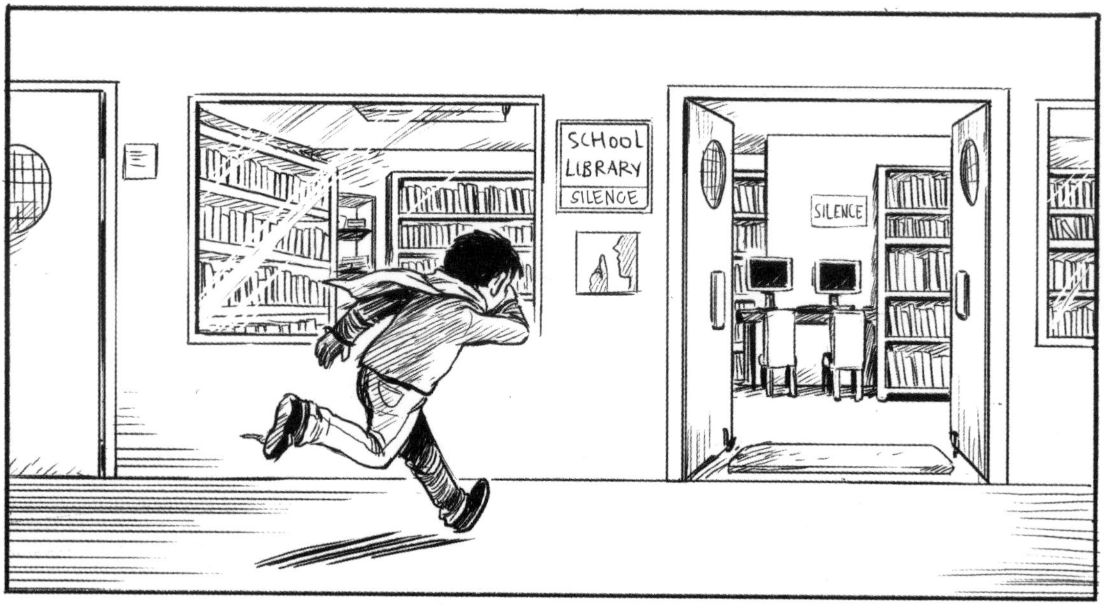
SCHOOL
LIBRARY
SILENCE
SILENCE

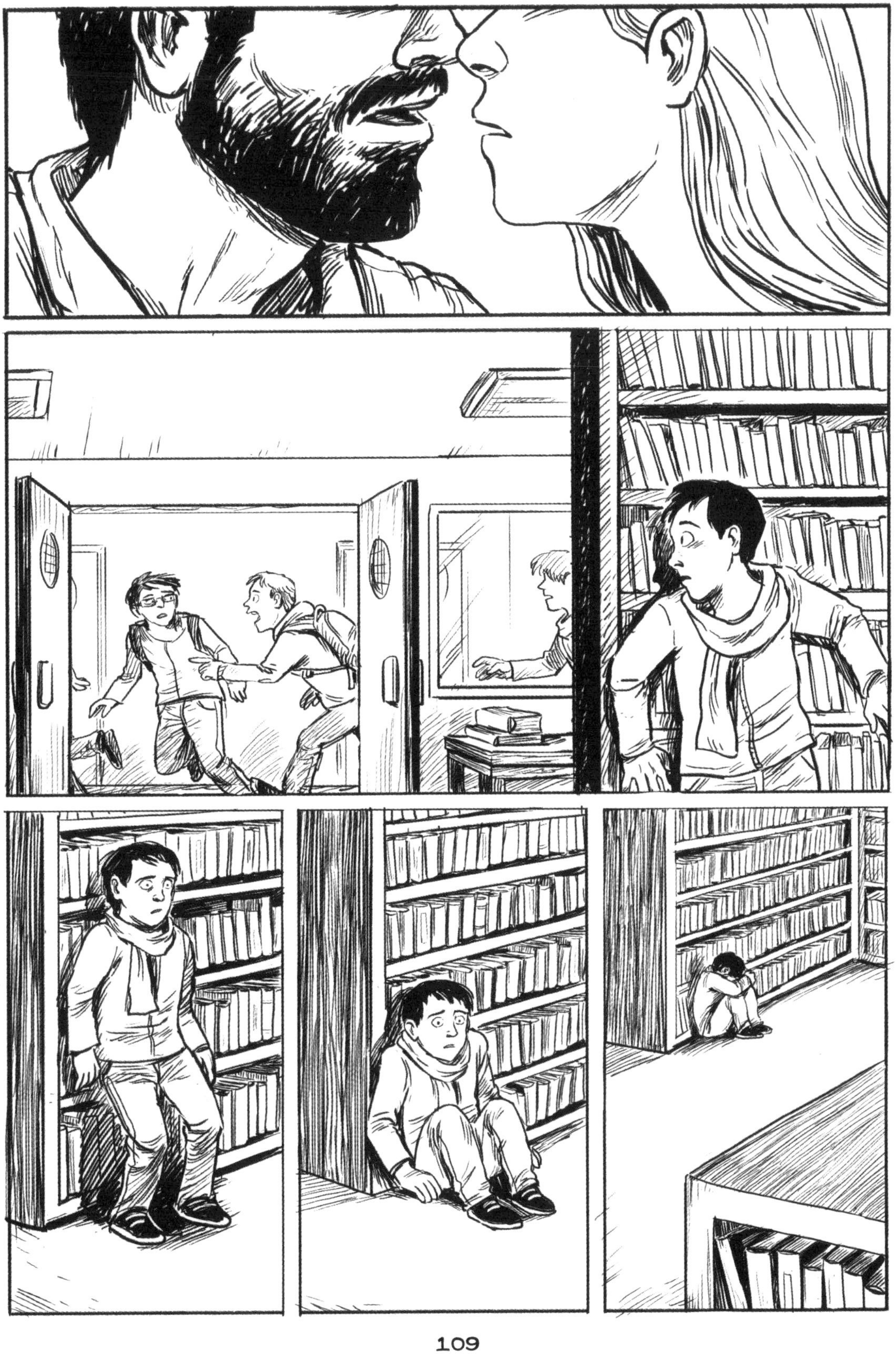

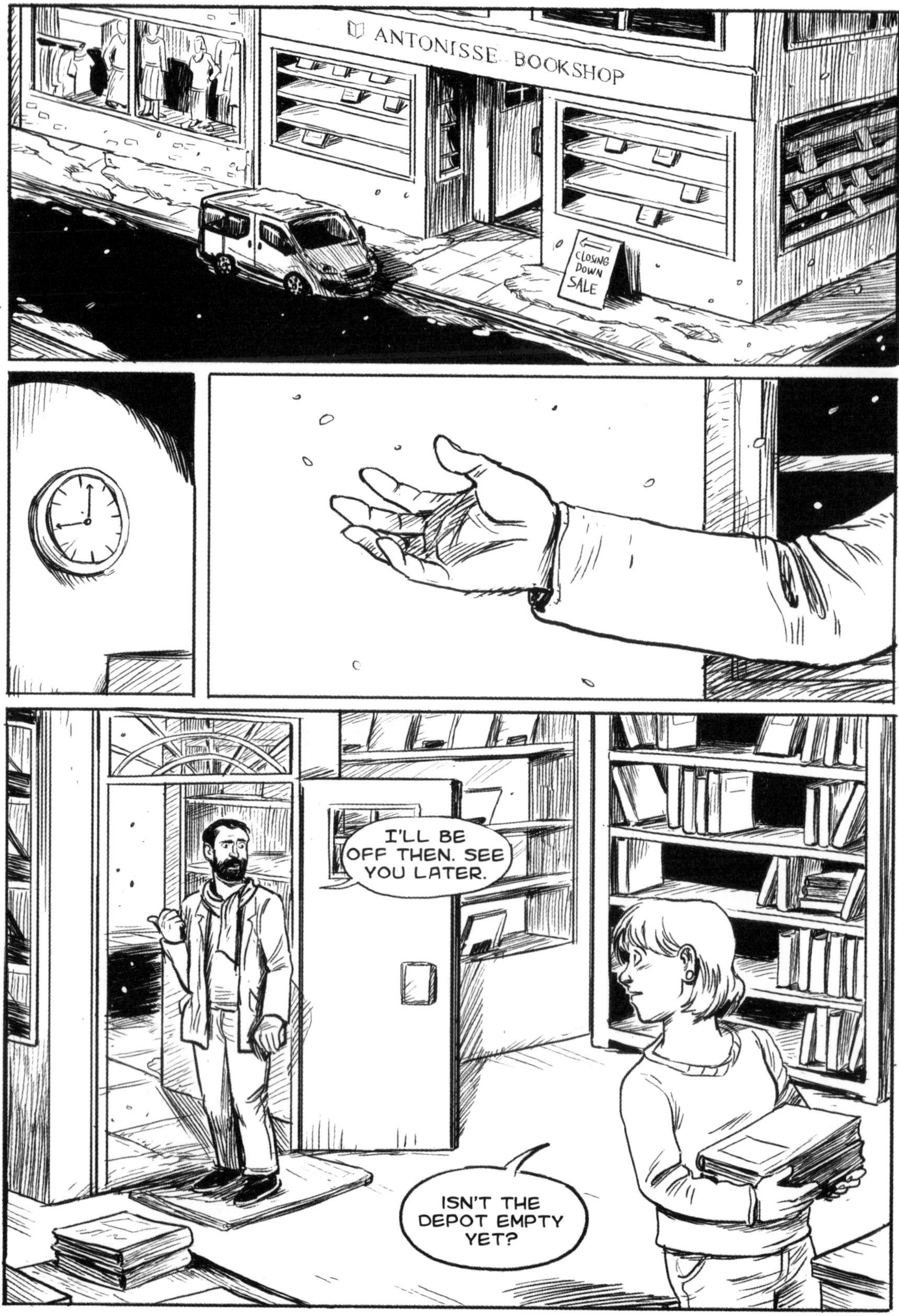
ANTONISSE BOOKSHOP
CLOSING DOWN SALE
I'LL BE OFF THEN. SEE YOU LATER.
ISN'T THE DEPOT EMPTY YET?

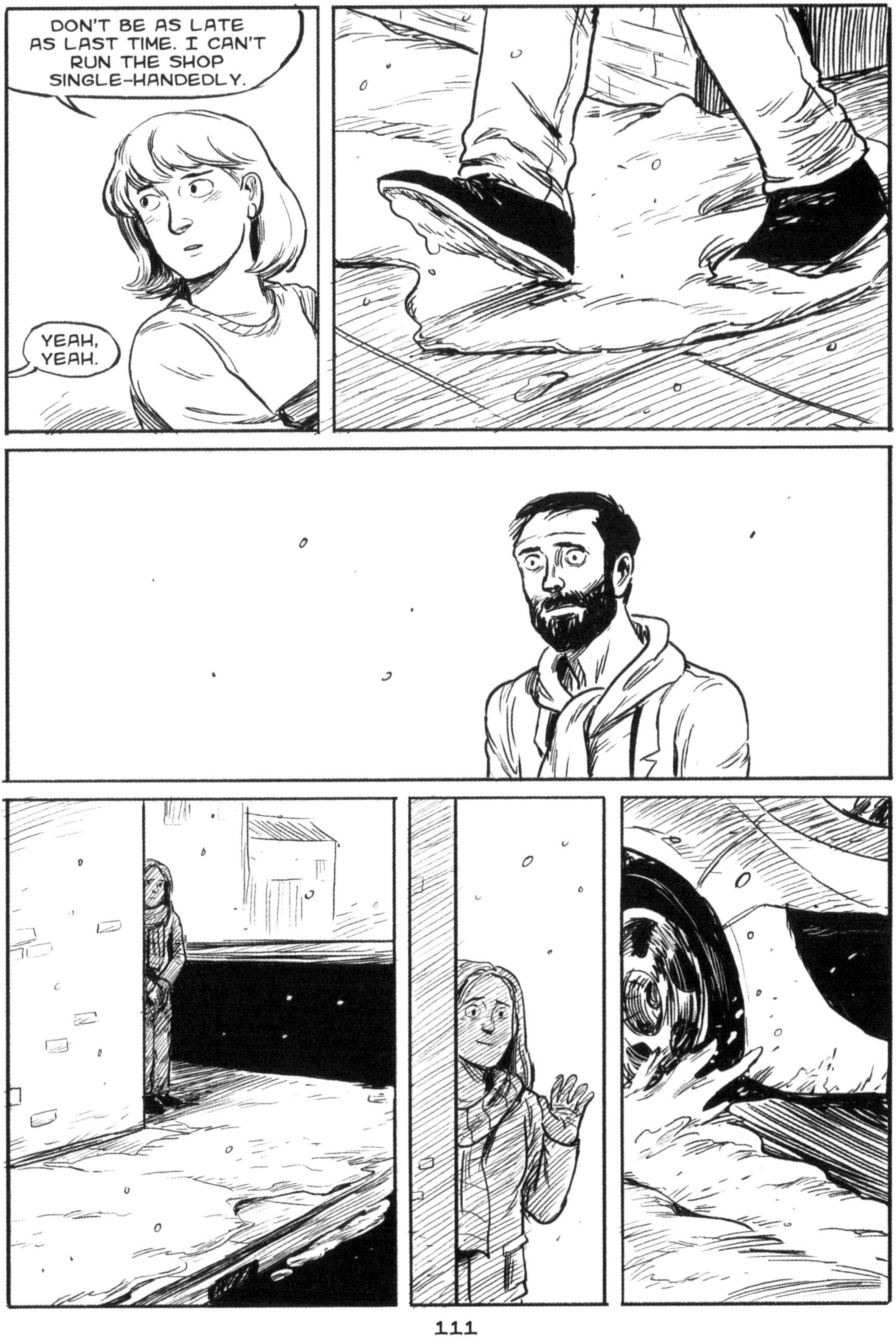
DON'T BE AS LATE AS LAST TIME. I CAN'T RUN THE SHOP SINGLE-HANDEDLY.
YEAH, YEAH.

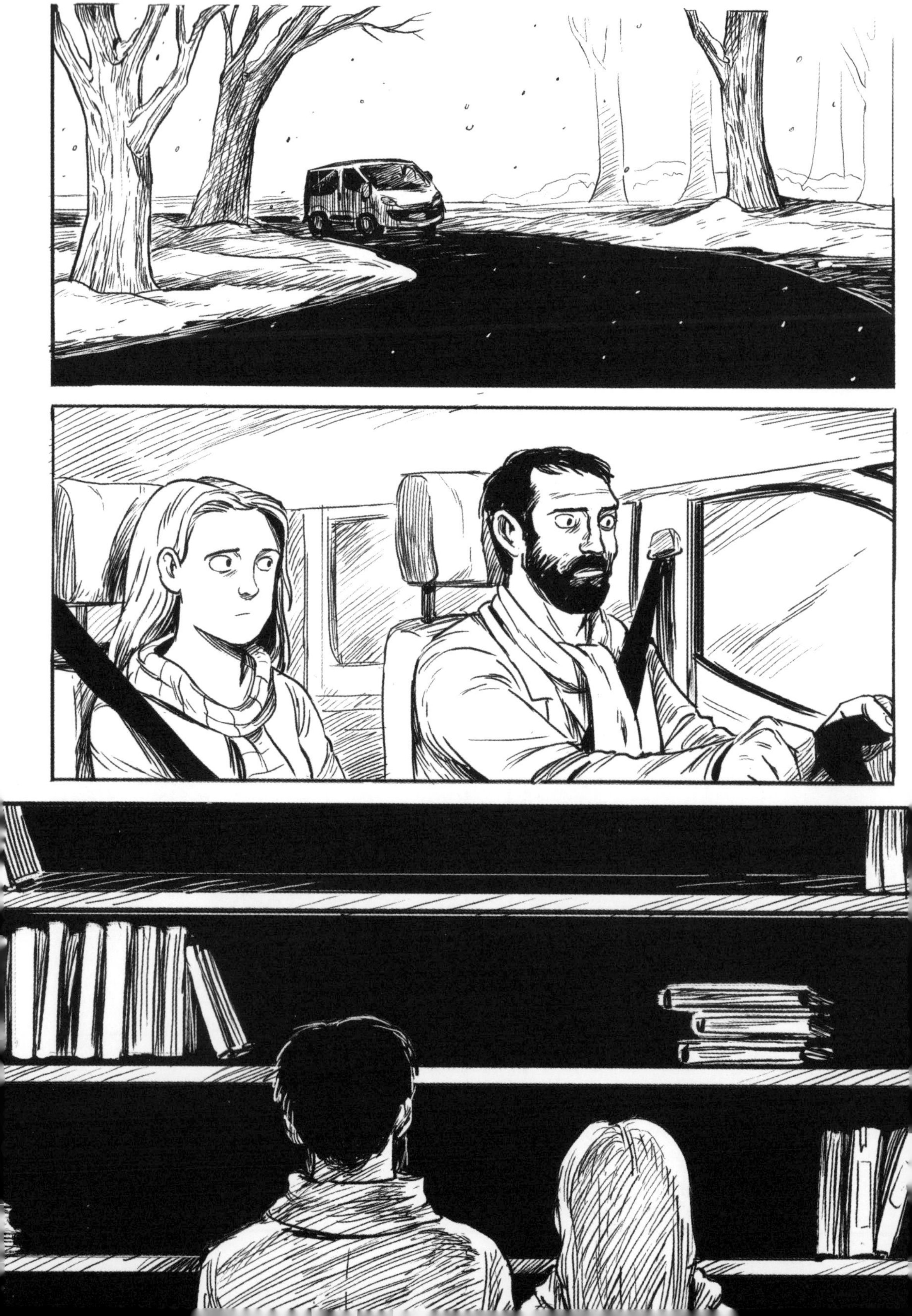

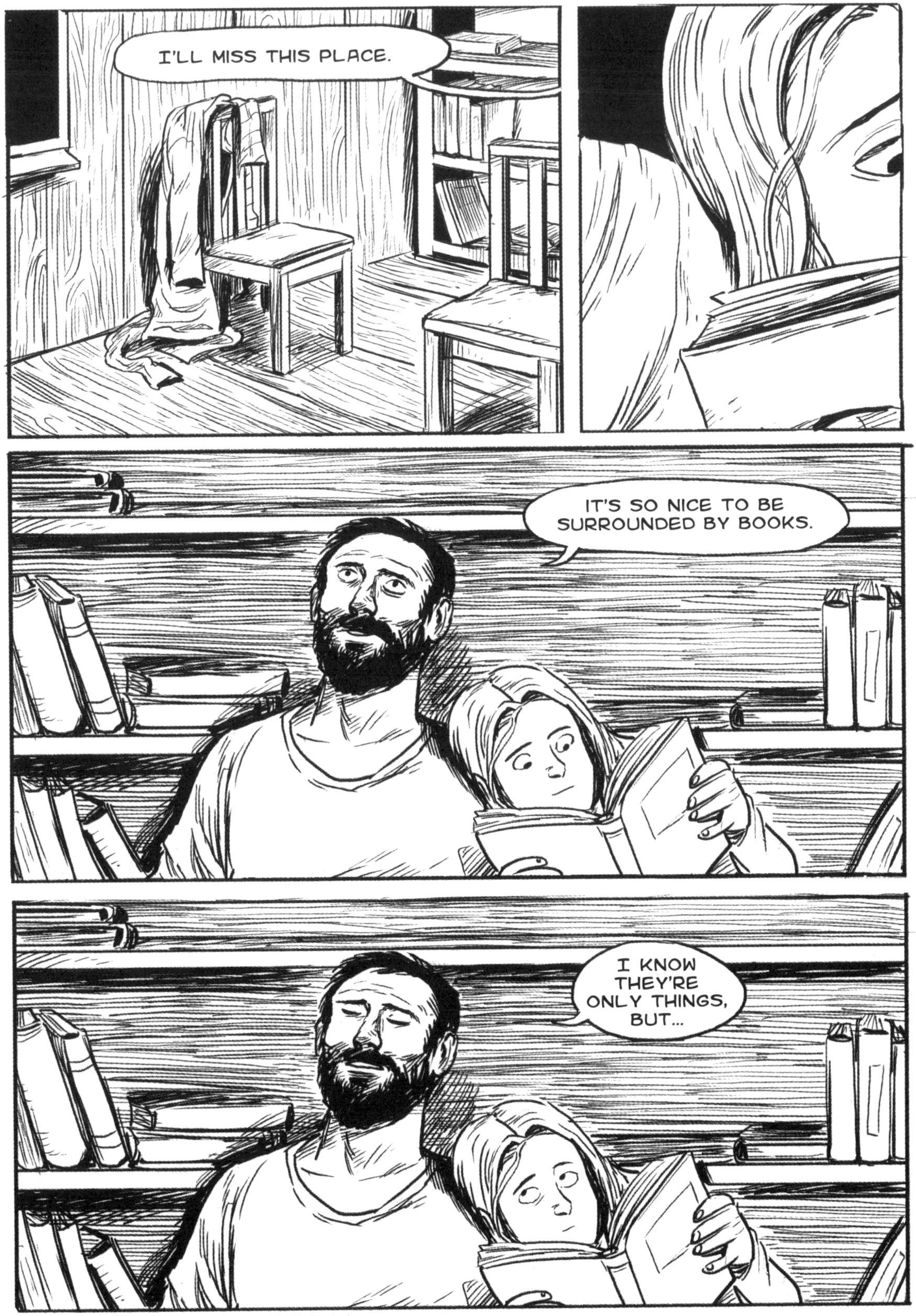
I'LL MISS THIS PLACE.
IT'S SO NICE TO BE SURROUNDED BY BOOKS.
I KNOW THEY'RE ONLY THINGS, BUT...

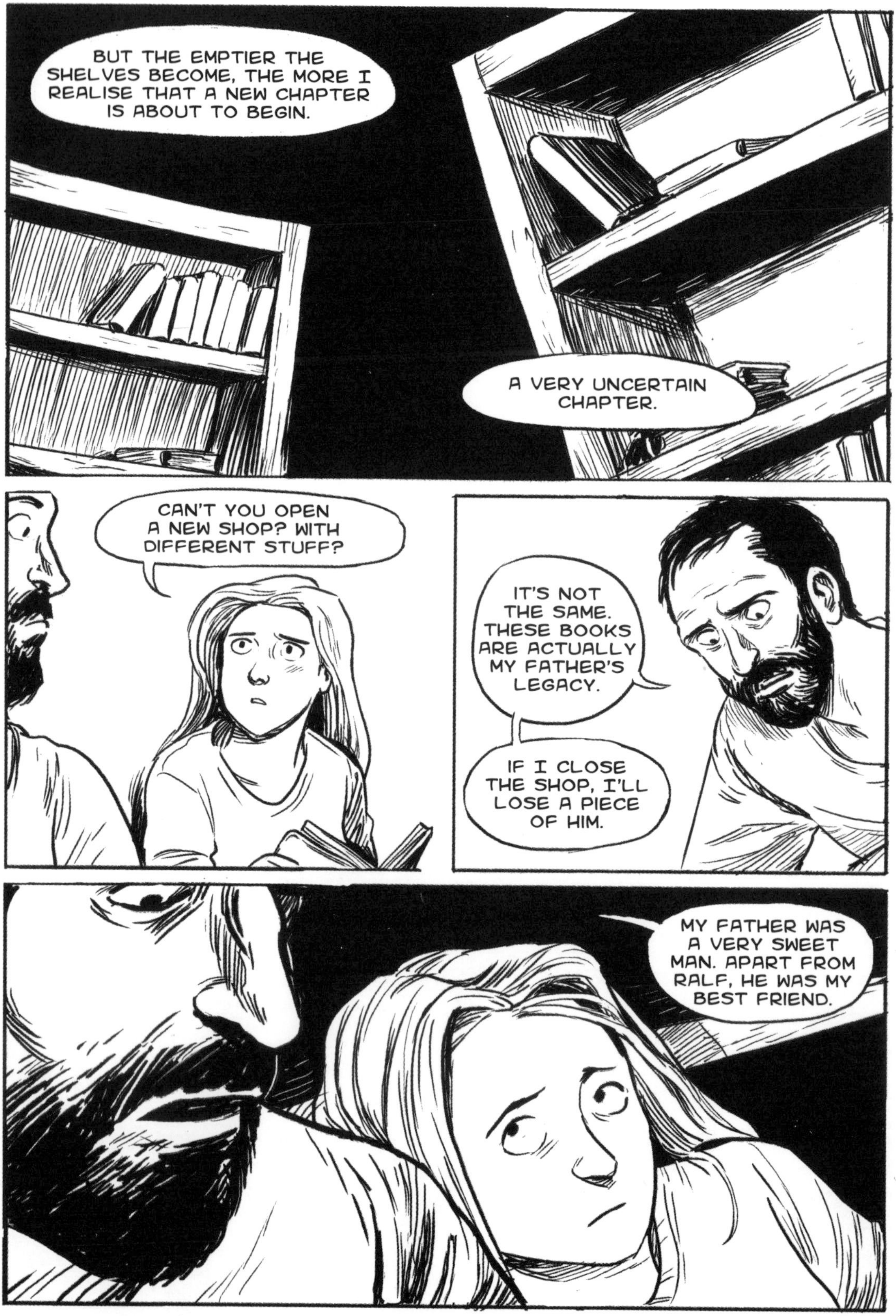
BUT THE EMPTIER THE SHELVES BECOME, THE MORE I REALISE THAT A NEW CHAPTER IS ABOUT TO BEGIN.
A VERY UNCERTAIN CHAPTER.
CAN'T YOU OPEN A NEW SHOP? WITH DIFFERENT STUFF?
IT'S NOT THE SAME. THESE BOOKS ARE ACTUALLY MY FATHER'S LEGACY.
IF I CLOSE THE SHOP, I'LL LOSE A PIECE OF HIM.
MY FATHER WAS A VERY SWEET MAN. APART FROM RALF, HE WAS MY BEST FRIEND.

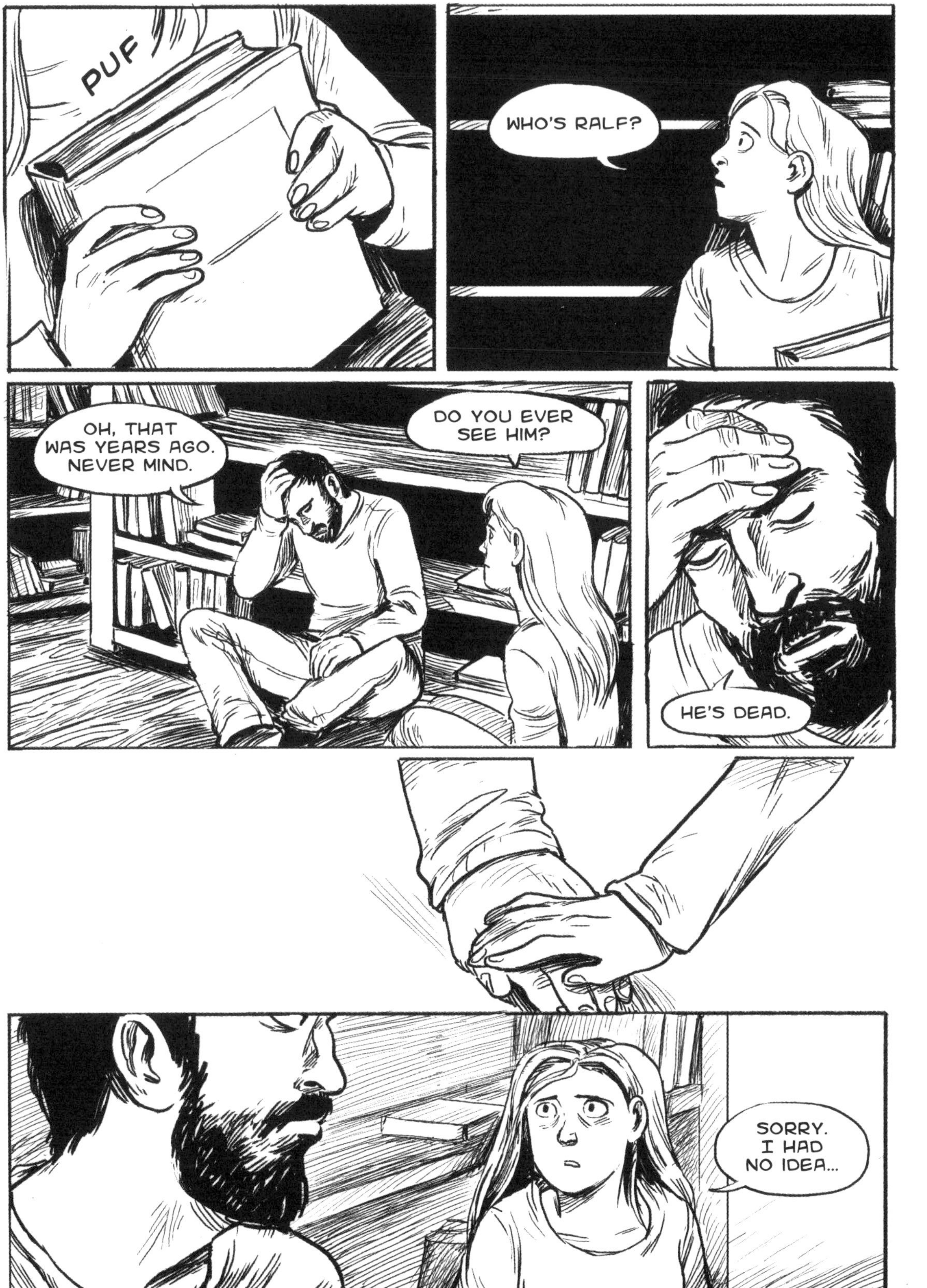
PUF
WHO'S RALF?
OH, THAT WAS YEARS AGO. NEVER MIND.
DO YOU EVER SEE HIM?
HE'S DEAD.
SORRY. I HAD NO IDEA...

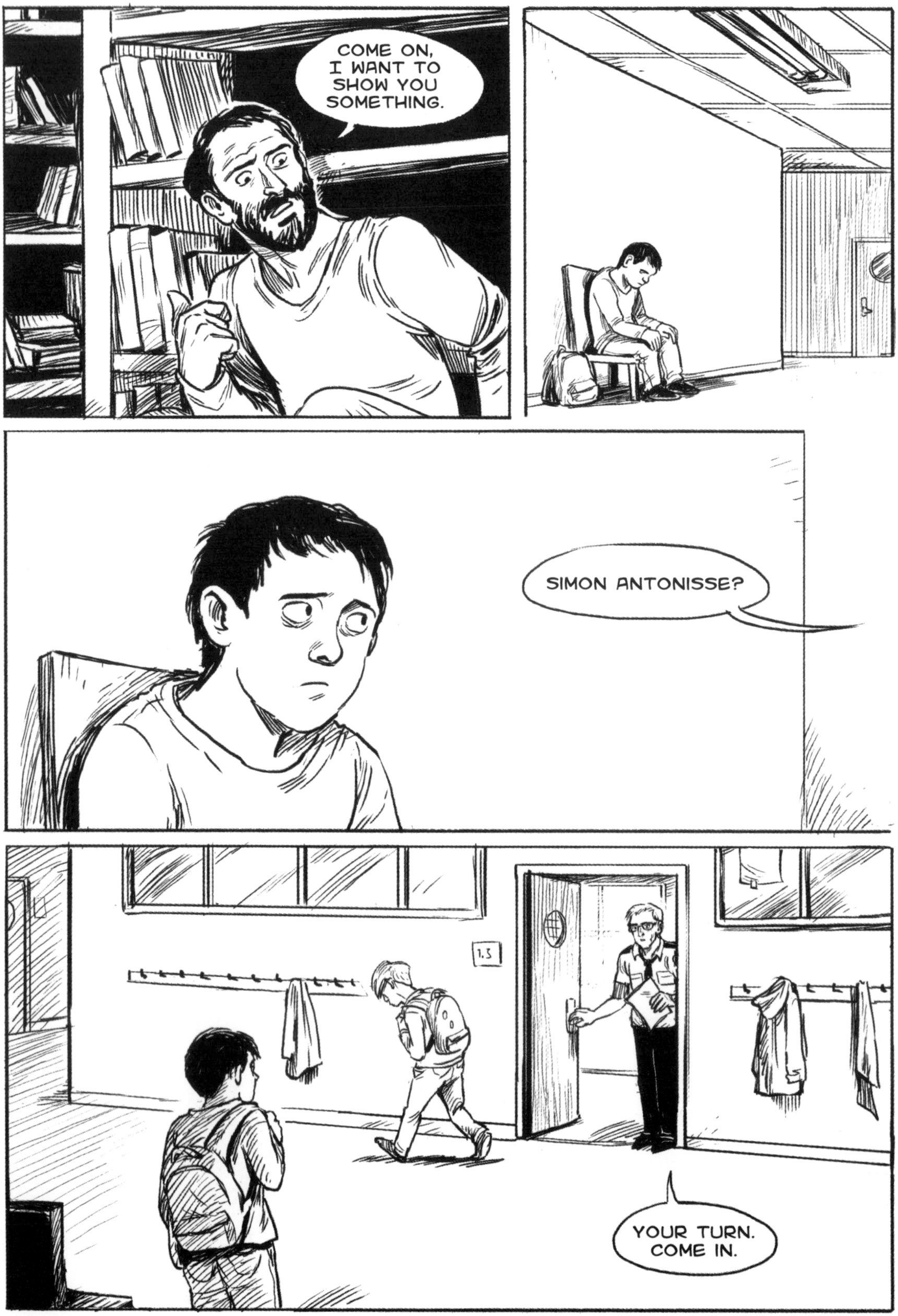
COME ON, I WANT TO SHOW YOU SOMETHING.
SIMON ANTONISSE?
1.3
YOUR TURN. COME IN.

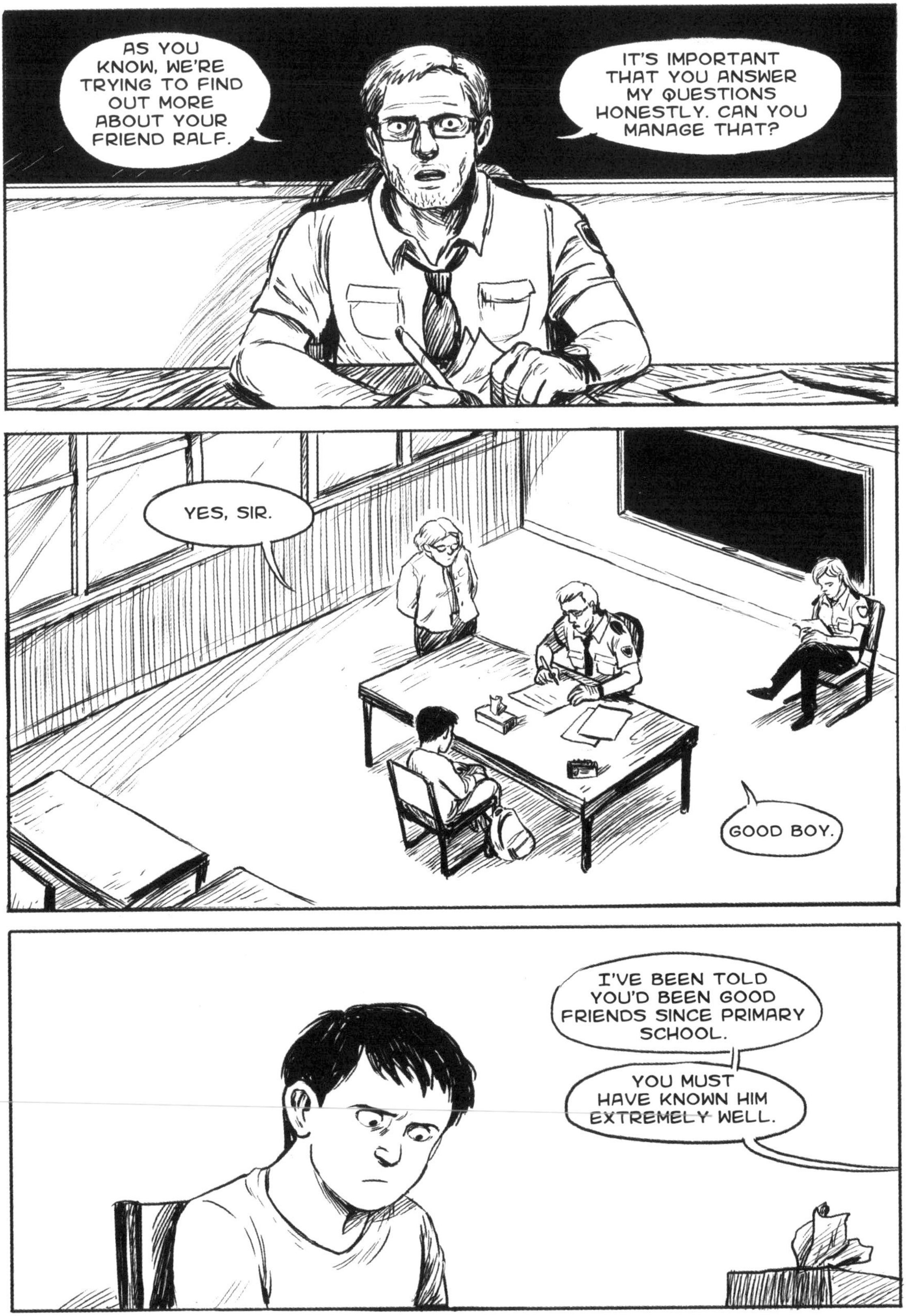
AS YOU KNOW, WE'RE TRYING TO FIND OUT MORE ABOUT YOUR FRIEND RALF.
IT'S IMPORTANT THAT YOU ANSWER MY QUESTIONS HONESTLY. CAN YOU MANAGE THAT?
YES, SIR.
GOOD BOY.
I'VE BEEN TOLD YOU'D BEEN GOOD FRIENDS SINCE PRIMARY SCHOOL.
YOU MUST HAVE KNOWN HIM EXTREMELY WELL.

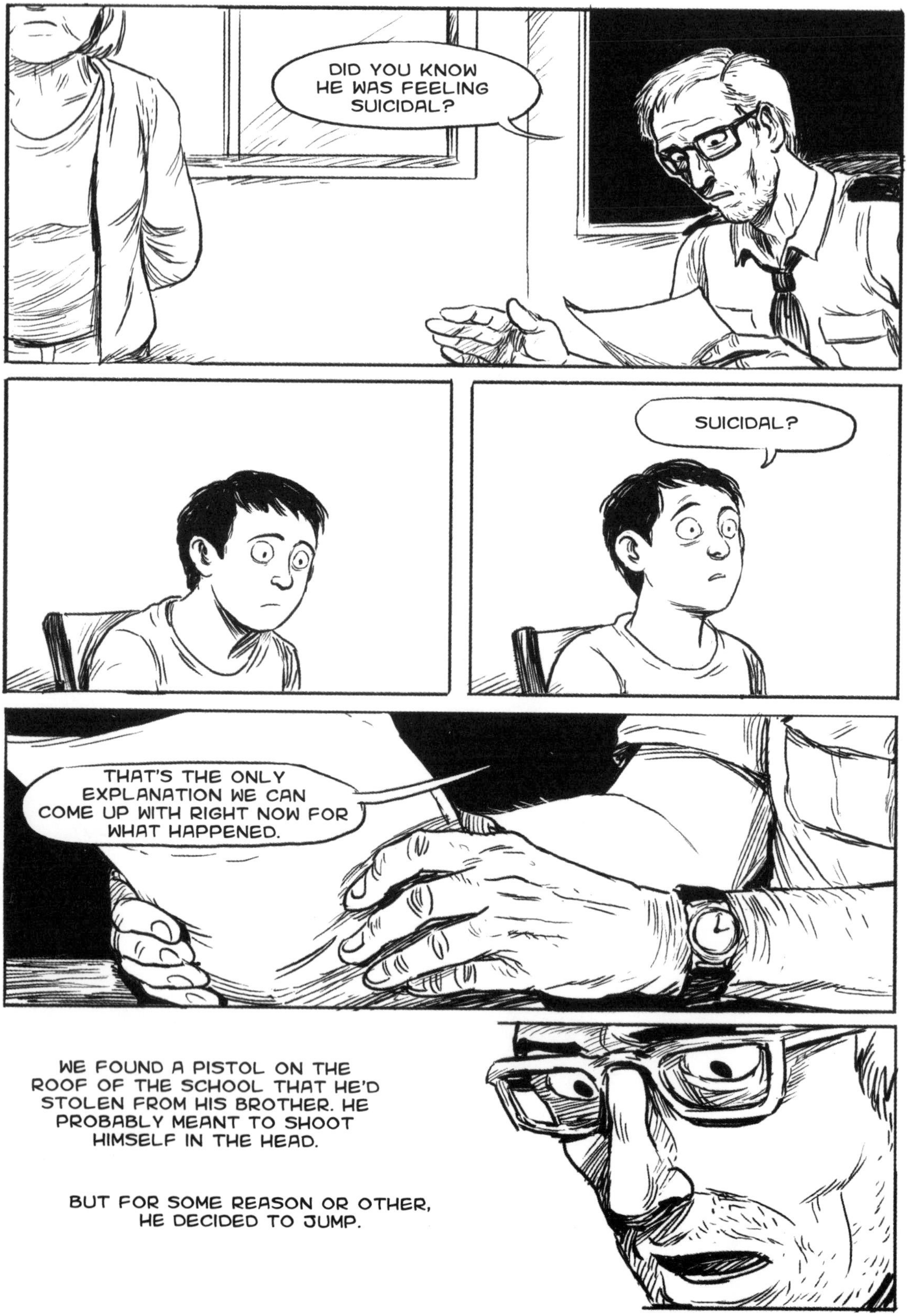
DID YOU KNOW HE WAS FEELING SUICIDAL?
SUICIDAL?
THAT'S THE ONLY EXPLANATION WE CAN COME UP WITH RIGHT NOW FOR WHAT HAPPENED.
WE FOUND A PISTOL ON THE ROOF OF THE SCHOOL THAT HE'D STOLEN FROM HIS BROTHER. HE PROBABLY MEANT TO SHOOT HIMSELF IN THE HEAD.
BUT FOR SOME REASON OR OTHER, HE DECIDED TO JUMP.

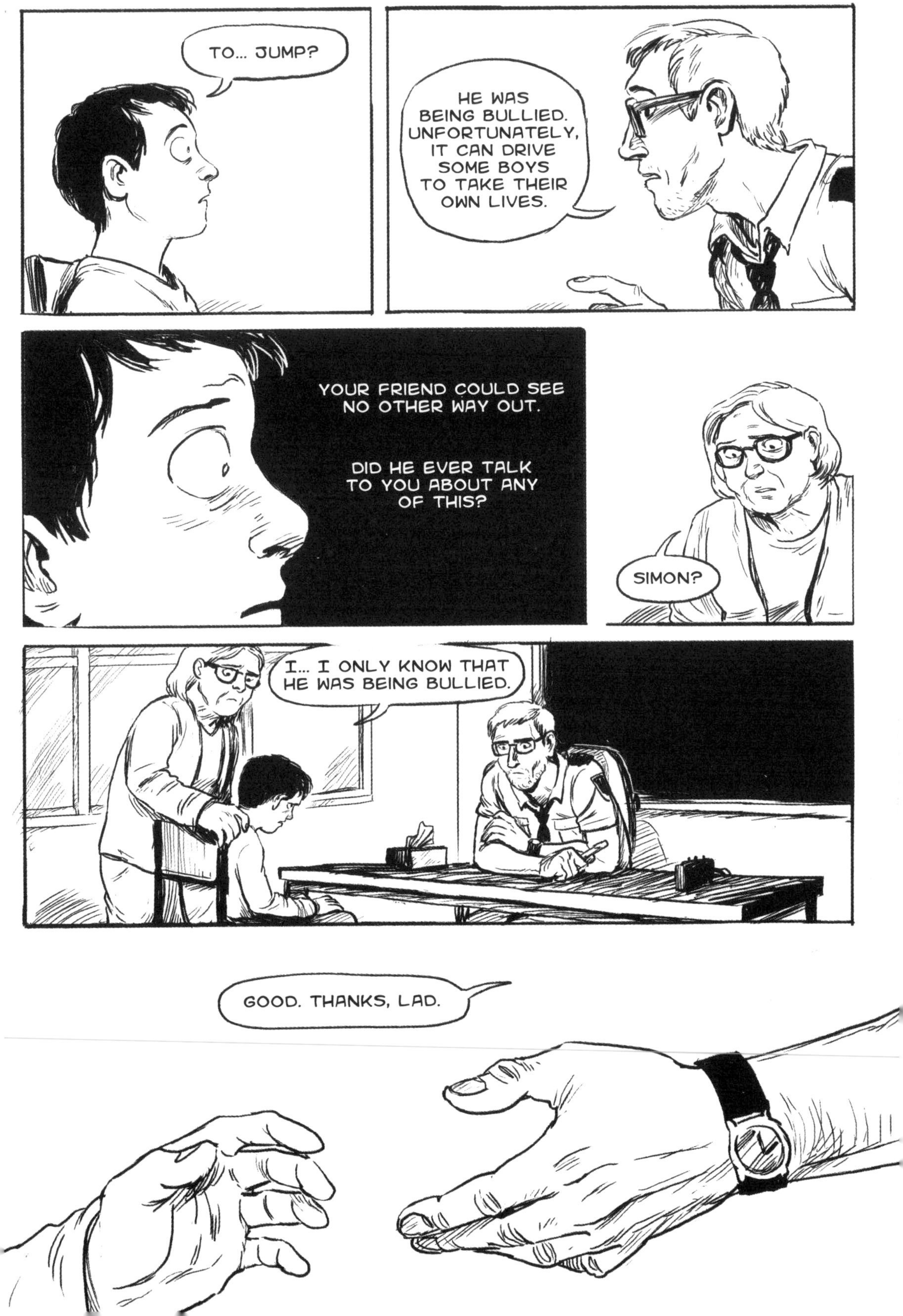
TO... JUMP?
HE WAS BEING BULLIED. UNFORTUNATELY, IT CAN DRIVE SOME BOYS TO TAKE THEIR OWN LIVES.
YOUR FRIEND COULD SEE NO OTHER WAY OUT.
DID HE EVER TALK TO YOU ABOUT ANY OF THIS?
SIMON?
I... I ONLY KNOW THAT HE WAS BEING BULLIED.
GOOD. THANKS, LAD.

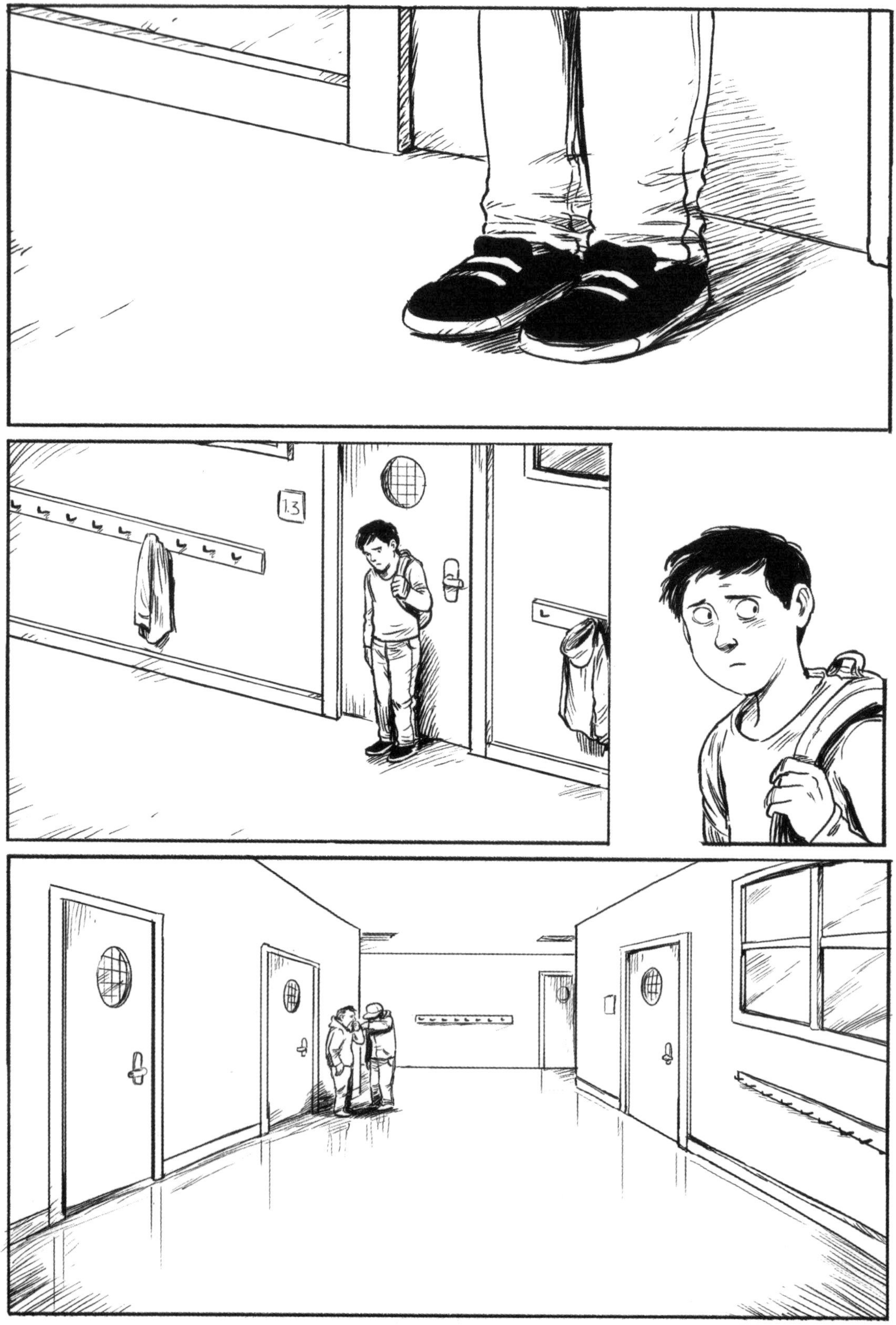
1.3

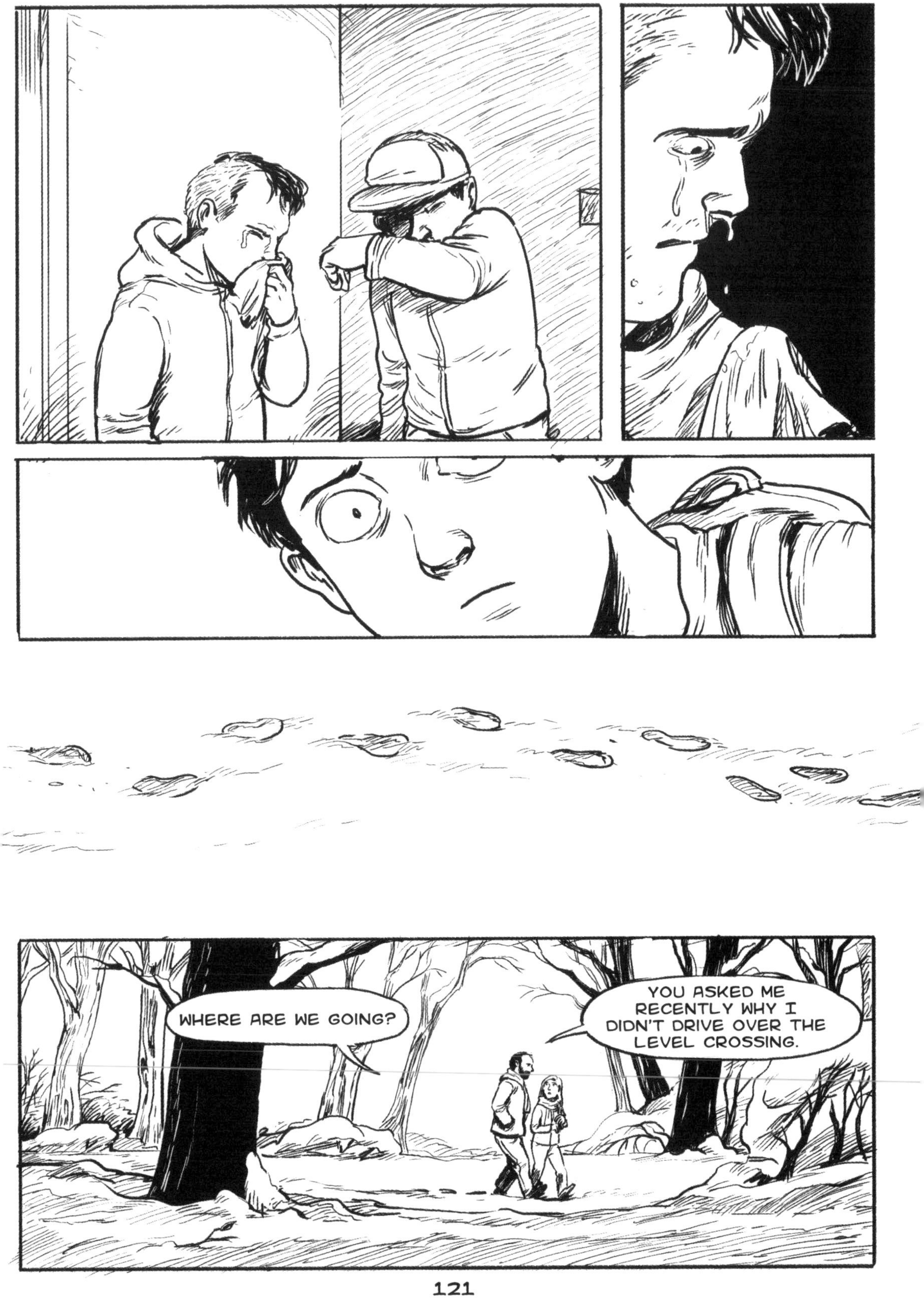
WHERE ARE WE GOING?
YOU ASKED ME RECENTLY WHY I DIDN'T DRIVE OVER THE LEVEL CROSSING.

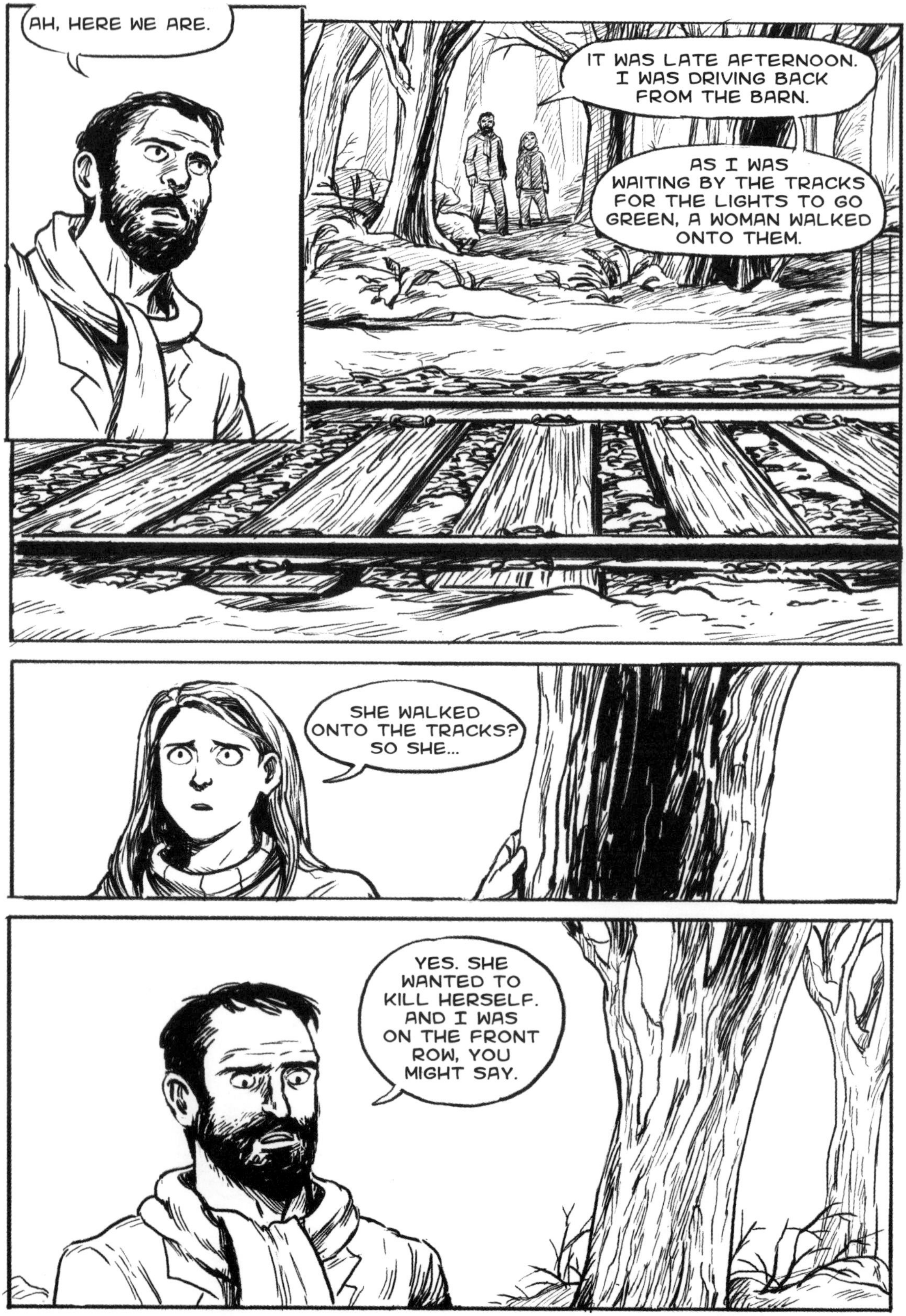
AH, HERE WE ARE.
IT WAS LATE AFTERNOON. I WAS DRIVING BACK FROM THE BARN.
AS I WAS WAITING BY THE TRACKS FOR THE LIGHTS TO GO GREEN, A WOMAN WALKED ONTO THEM.
SHE WALKED ONTO THE TRACKS? SO SHE...
YES. SHE WANTED TO KILL HERSELF. AND I WAS ON THE FRONT ROW, YOU MIGHT SAY.

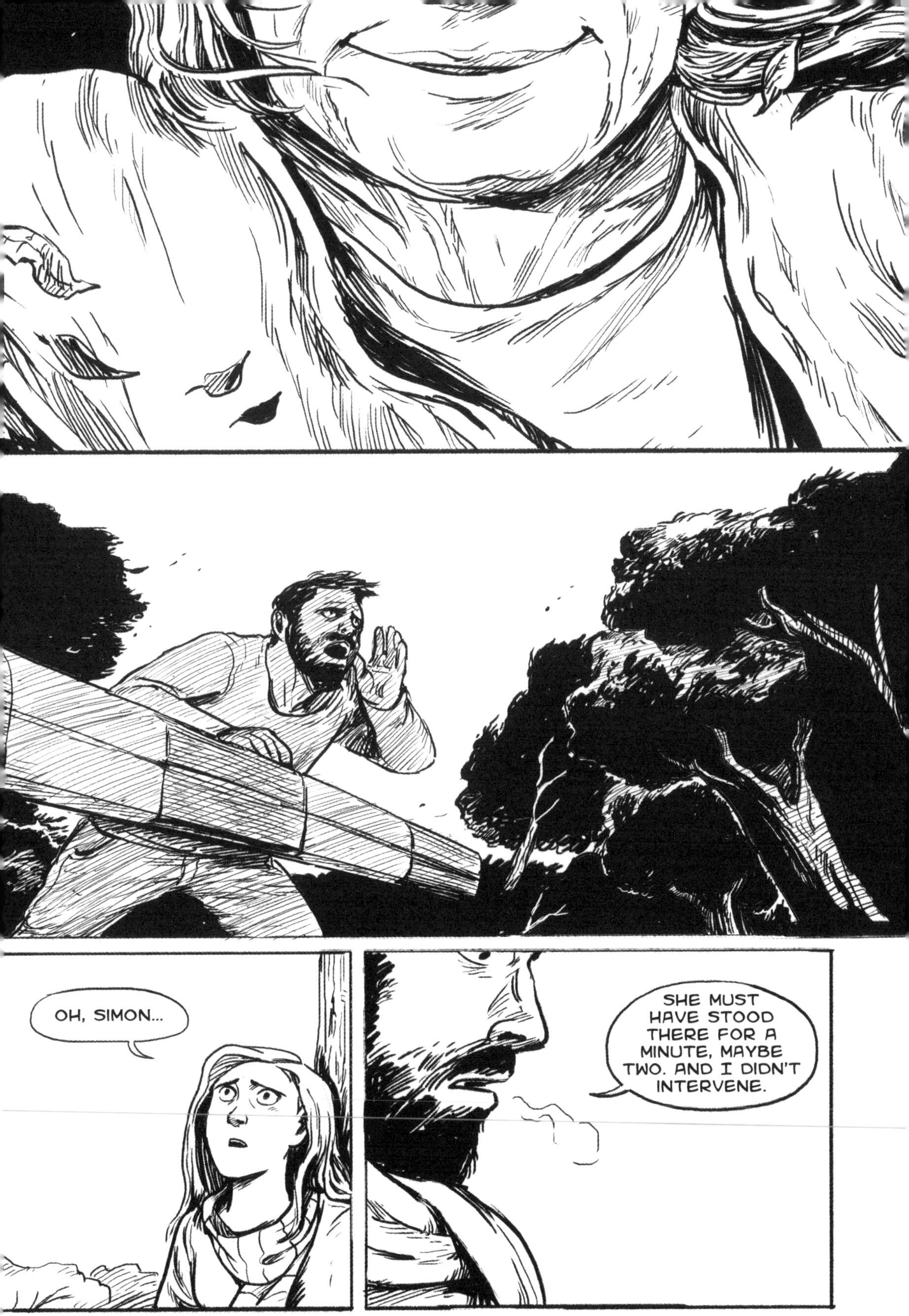
OH, SIMON...
SHE MUST HAVE STOOD THERE FOR A MINUTE, MAYBE TWO. AND I DIDN'T INTERVENE.

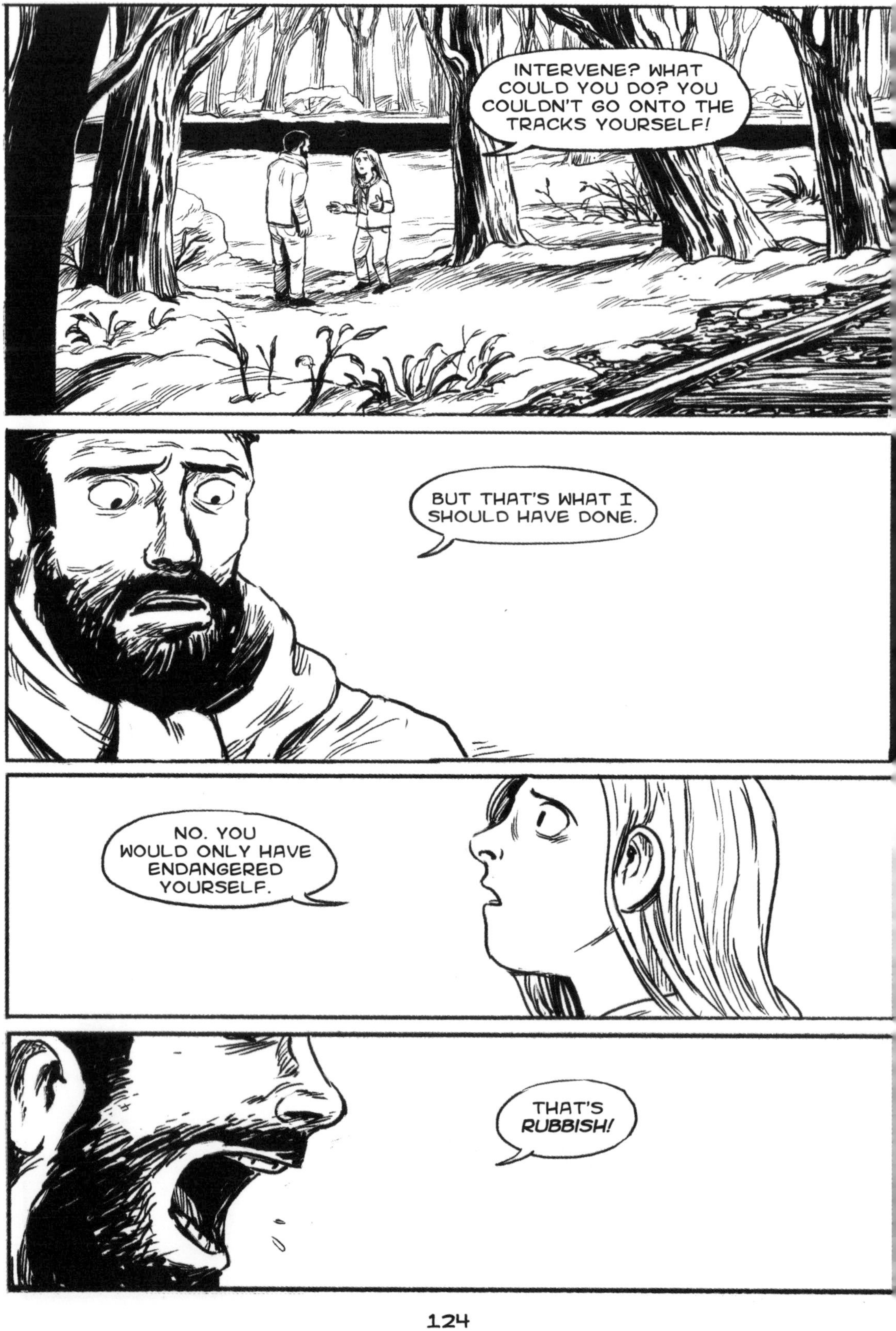
INTERVENE? WHAT COULD YOU DO? YOU COULDN'T GO ONTO THE TRACKS YOURSELF!
BUT THAT'S WHAT I SHOULD HAVE DONE.
NO. YOU WOULD ONLY HAVE ENDANGERED YOURSELF.
THAT'S *RUBBISH!*

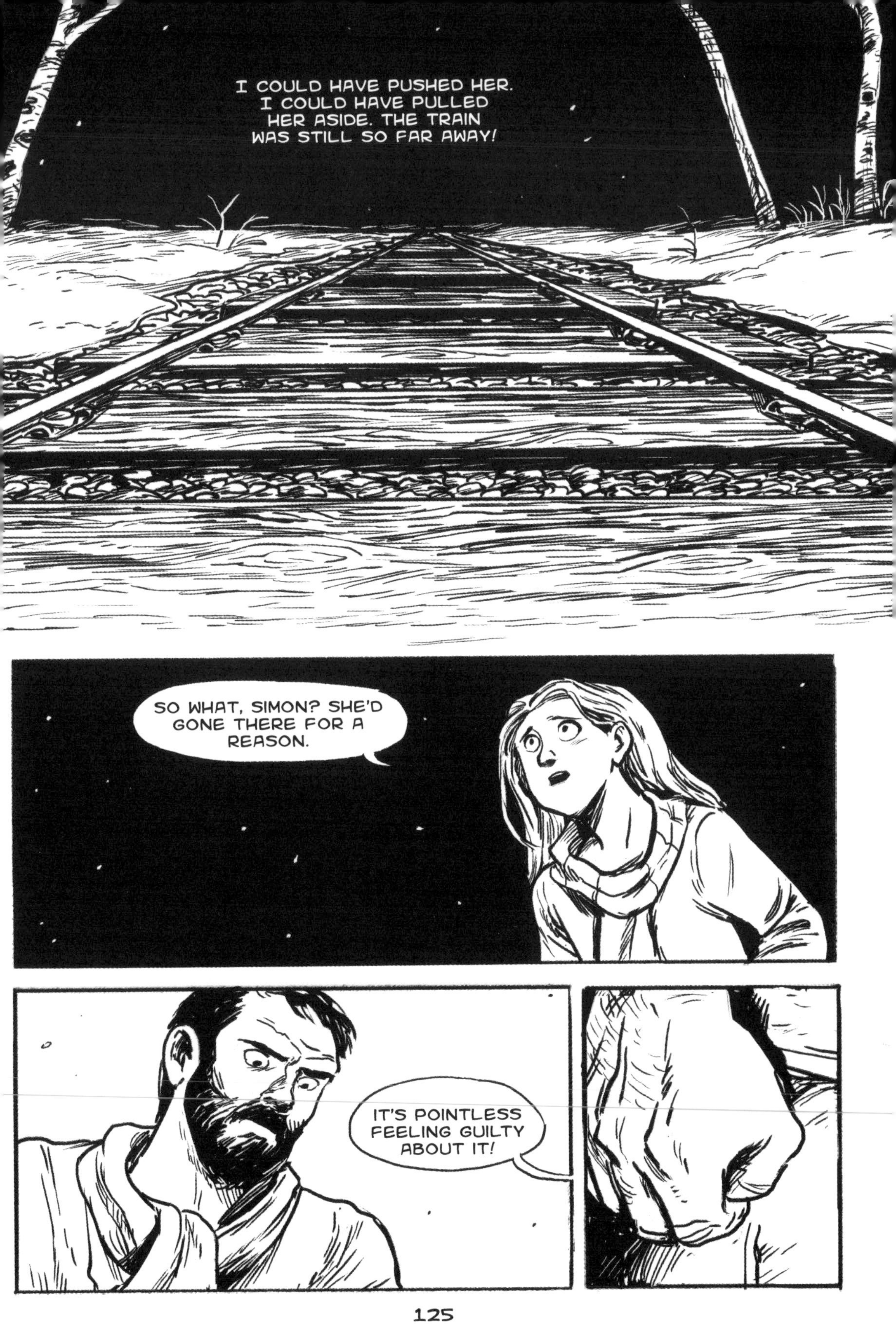
I COULD HAVE PUSHED HER. I COULD HAVE PULLED HER ASIDE. THE TRAIN WAS STILL SO FAR AWAY!
SO WHAT, SIMON? SHE'D GONE THERE FOR A REASON.
IT'S POINTLESS FEELING GUILTY ABOUT IT!

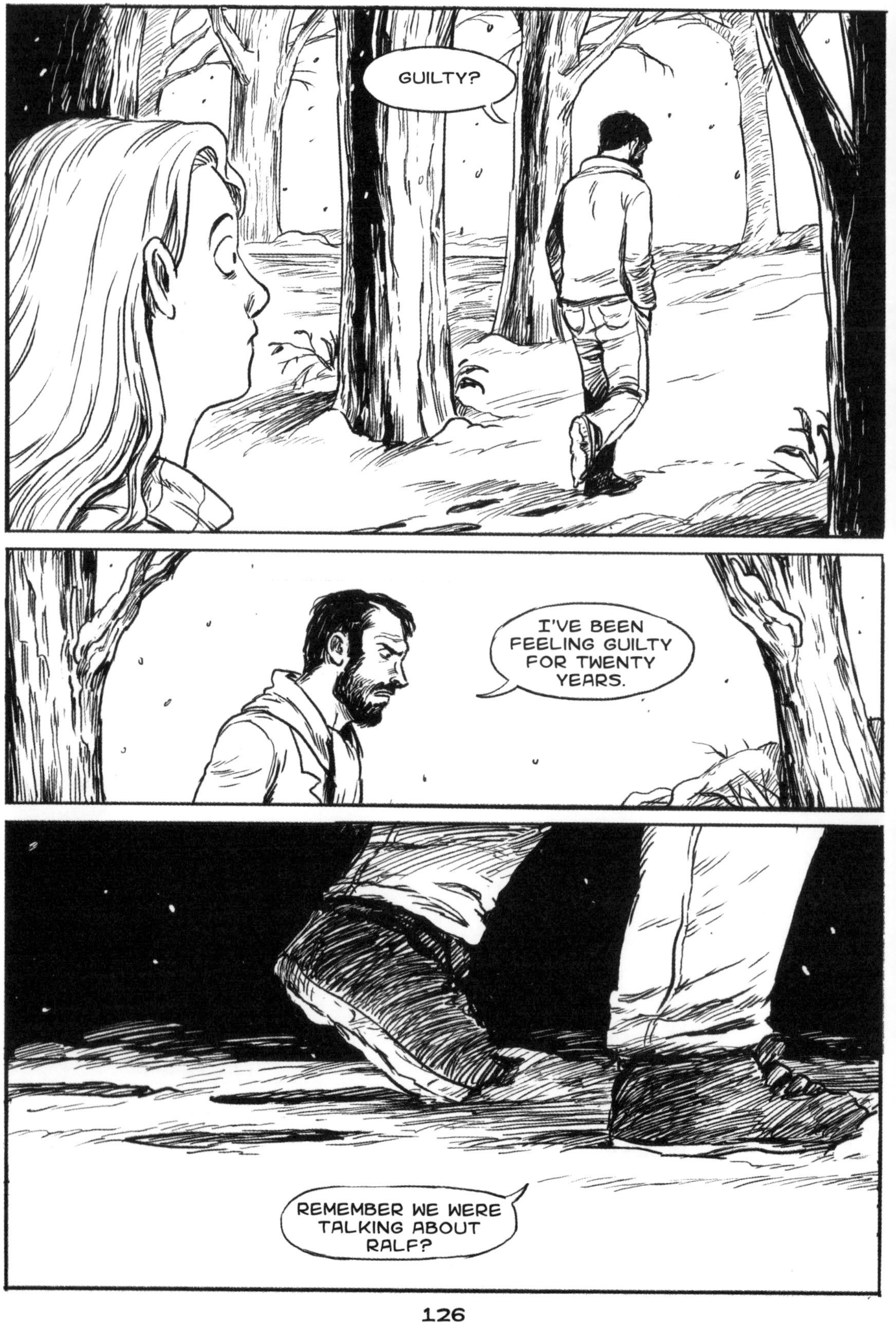
GUILTY?
I'VE BEEN FEELING GUILTY FOR TWENTY YEARS.
REMEMBER WE WERE TALKING ABOUT RALF?

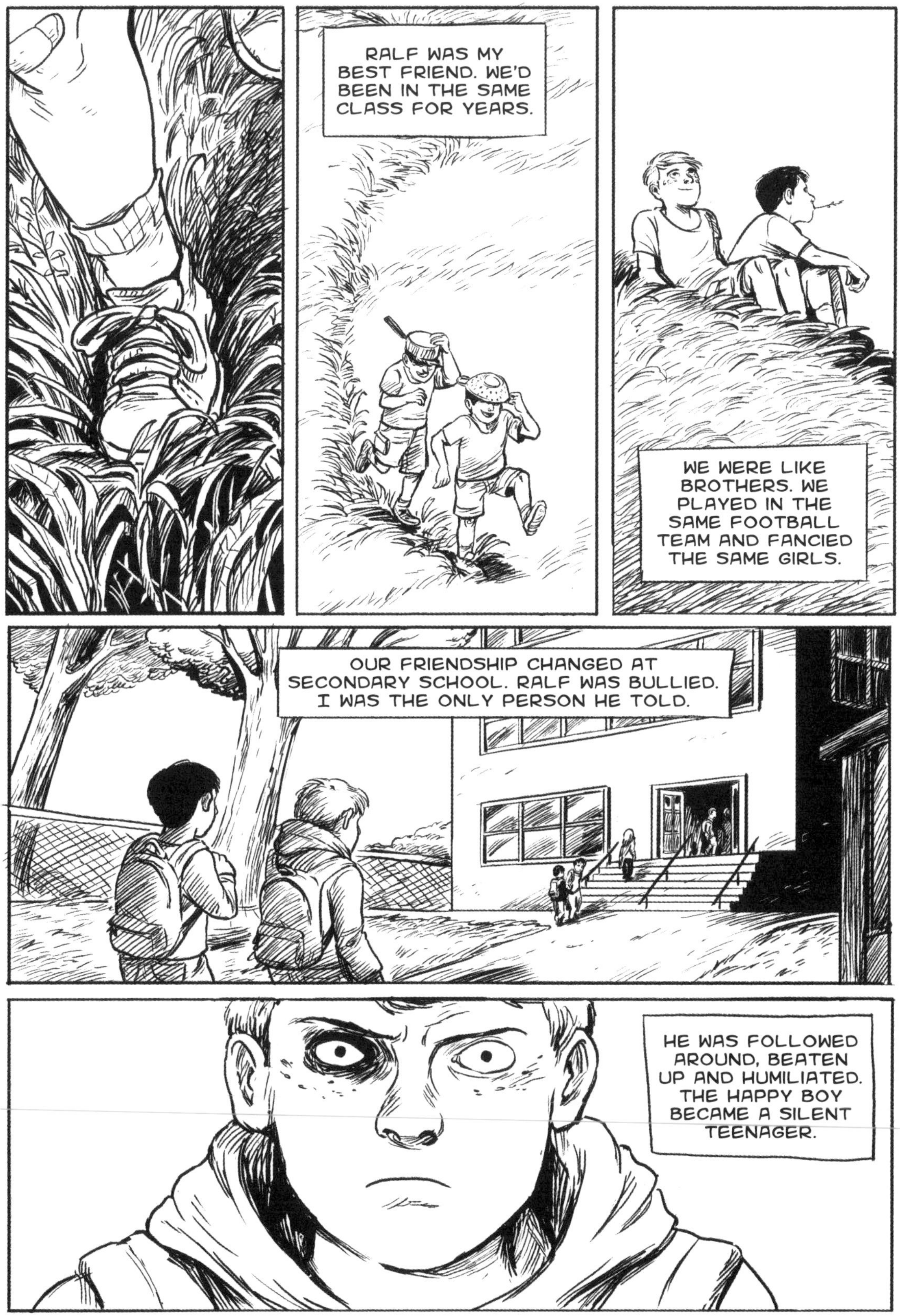
RALF WAS MY BEST FRIEND. WE'D BEEN IN THE SAME CLASS FOR YEARS.
WE WERE LIKE BROTHERS. WE PLAYED IN THE SAME FOOTBALL TEAM AND FANCIED THE SAME GIRLS.
OUR FRIENDSHIP CHANGED AT SECONDARY SCHOOL. RALF WAS BULLIED. I WAS THE ONLY PERSON HE TOLD.
HE WAS FOLLOWED AROUND, BEATEN UP AND HUMILIATED. THE HAPPY BOY BECAME A SILENT TEENAGER.

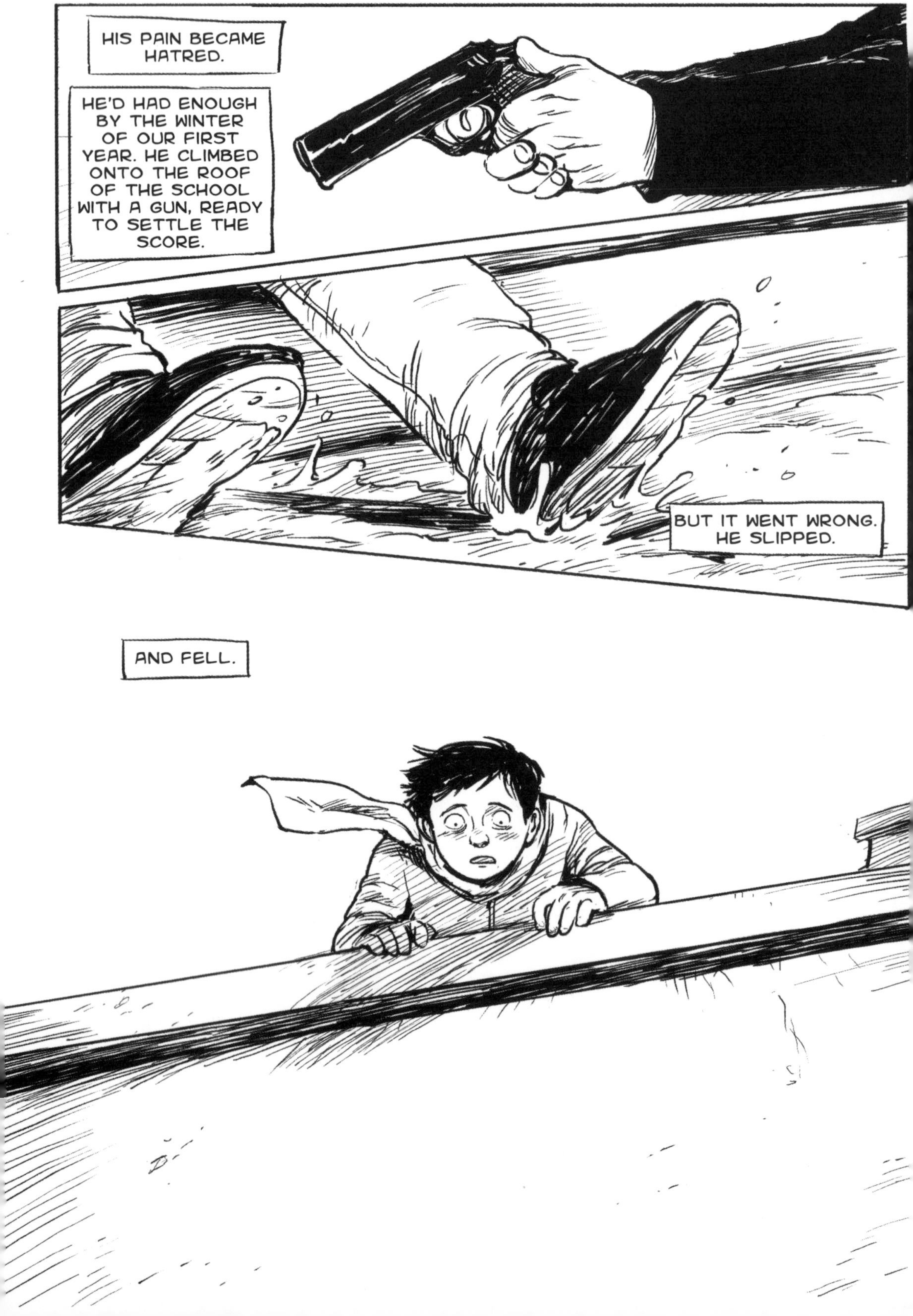
HIS PAIN BECAME HATRED.
HE'D HAD ENOUGH BY THE WINTER OF OUR FIRST YEAR. HE CLIMBED ONTO THE ROOF OF THE SCHOOL WITH A GUN, READY TO SETTLE THE SCORE.
BUT IT WENT WRONG. HE SLIPPED.
AND FELL.

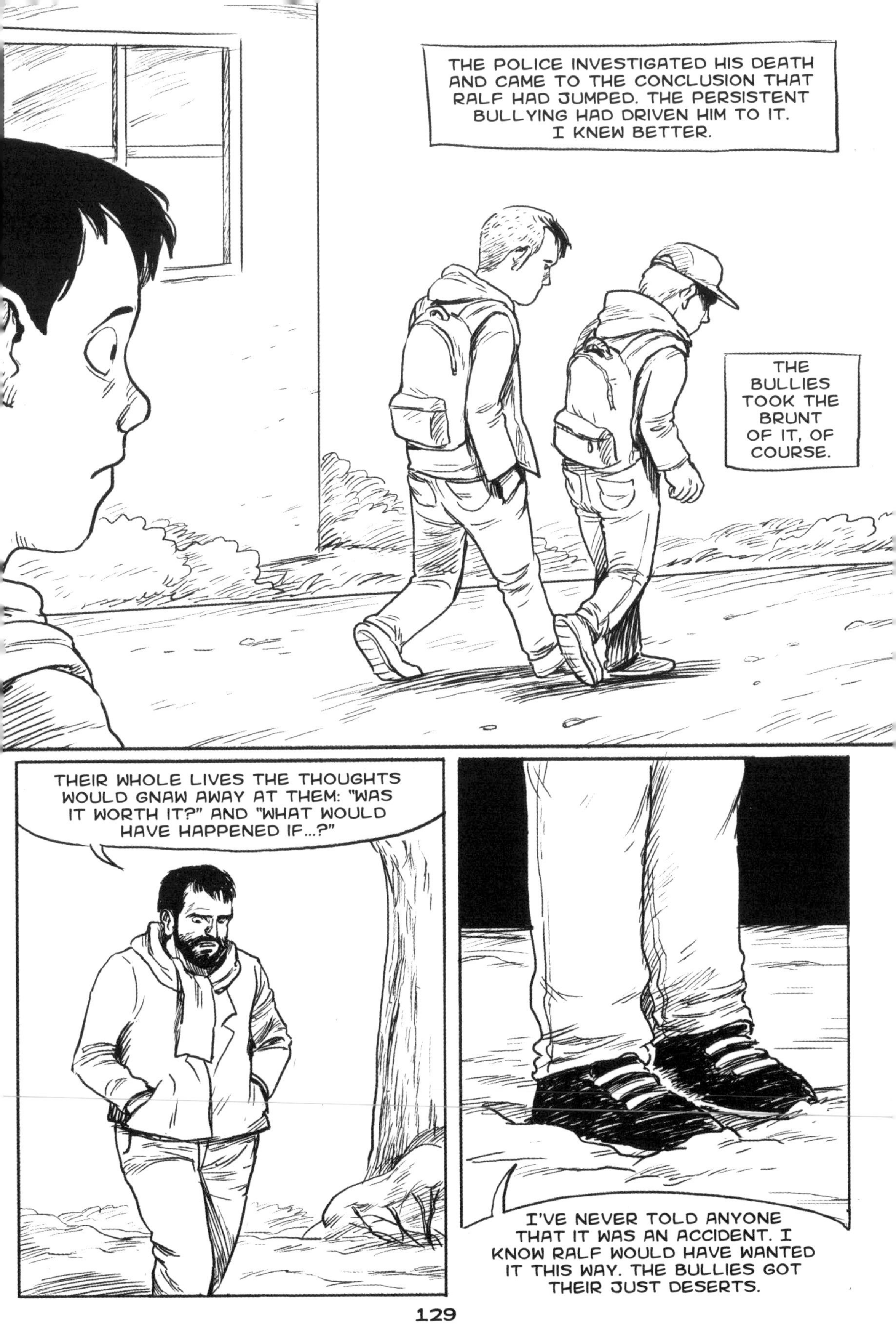
THE POLICE INVESTIGATED HIS DEATH AND CAME TO THE CONCLUSION THAT RALF HAD JUMPED. THE PERSISTENT BULLYING HAD DRIVEN HIM TO IT. I KNEW BETTER.
THE BULLIES TOOK THE BRUNT OF IT, OF COURSE.
THEIR WHOLE LIVES THE THOUGHTS WOULD GNAW AWAY AT THEM: "WAS IT WORTH IT?" AND "WHAT WOULD HAVE HAPPENED IF...?"
I'VE NEVER TOLD ANYONE THAT IT WAS AN ACCIDENT. I KNOW RALF WOULD HAVE WANTED IT THIS WAY. THE BULLIES GOT THEIR JUST DESERTS.

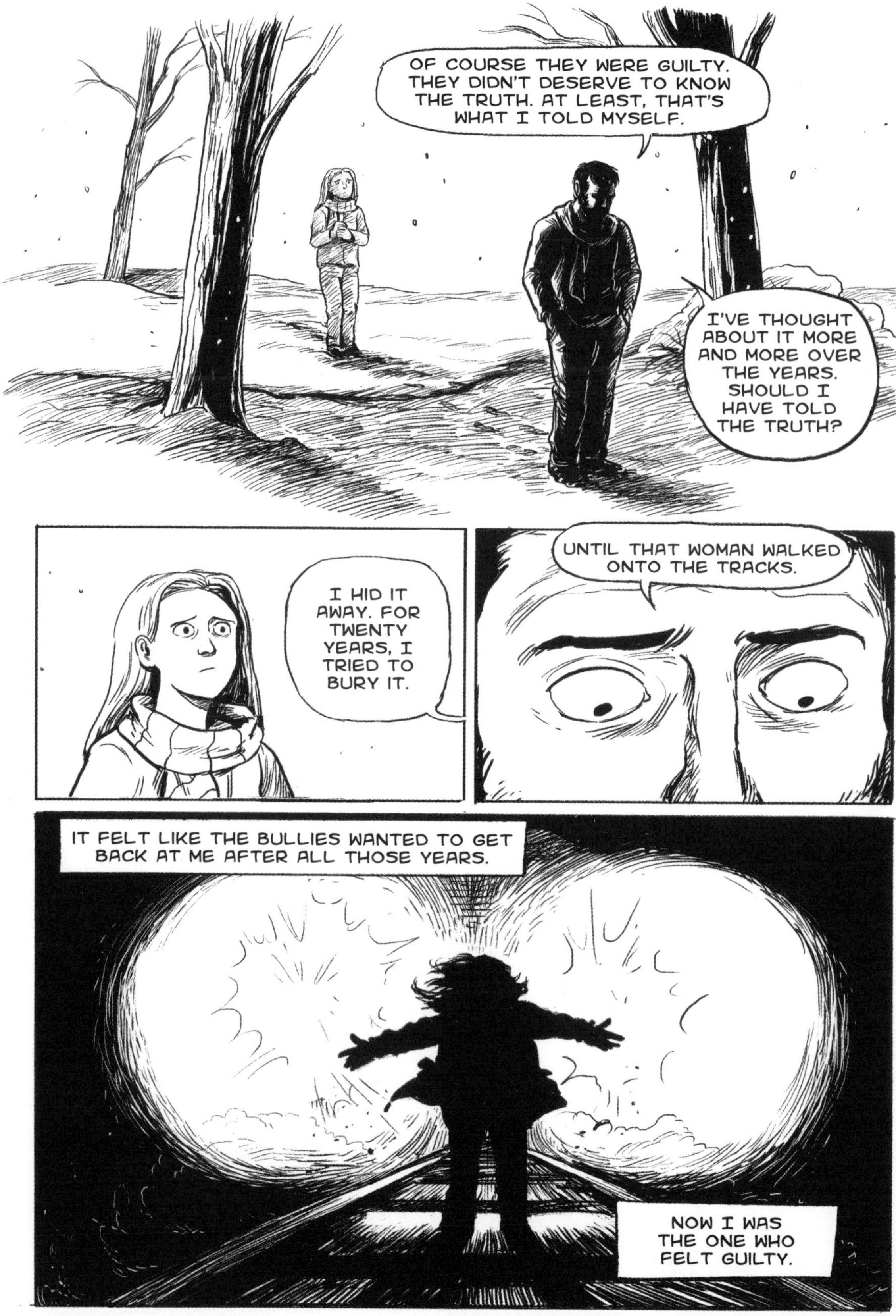
OF COURSE THEY WERE GUILTY. THEY DIDN'T DESERVE TO KNOW THE TRUTH. AT LEAST, THAT'S WHAT I TOLD MYSELF.
I'VE THOUGHT ABOUT IT MORE AND MORE OVER THE YEARS. SHOULD I HAVE TOLD THE TRUTH?
I HID IT AWAY. FOR TWENTY YEARS, I TRIED TO BURY IT.
UNTIL THAT WOMAN WALKED ONTO THE TRACKS.
IT FELT LIKE THE BULLIES WANTED TO GET BACK AT ME AFTER ALL THOSE YEARS.
NOW I WAS THE ONE WHO FELT GUILTY.

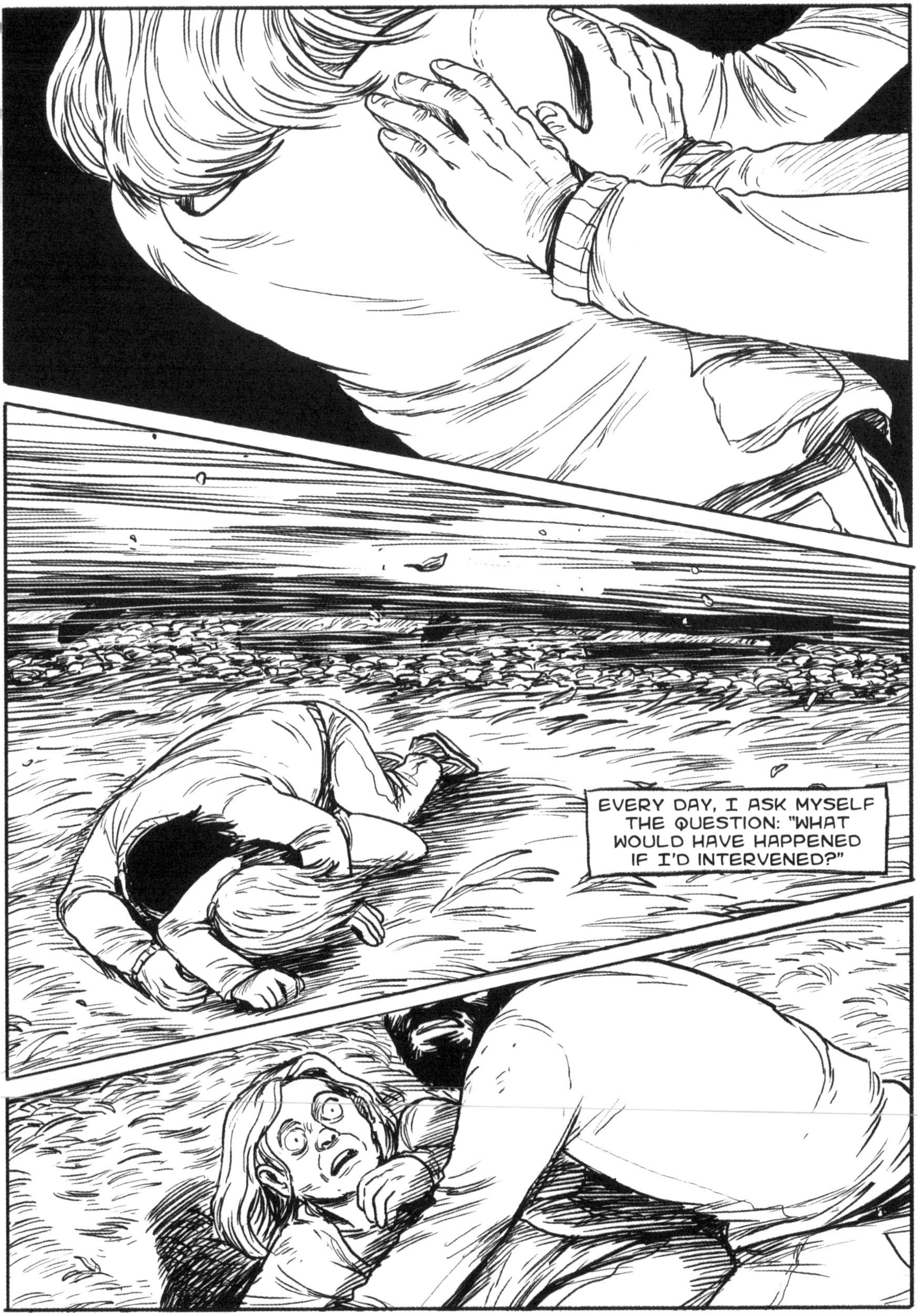
EVERY DAY, I ASK MYSELF THE QUESTION: "WHAT WOULD HAVE HAPPENED IF I'D INTERVENED?"

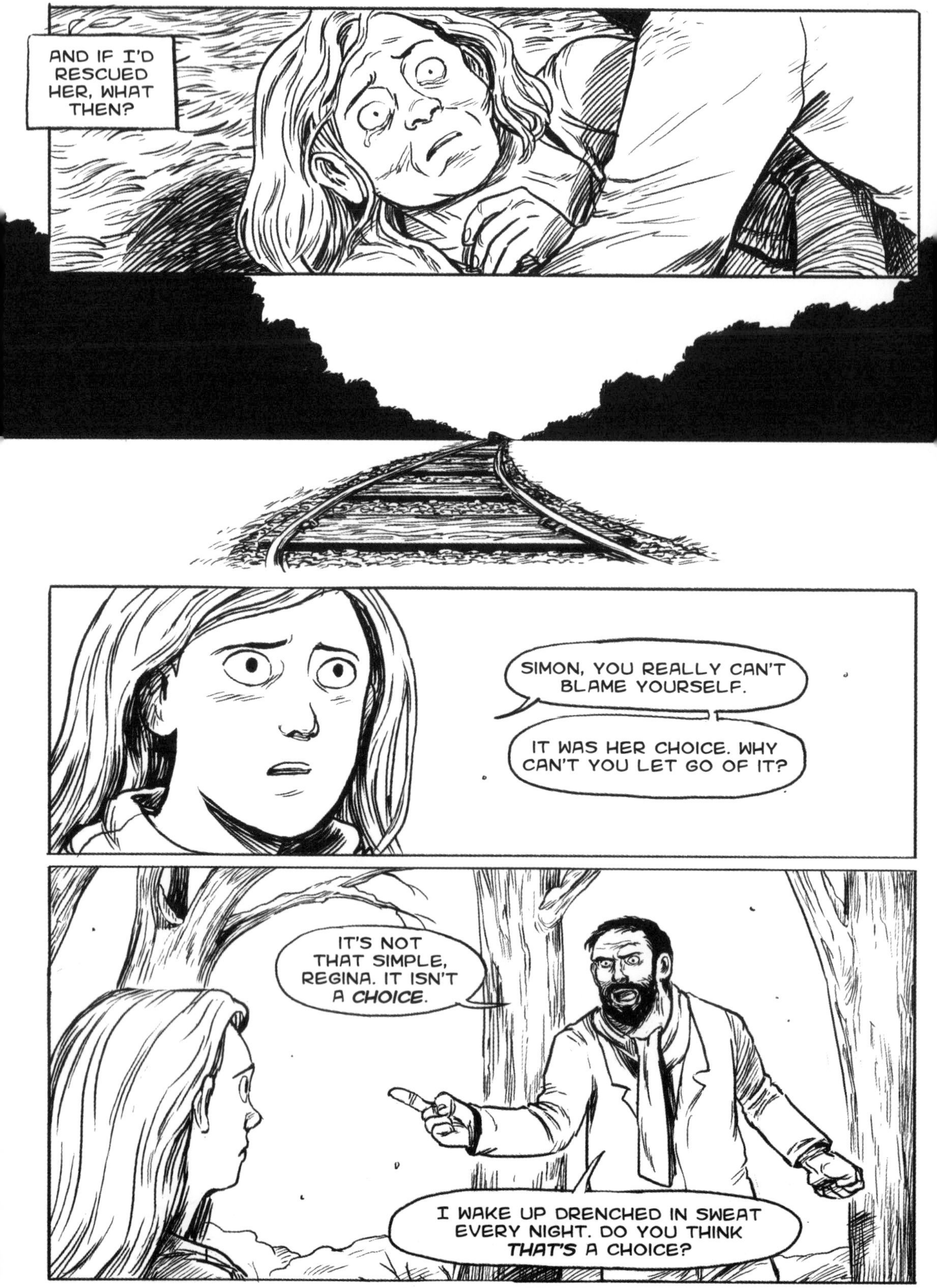
AND IF I'D RESCUED HER, WHAT THEN?
SIMON, YOU REALLY CAN'T BLAME YOURSELF.
IT WAS HER CHOICE. WHY CAN'T YOU LET GO OF IT?
IT'S NOT THAT SIMPLE, REGINA. IT ISN'T A *CHOICE*.
I WAKE UP DRENCHED IN SWEAT EVERY NIGHT. DO YOU THINK *THAT'S* A CHOICE?

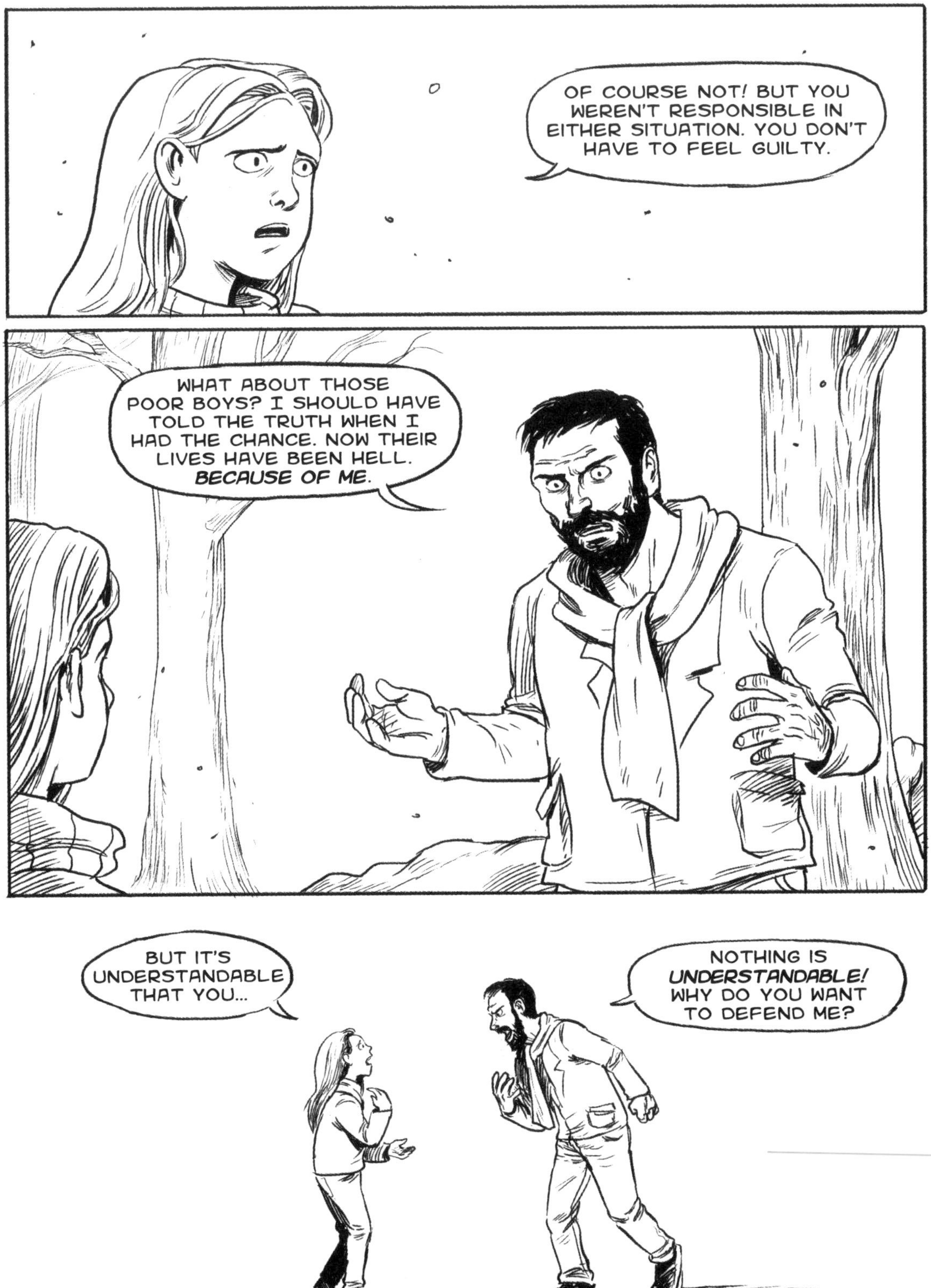
OF COURSE NOT! BUT YOU WEREN'T RESPONSIBLE IN EITHER SITUATION. YOU DON'T HAVE TO FEEL GUILTY.
WHAT ABOUT THOSE POOR BOYS? I SHOULD HAVE TOLD THE TRUTH WHEN I HAD THE CHANCE. NOW THEIR LIVES HAVE BEEN HELL. *BECAUSE OF ME*.
BUT IT'S UNDERSTANDABLE THAT YOU...
NOTHING IS *UNDERSTANDABLE!* WHY DO YOU WANT TO DEFEND ME?

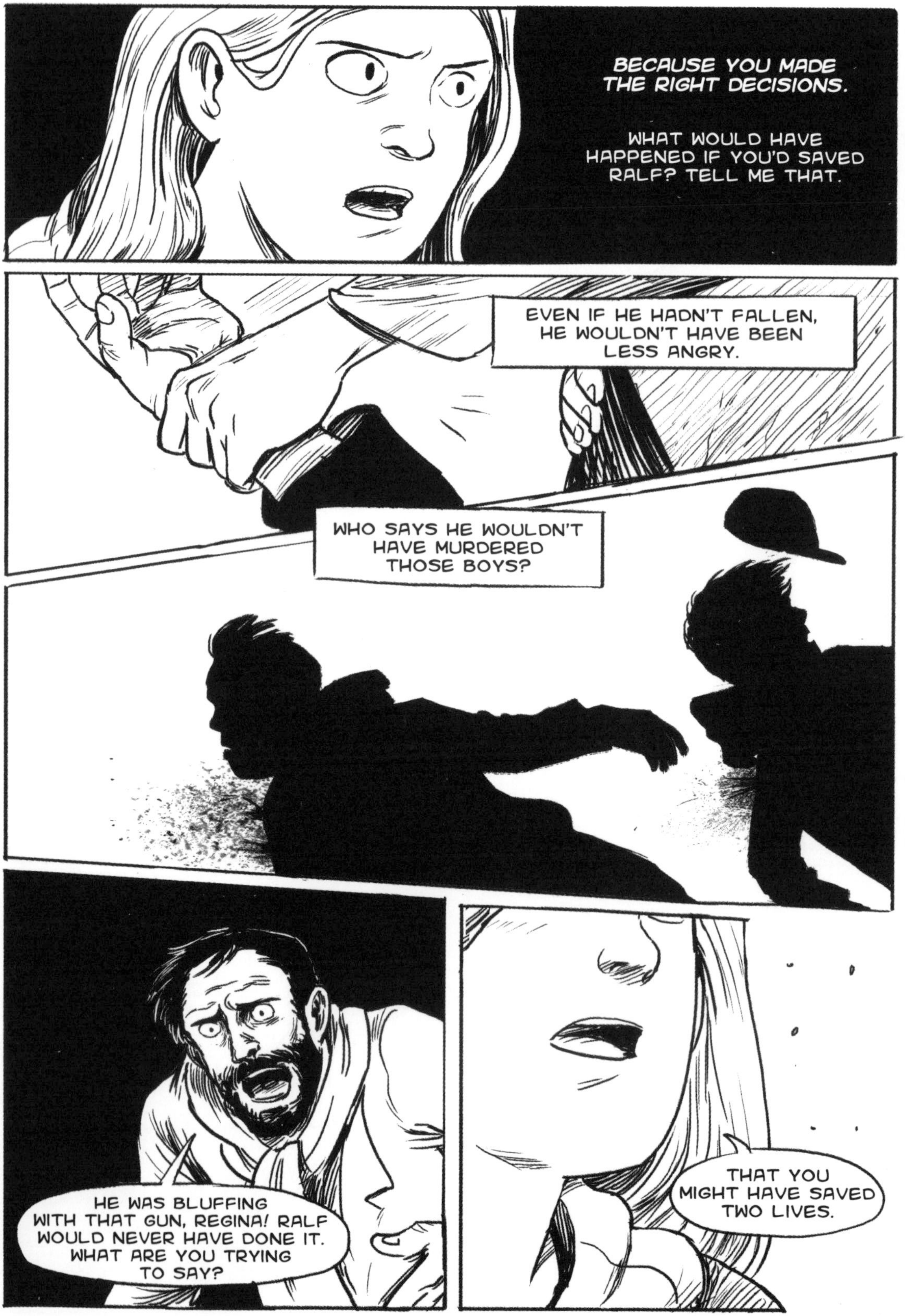

BECAUSE YOU MADE THE RIGHT DECISIONS.
WHAT WOULD HAVE HAPPENED IF YOU'D SAVED RALF? TELL ME THAT.
EVEN IF HE HADN'T FALLEN, HE WOULDN'T HAVE BEEN LESS ANGRY.
WHO SAYS HE WOULDN'T HAVE MURDERED THOSE BOYS?
HE WAS BLUFFING WITH THAT GUN, REGINA! RALF WOULD NEVER HAVE DONE IT. WHAT ARE YOU TRYING TO SAY?
THAT YOU MIGHT HAVE SAVED TWO LIVES.

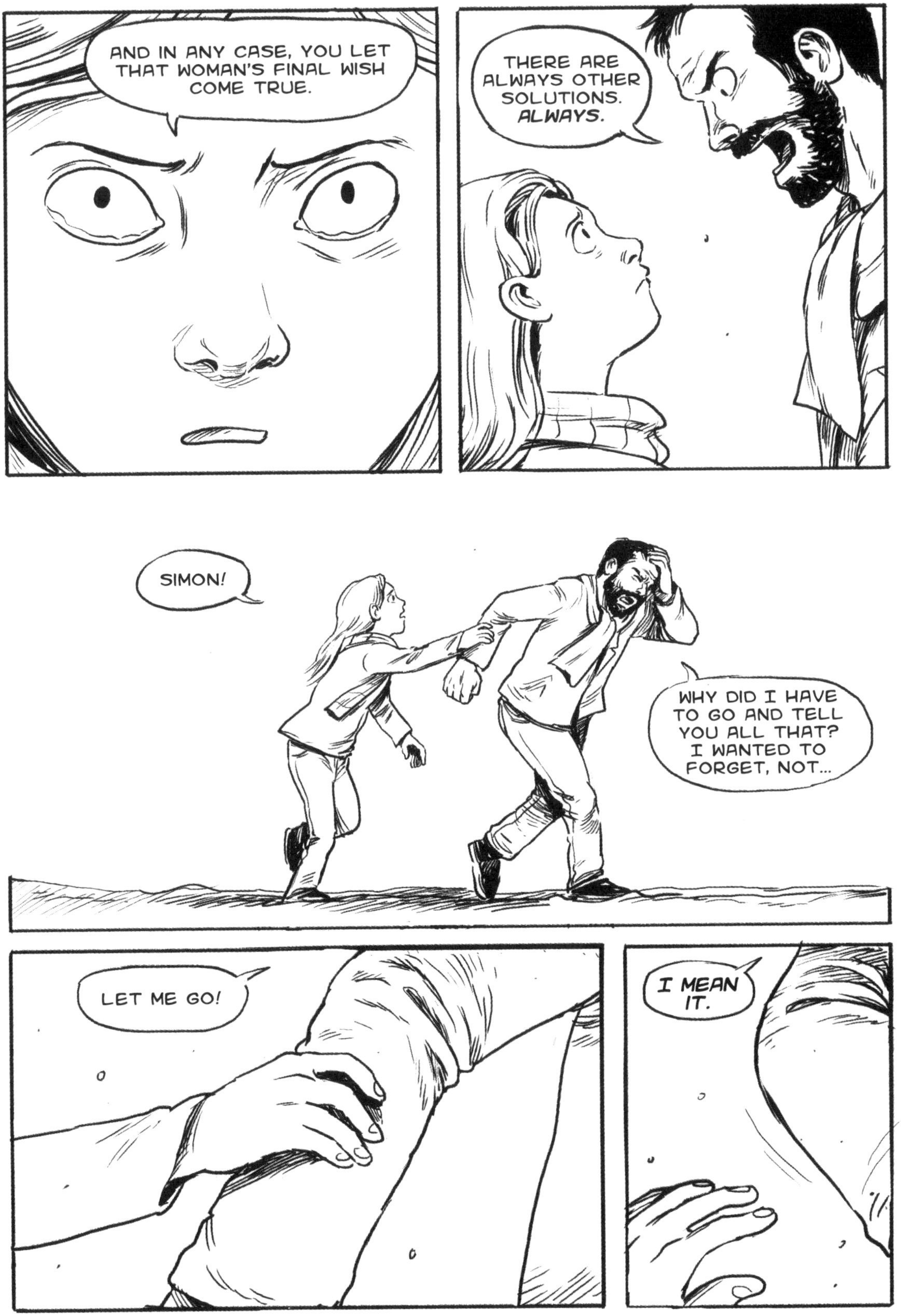
AND IN ANY CASE, YOU LET THAT WOMAN'S FINAL WISH COME TRUE.
THERE ARE ALWAYS OTHER SOLUTIONS. *ALWAYS.*
SIMON!
WHY DID I HAVE TO GO AND TELL YOU ALL THAT? I WANTED TO FORGET, NOT...
LET ME GO!
I MEAN IT.

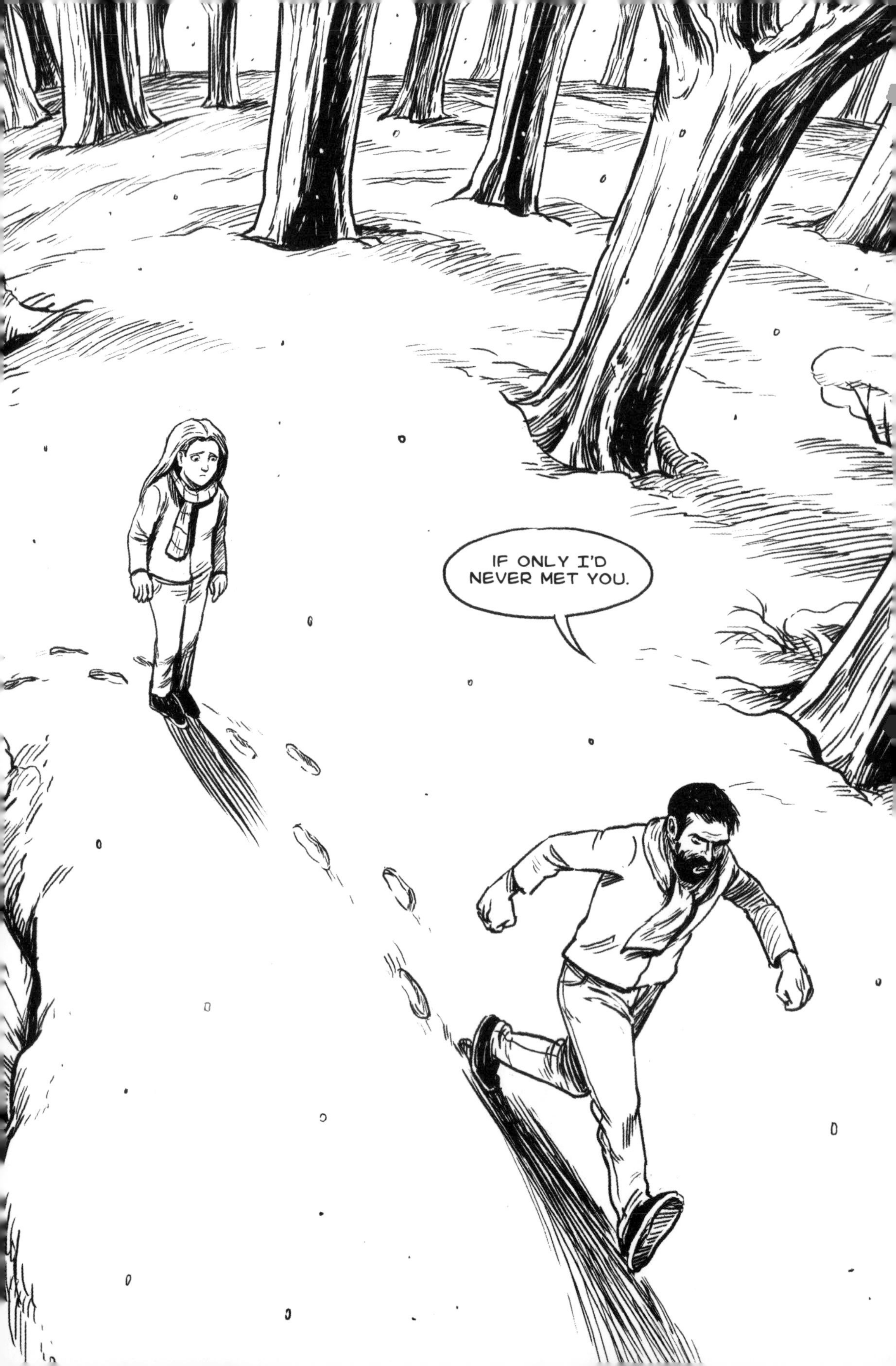
IF ONLY I'D NEVER MET YOU.

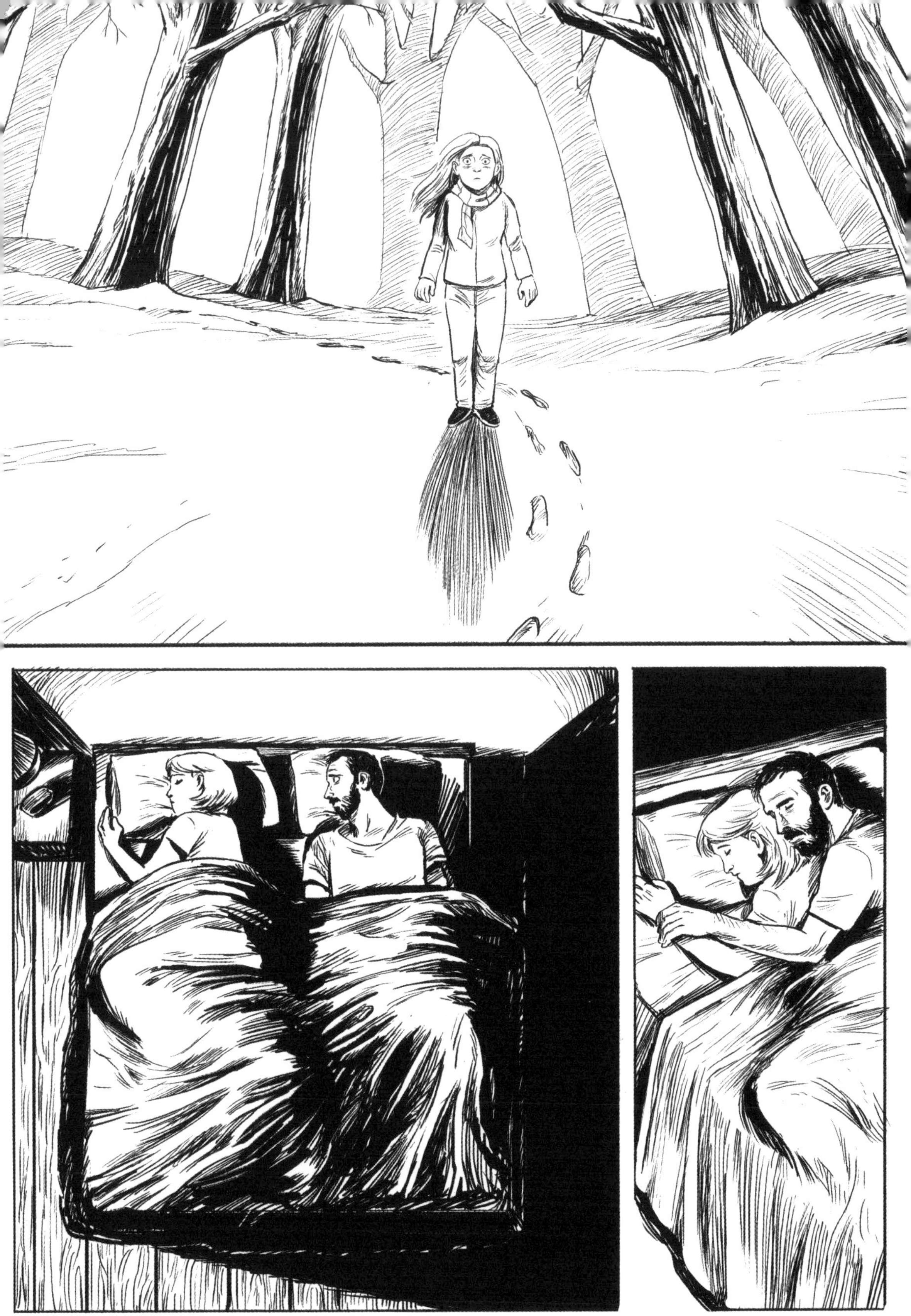

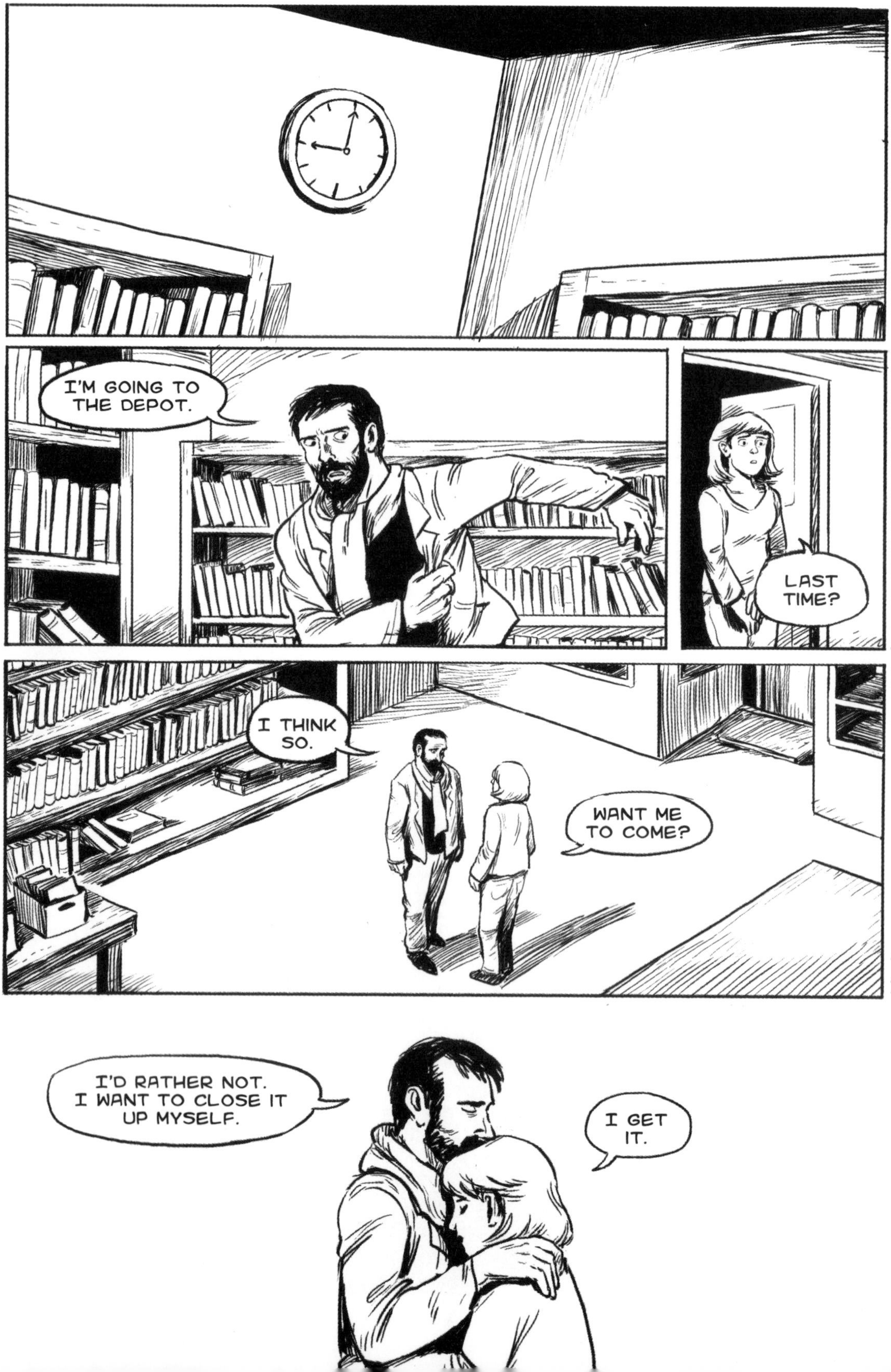
I'M GOING TO THE DEPOT.
LAST TIME?
I THINK SO.
WANT ME TO COME?
I'D RATHER NOT. I WANT TO CLOSE IT UP MYSELF.
I GET IT.

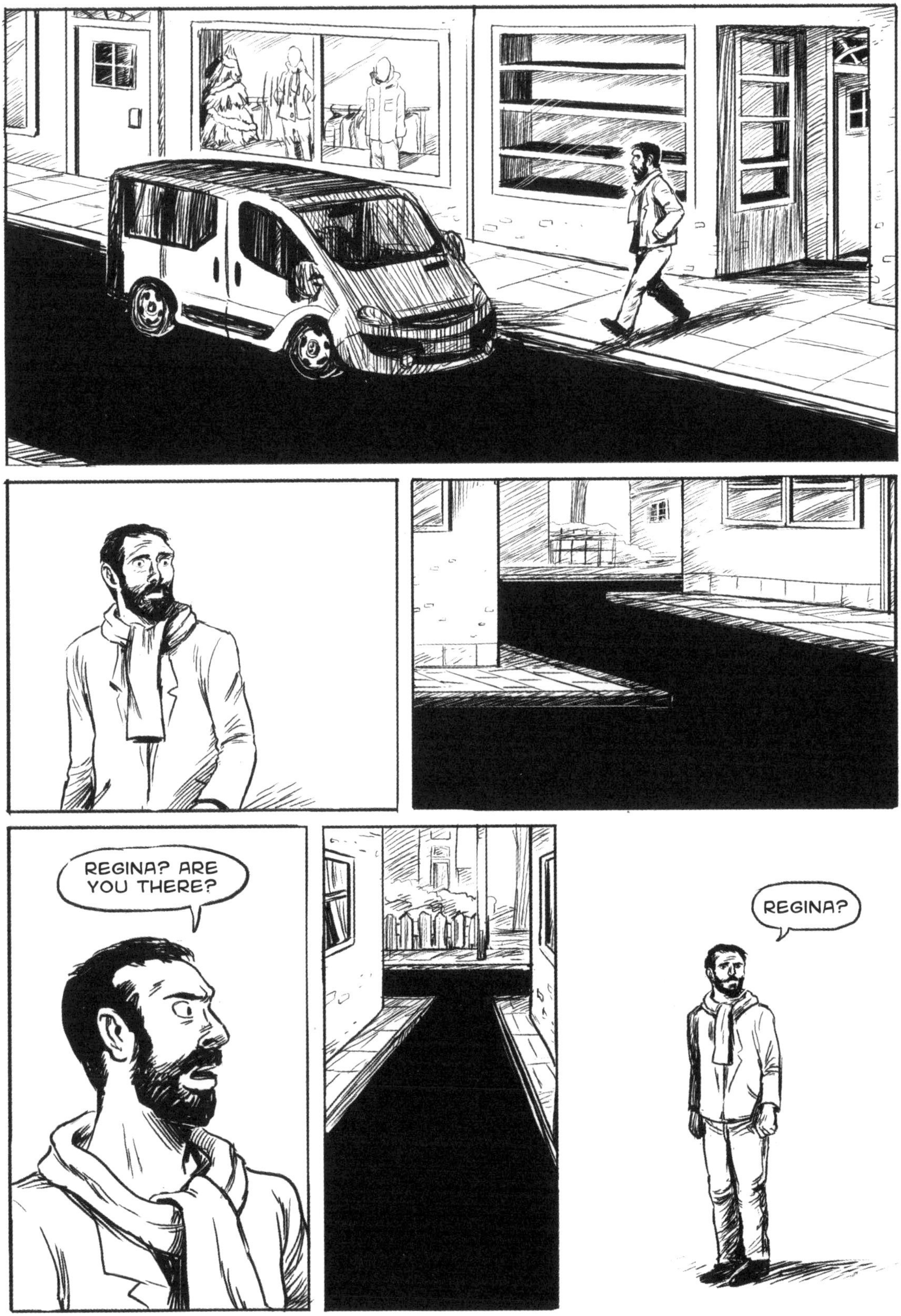
REGINA? ARE YOU THERE?
REGINA?

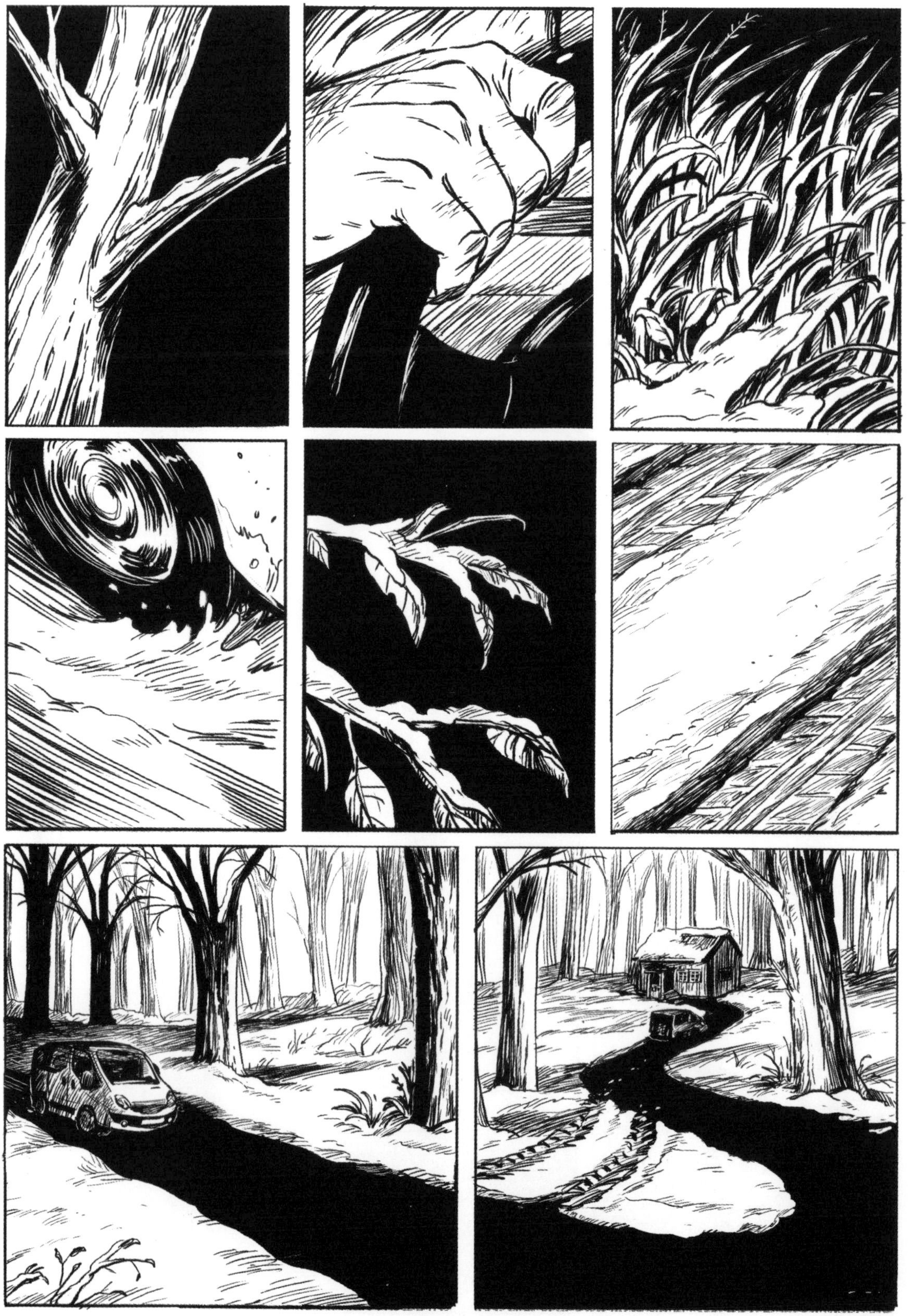

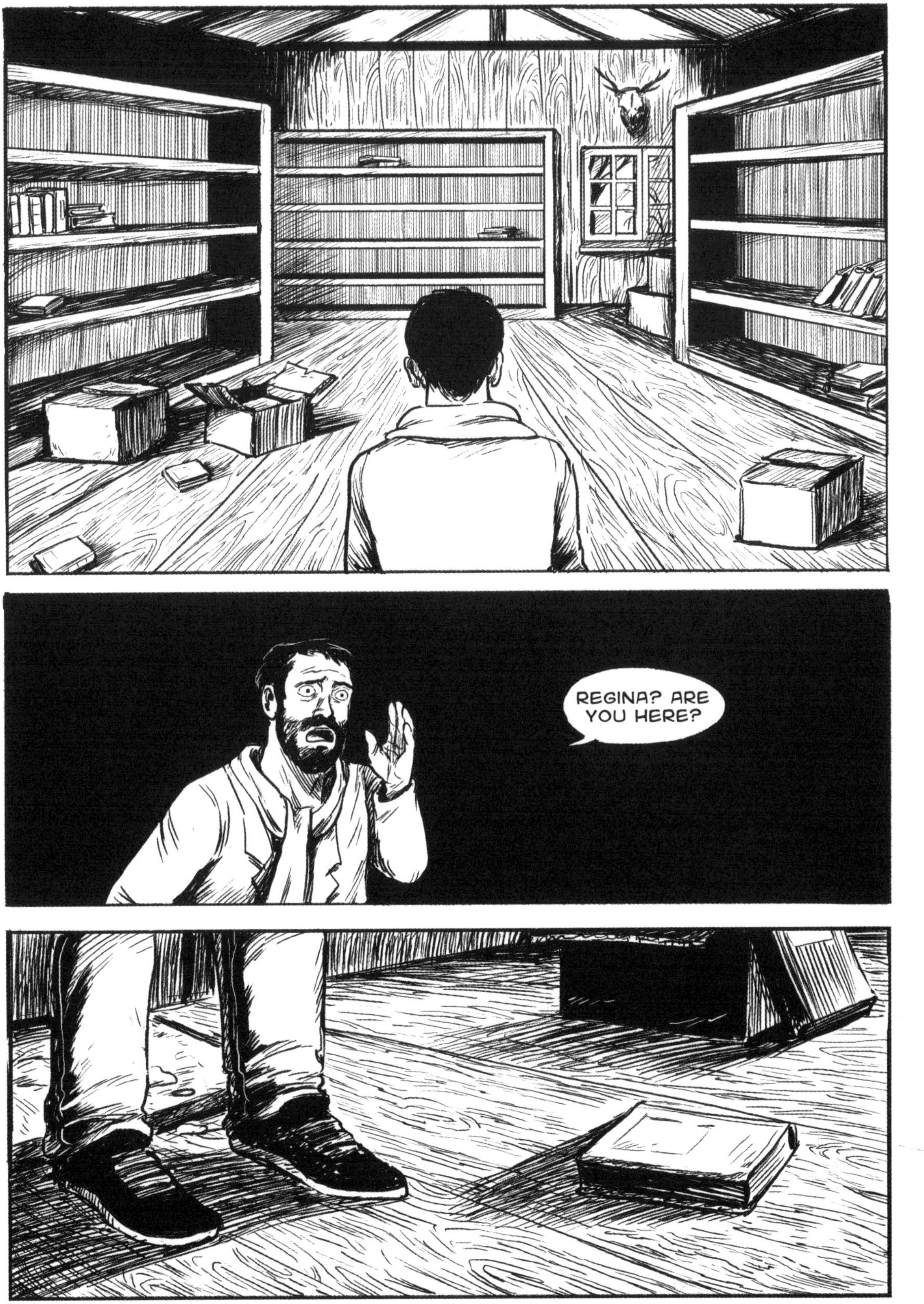
REGINA? ARE YOU HERE?

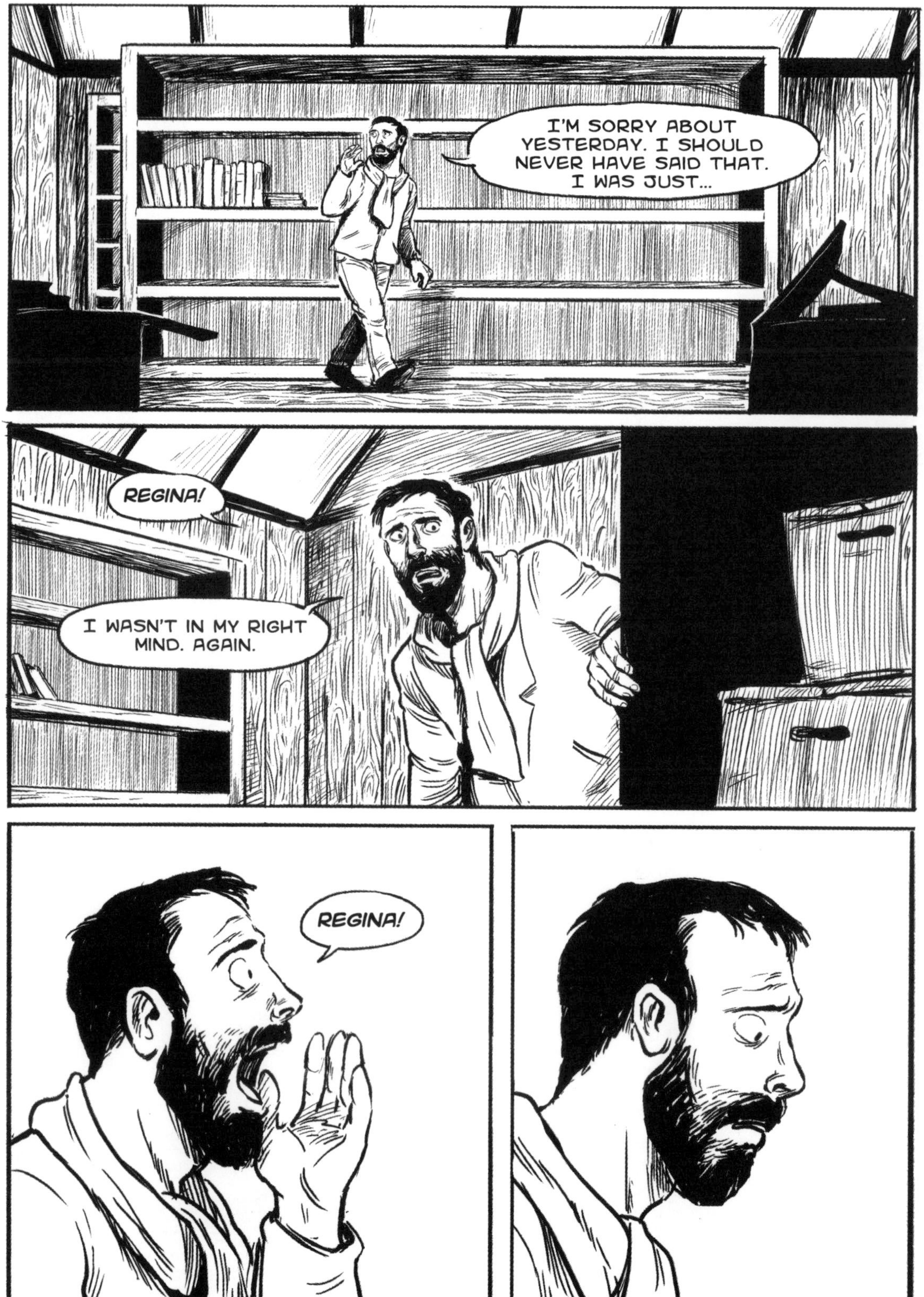
I'M SORRY ABOUT YESTERDAY. I SHOULD NEVER HAVE SAID THAT. I WAS JUST...
REGINA!
I WASN'T IN MY RIGHT MIND. AGAIN.
REGINA!

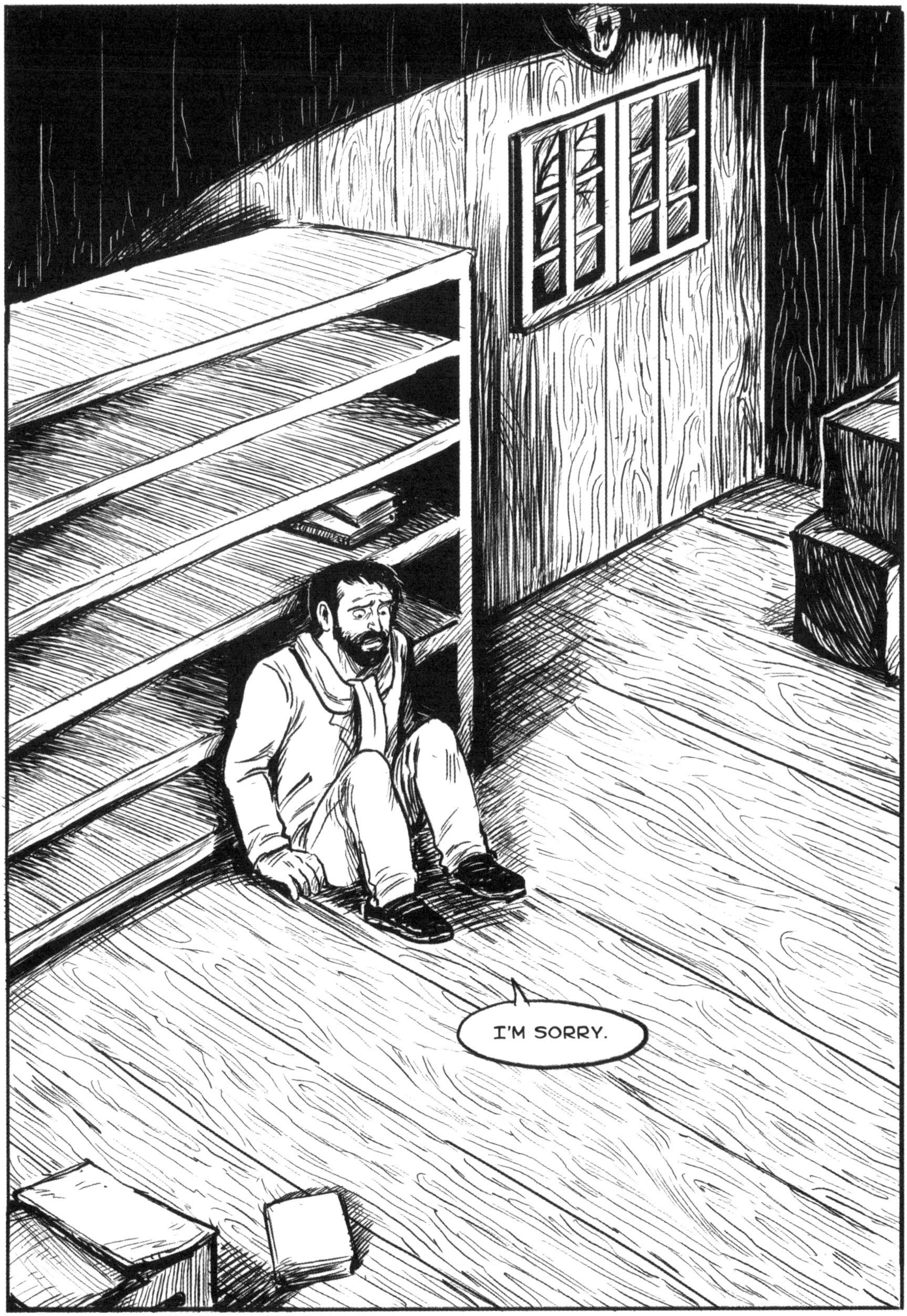
I'M SORRY.

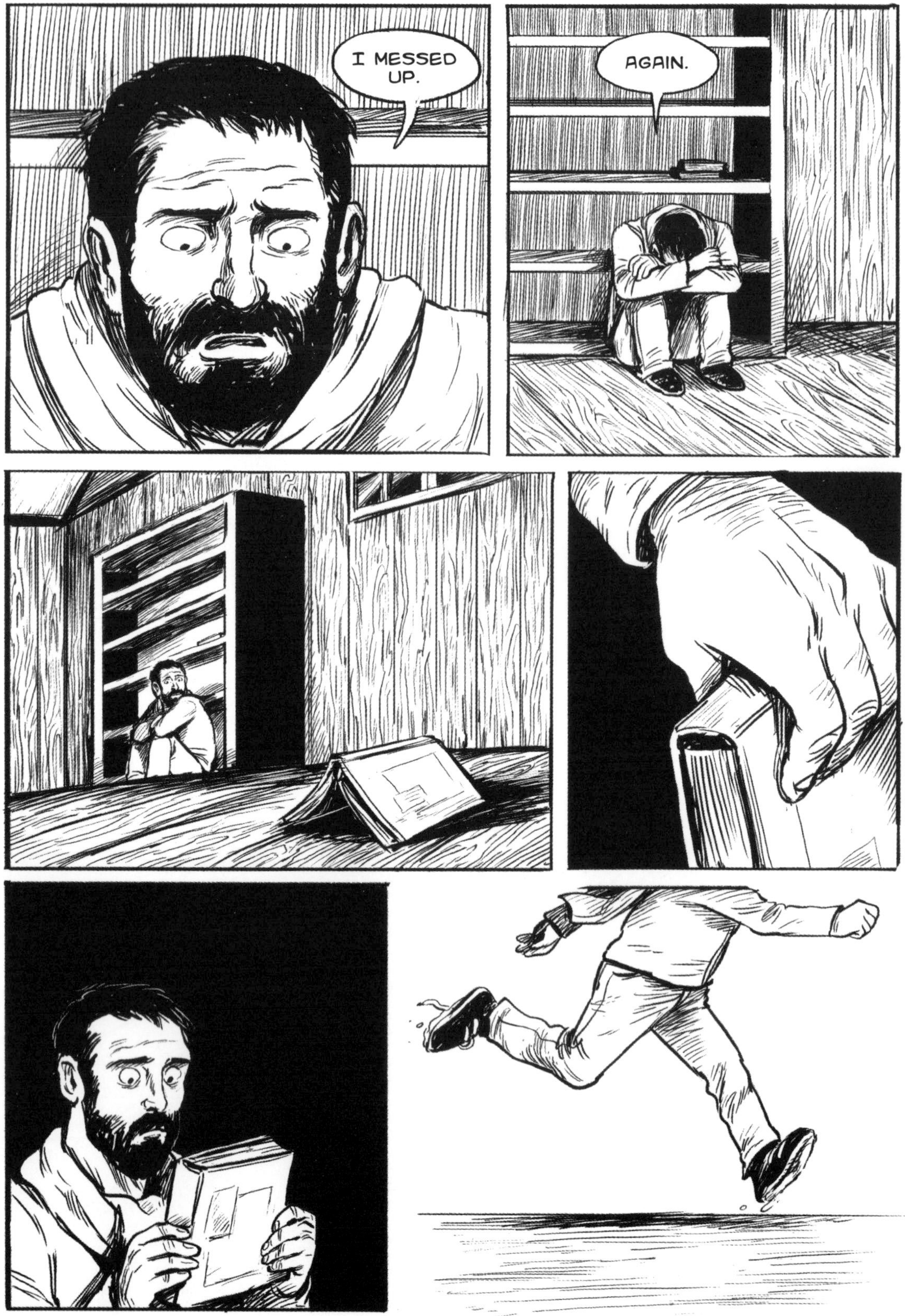
I MESSED UP.
AGAIN.

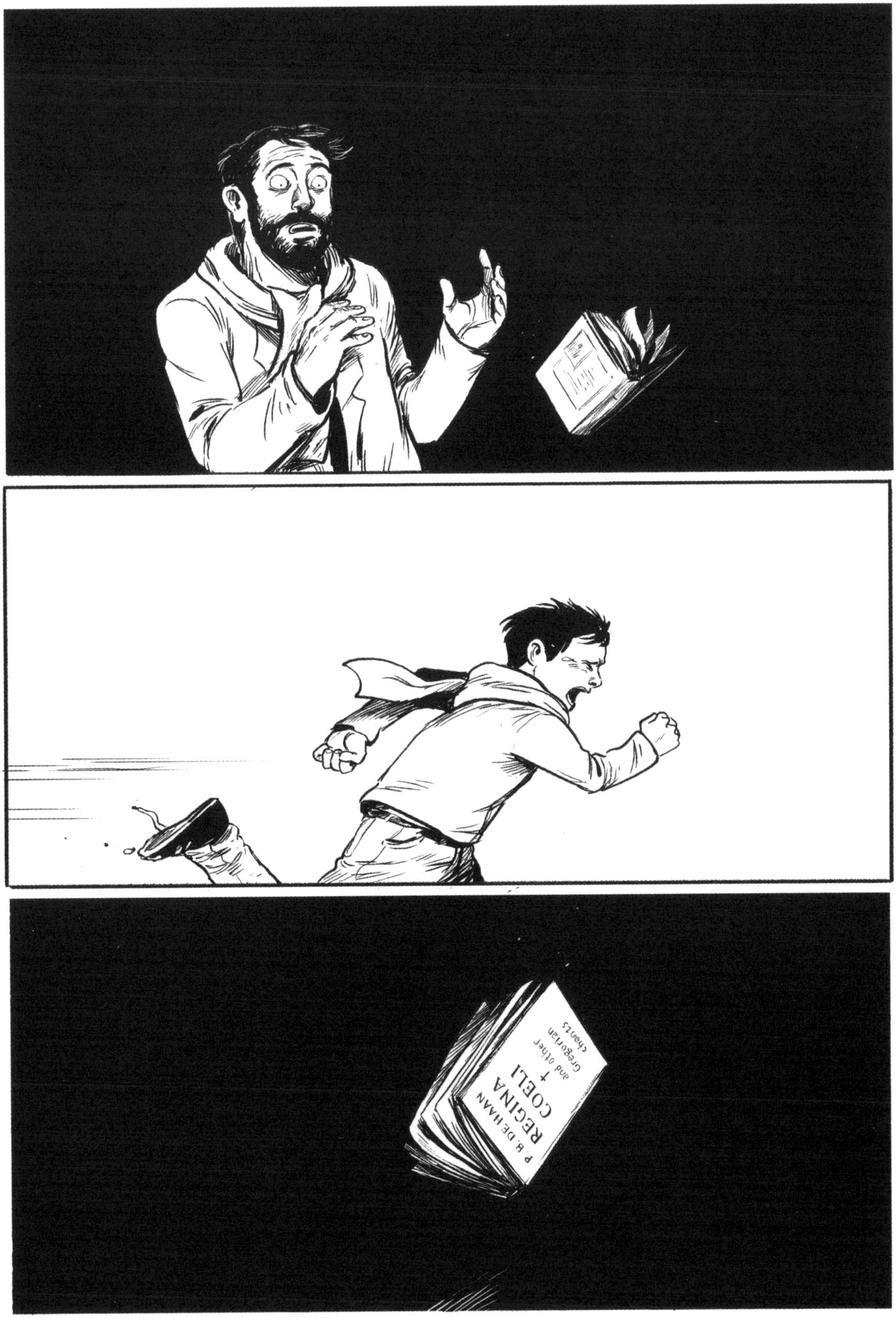
P. B. DE HAAN
REGINA
+
COELI
and other
Gregorian
chants

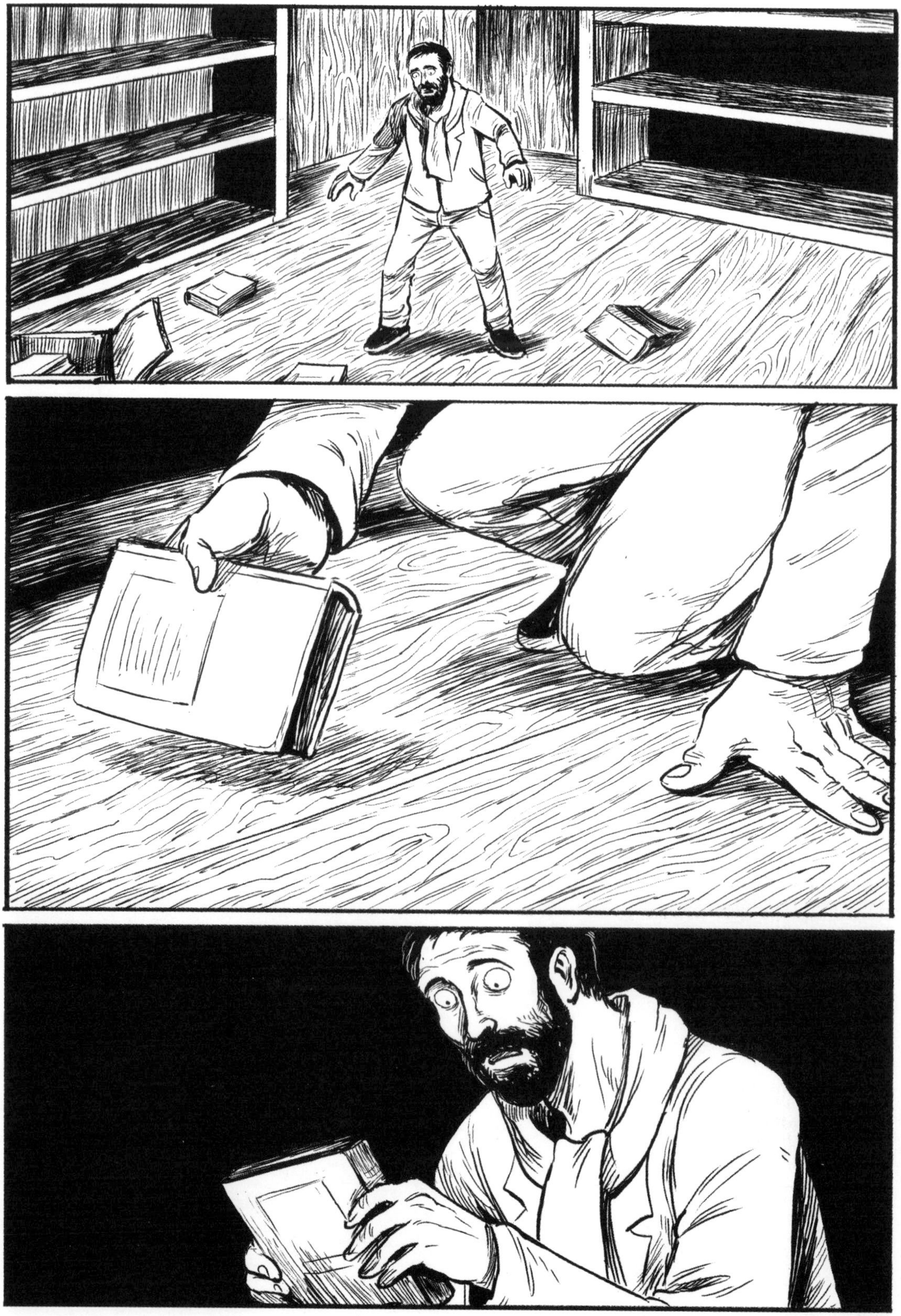

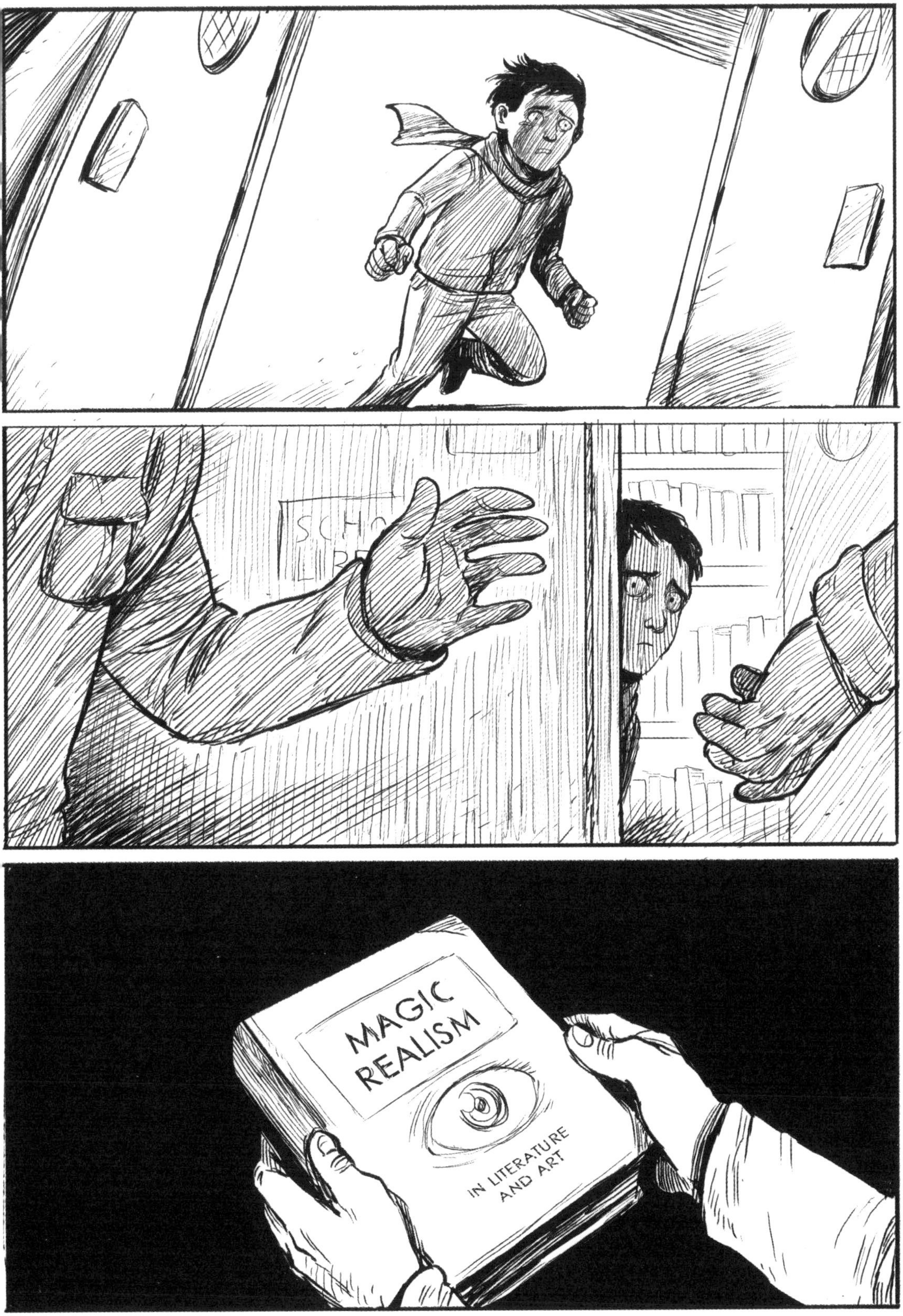
MAGIC REALISM
IN LITERATURE AND ART

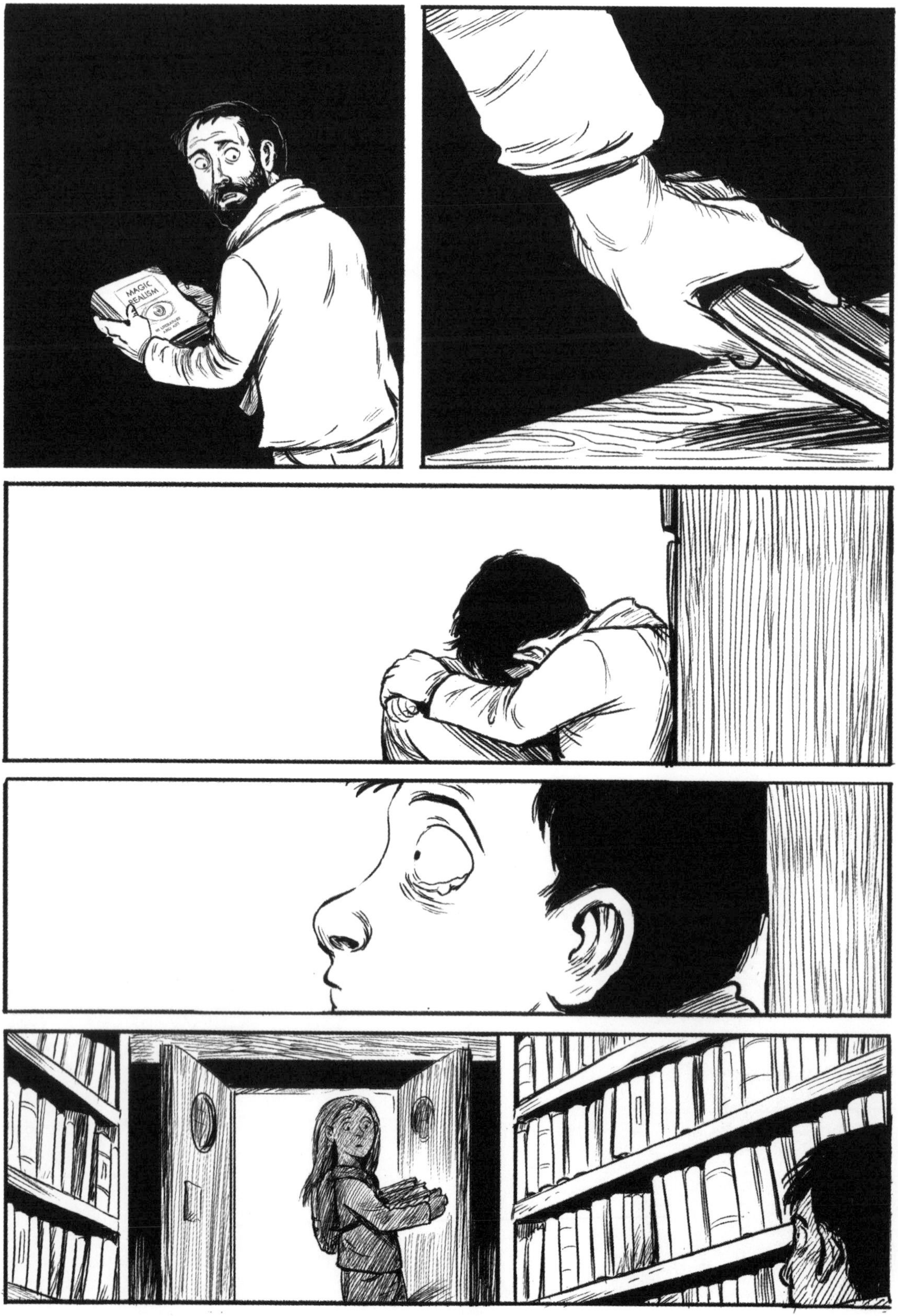
MAGIC REALISM
IN LITERATURE AND ART

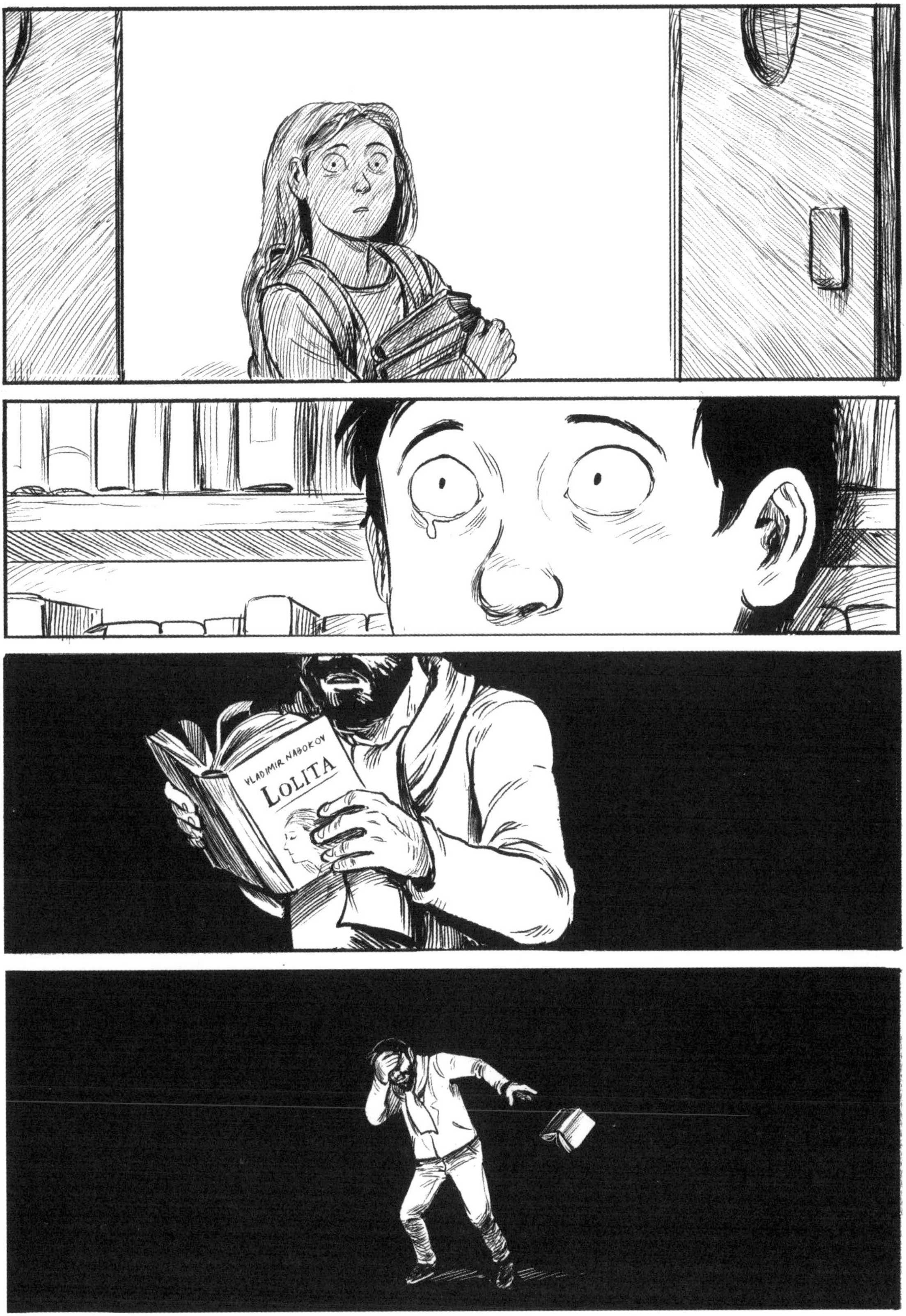
VLADIMIR NABOKOV
LOLITA

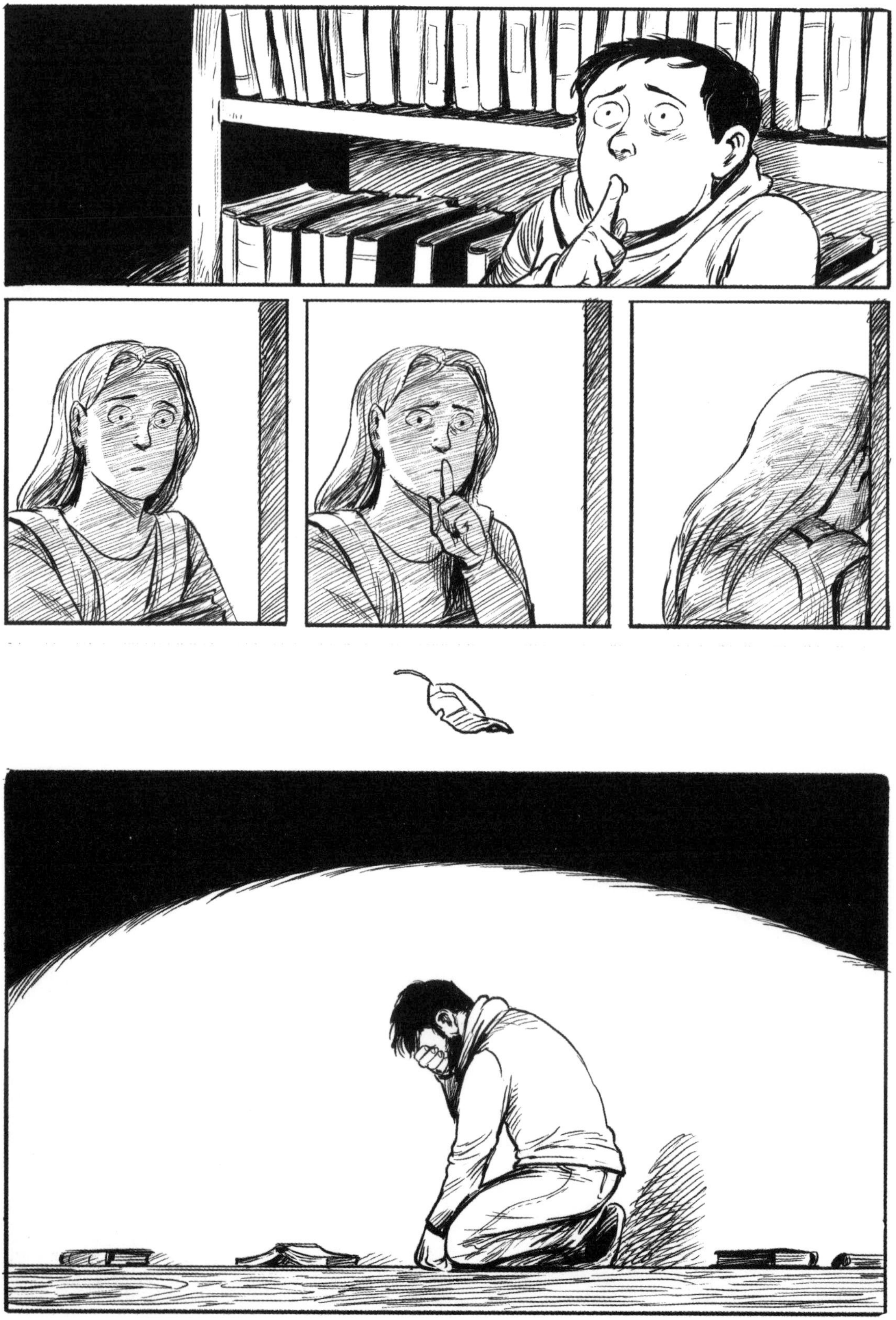

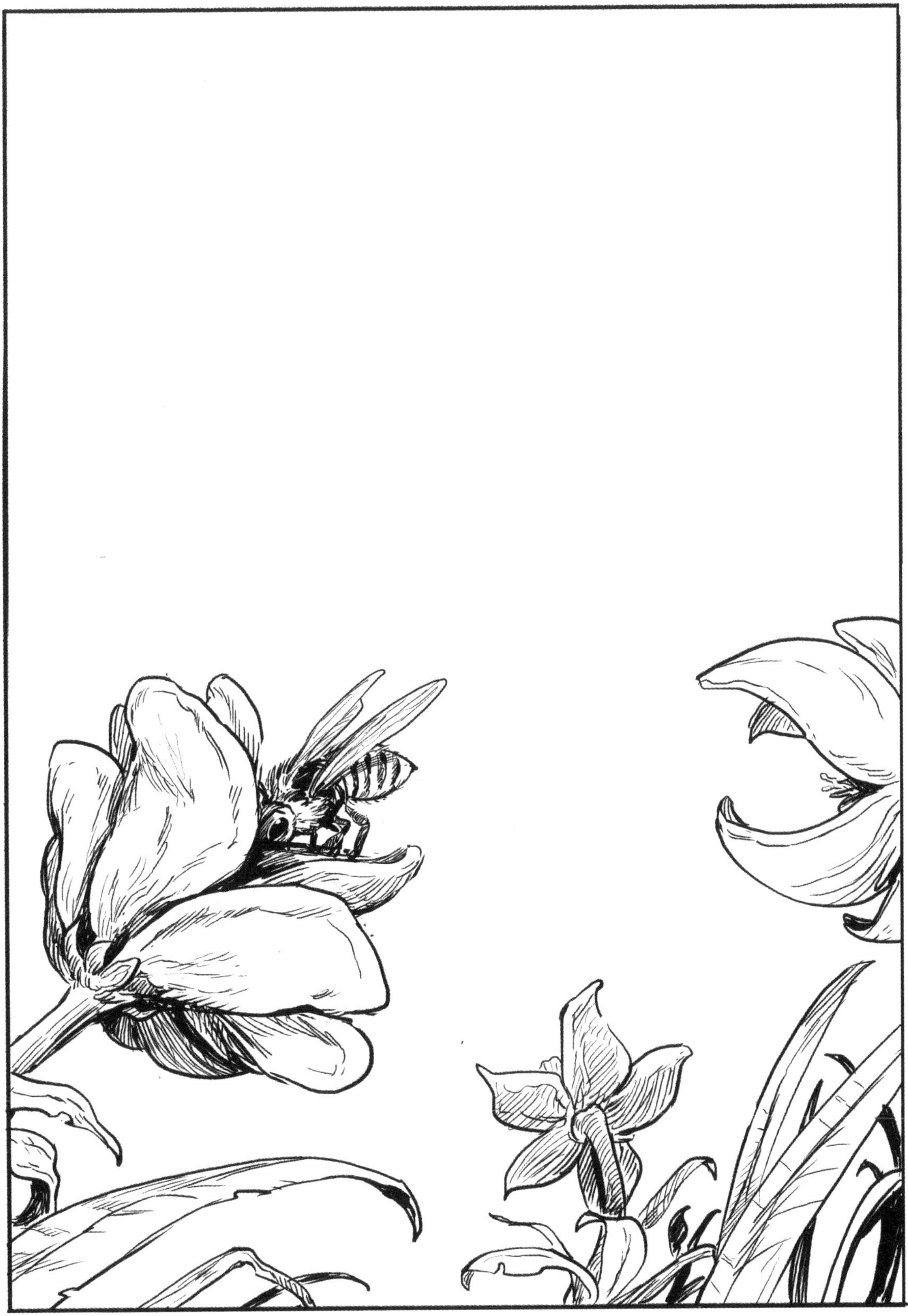

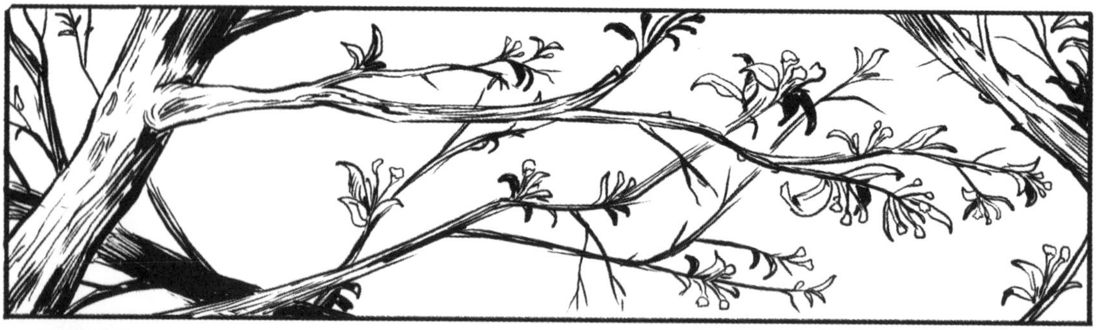
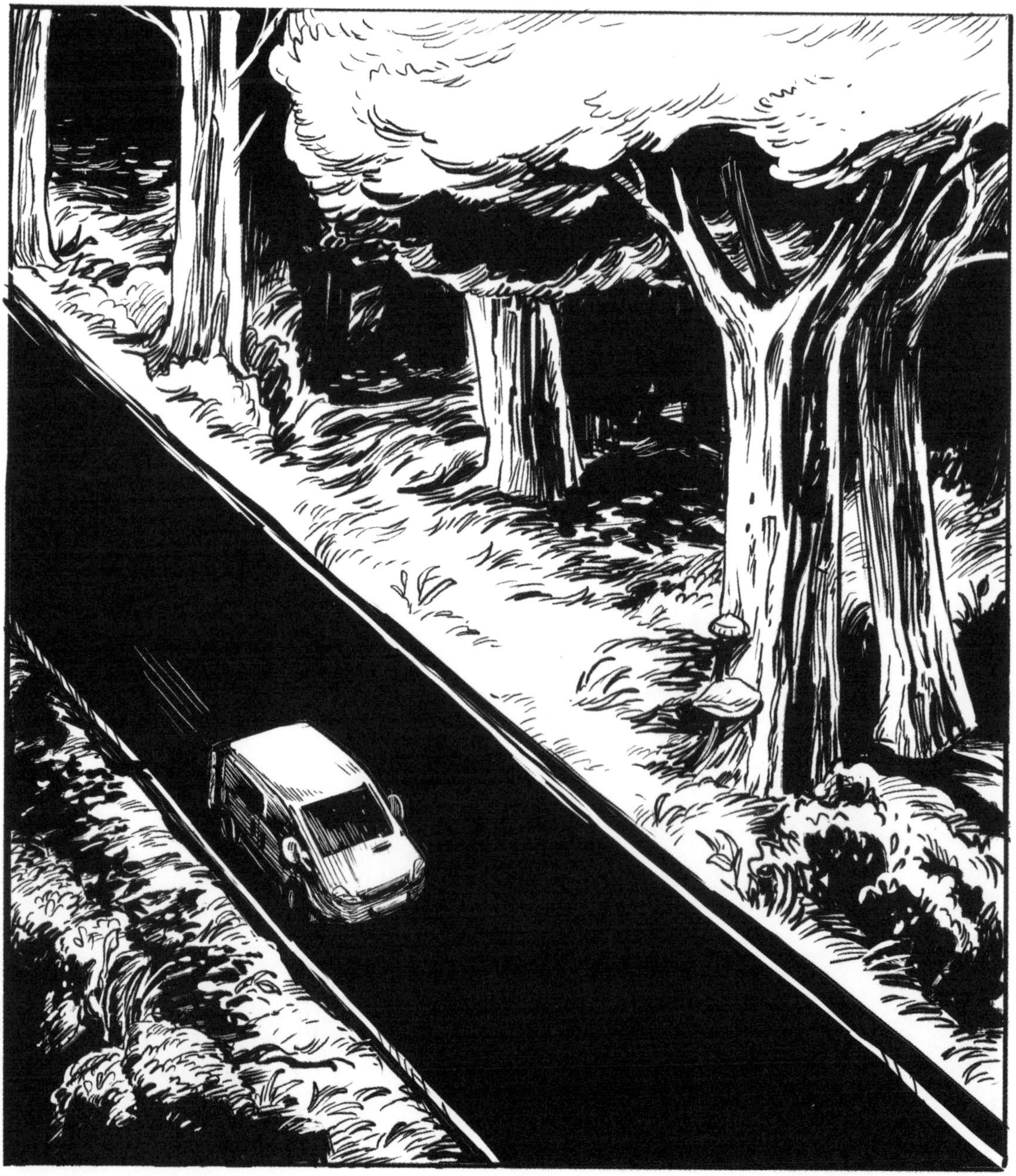

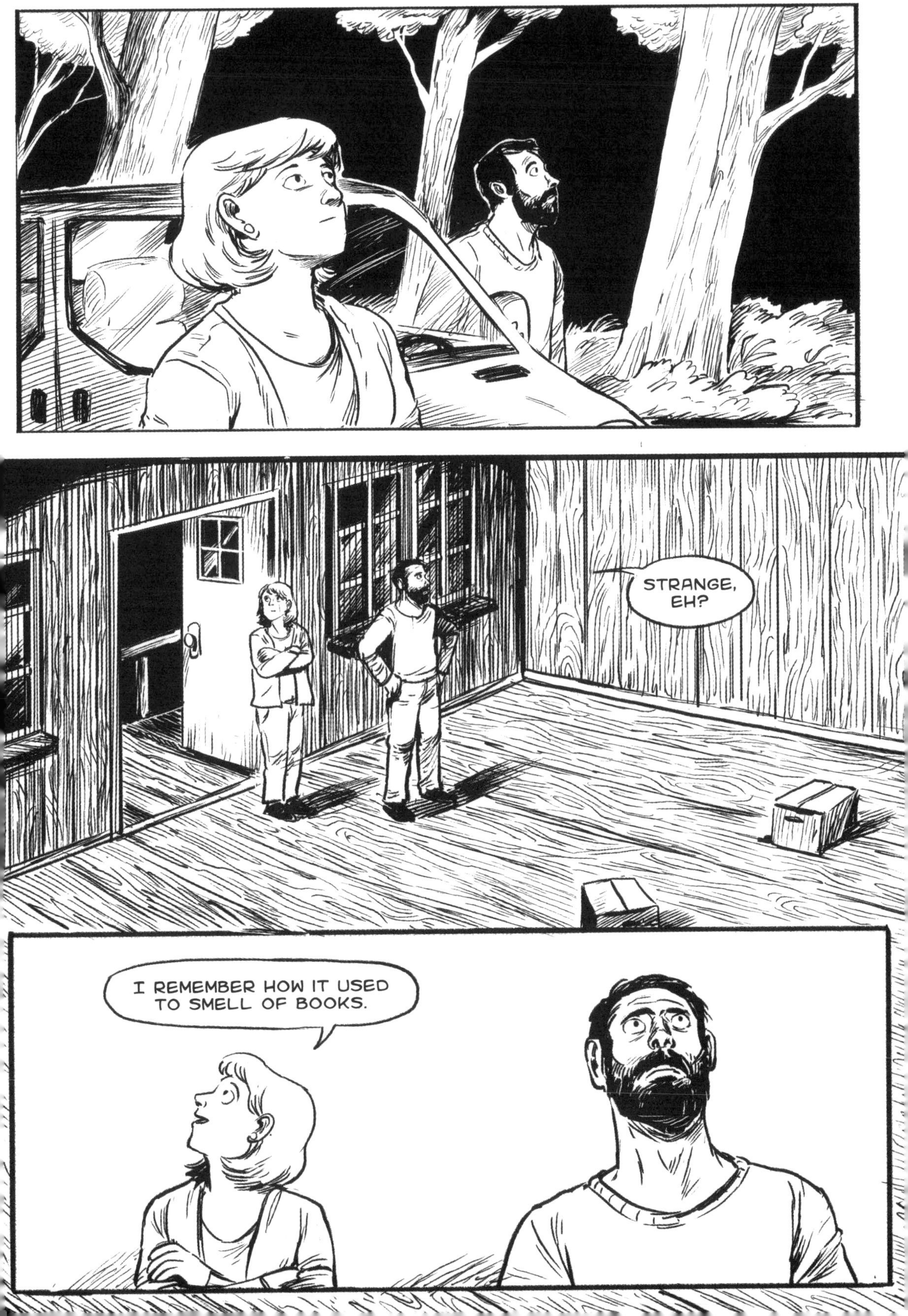
STRANGE, EH?
I REMEMBER HOW IT USED TO SMELL OF BOOKS.

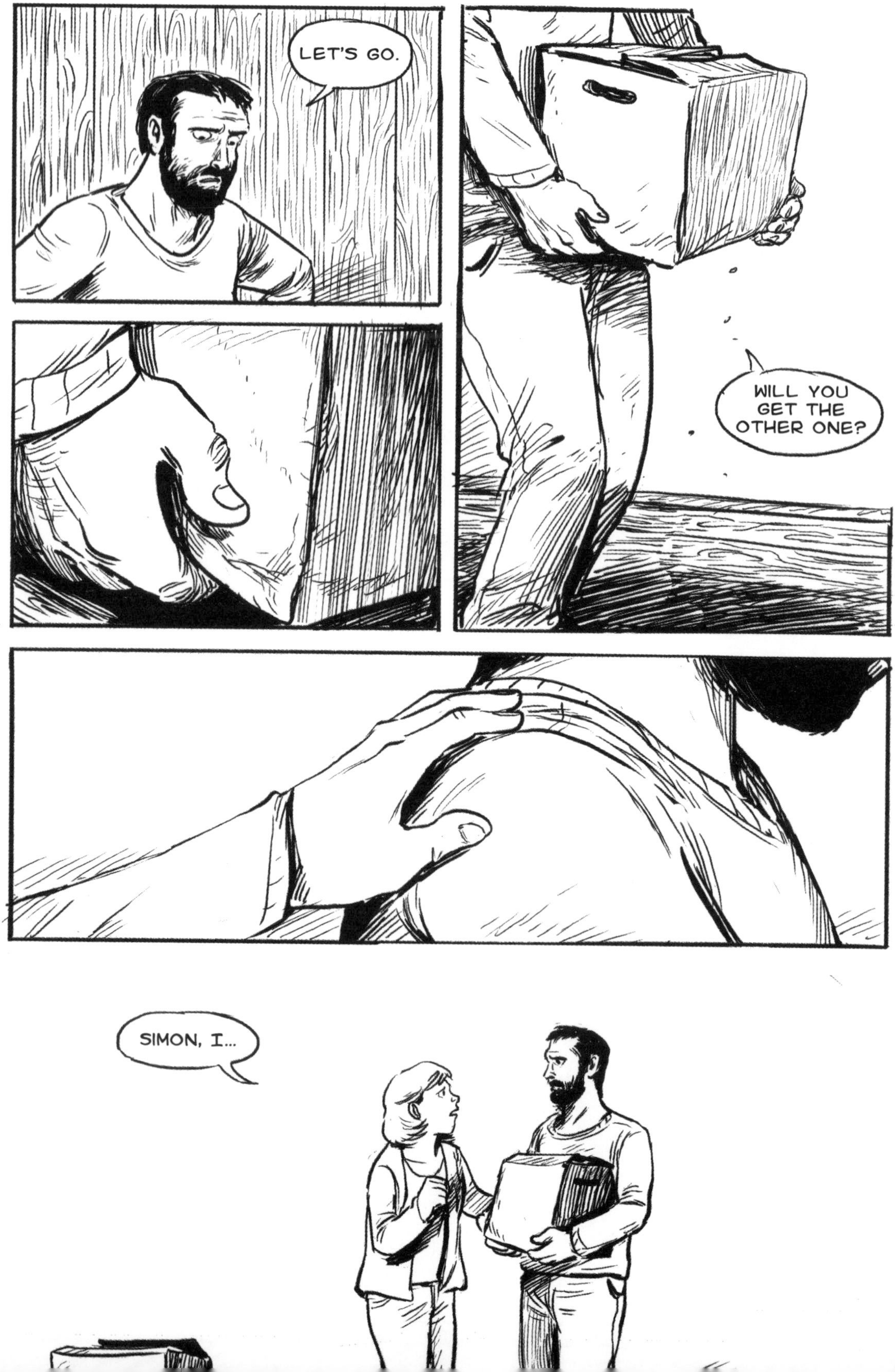
LET'S GO.
WILL YOU GET THE OTHER ONE?
SIMON, I...

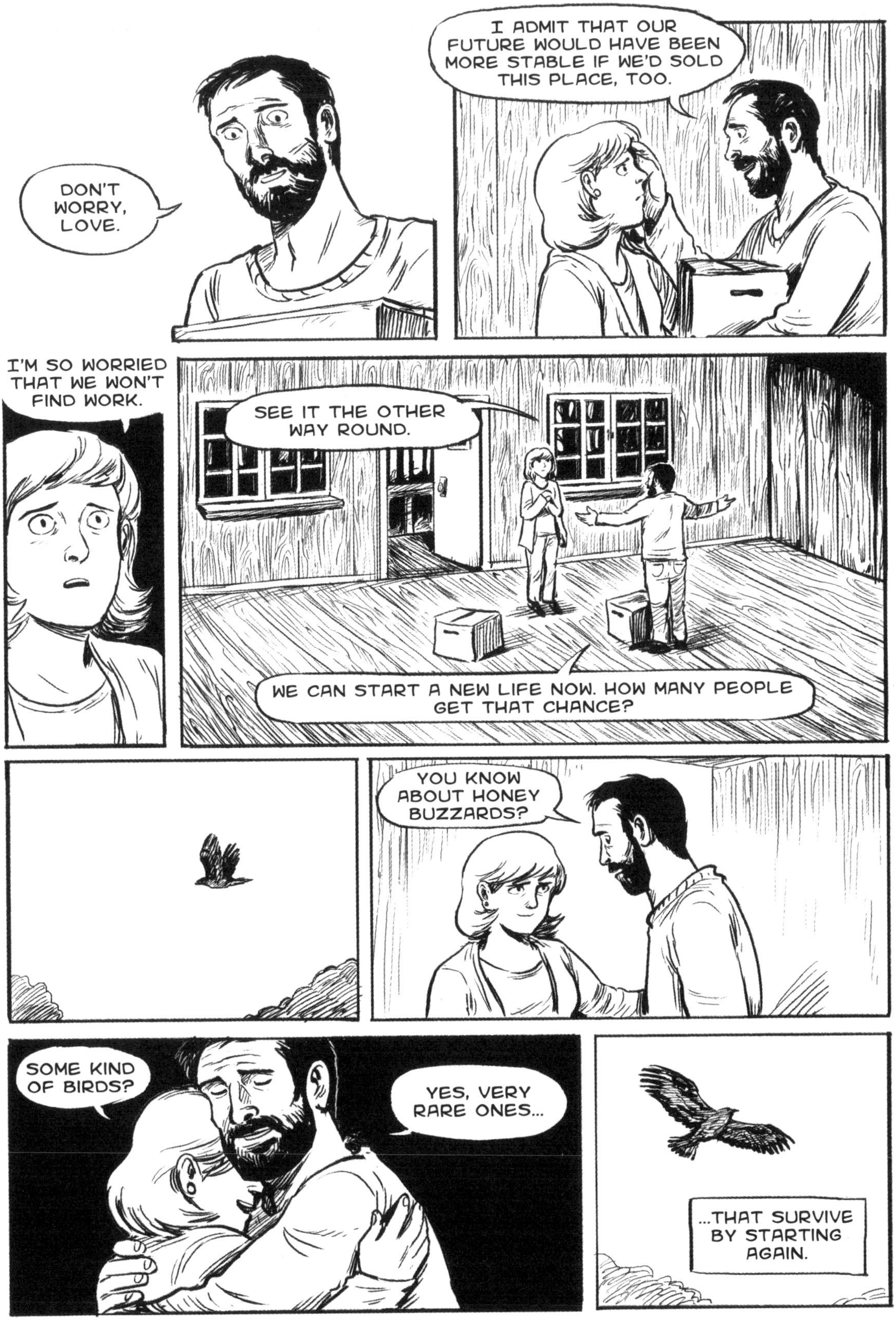
DON'T WORRY, LOVE.
I ADMIT THAT OUR FUTURE WOULD HAVE BEEN MORE STABLE IF WE'D SOLD THIS PLACE, TOO.
I'M SO WORRIED THAT WE WON'T FIND WORK.
SEE IT THE OTHER WAY ROUND.
WE CAN START A NEW LIFE NOW. HOW MANY PEOPLE GET THAT CHANCE?
YOU KNOW ABOUT HONEY BUZZARDS?
SOME KIND OF BIRDS?
YES, VERY RARE ONES...
...THAT SURVIVE BY STARTING AGAIN.

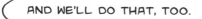

AND WE'LL DO THAT, TOO.

COMING?

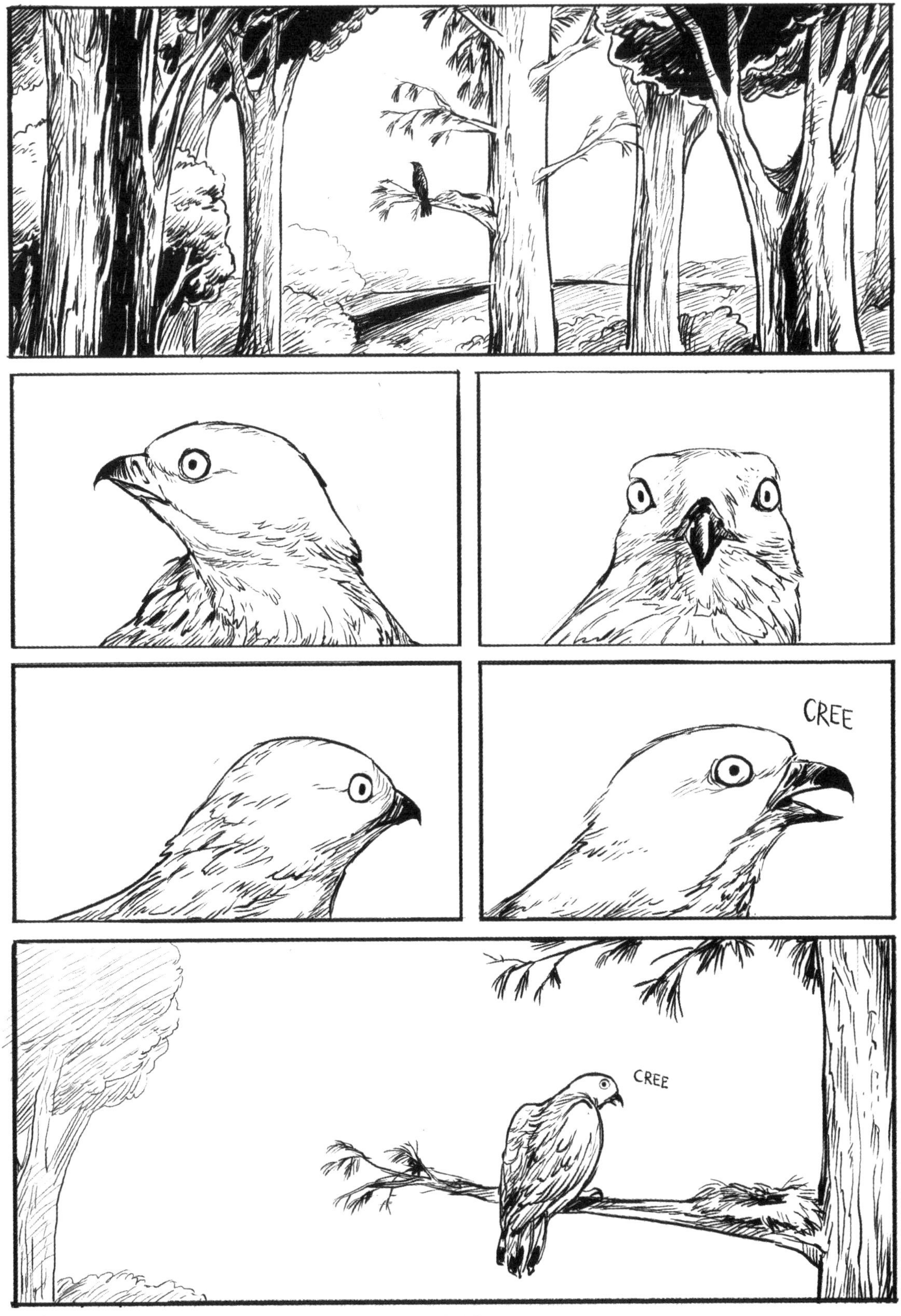
CREE
CREE

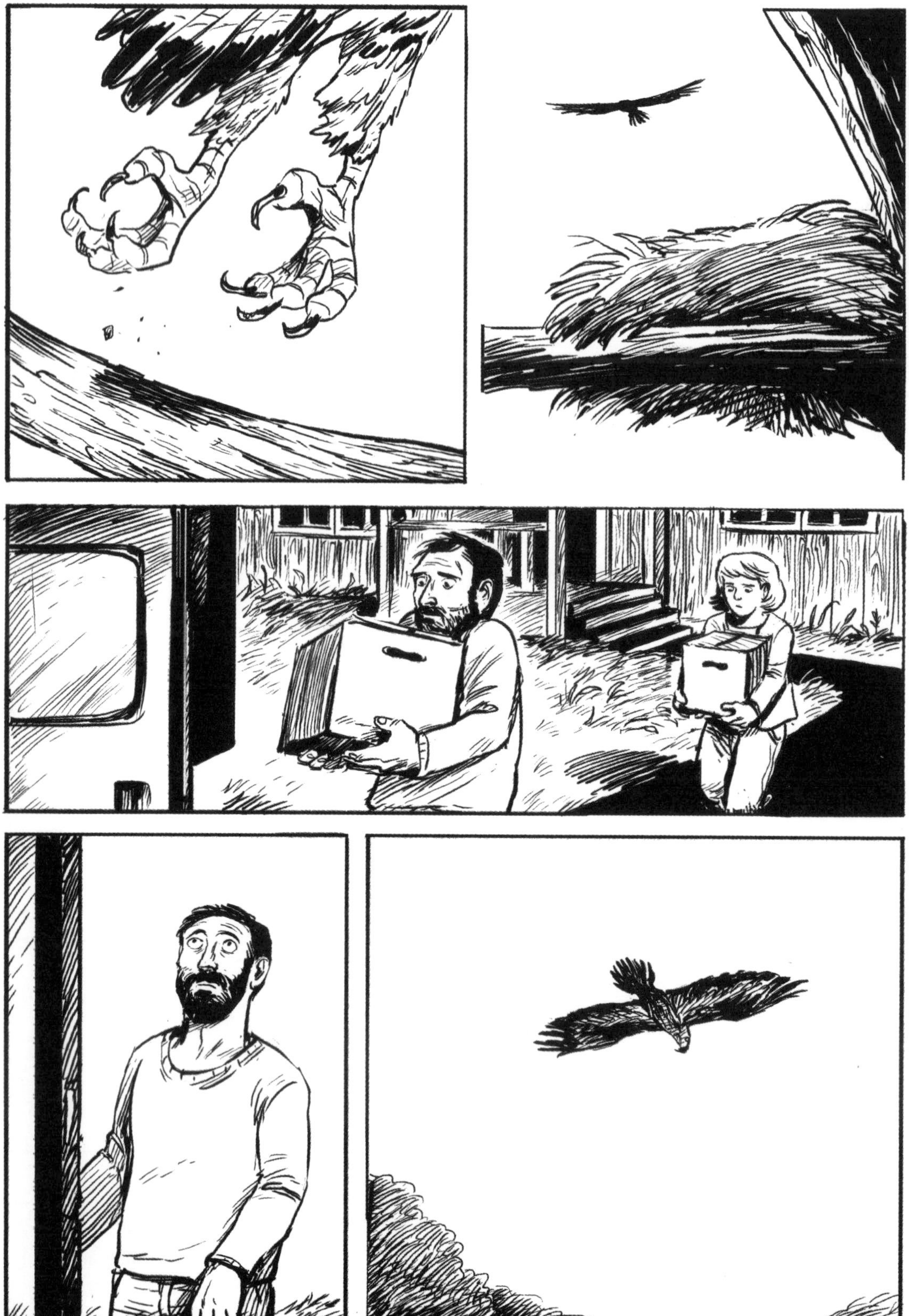

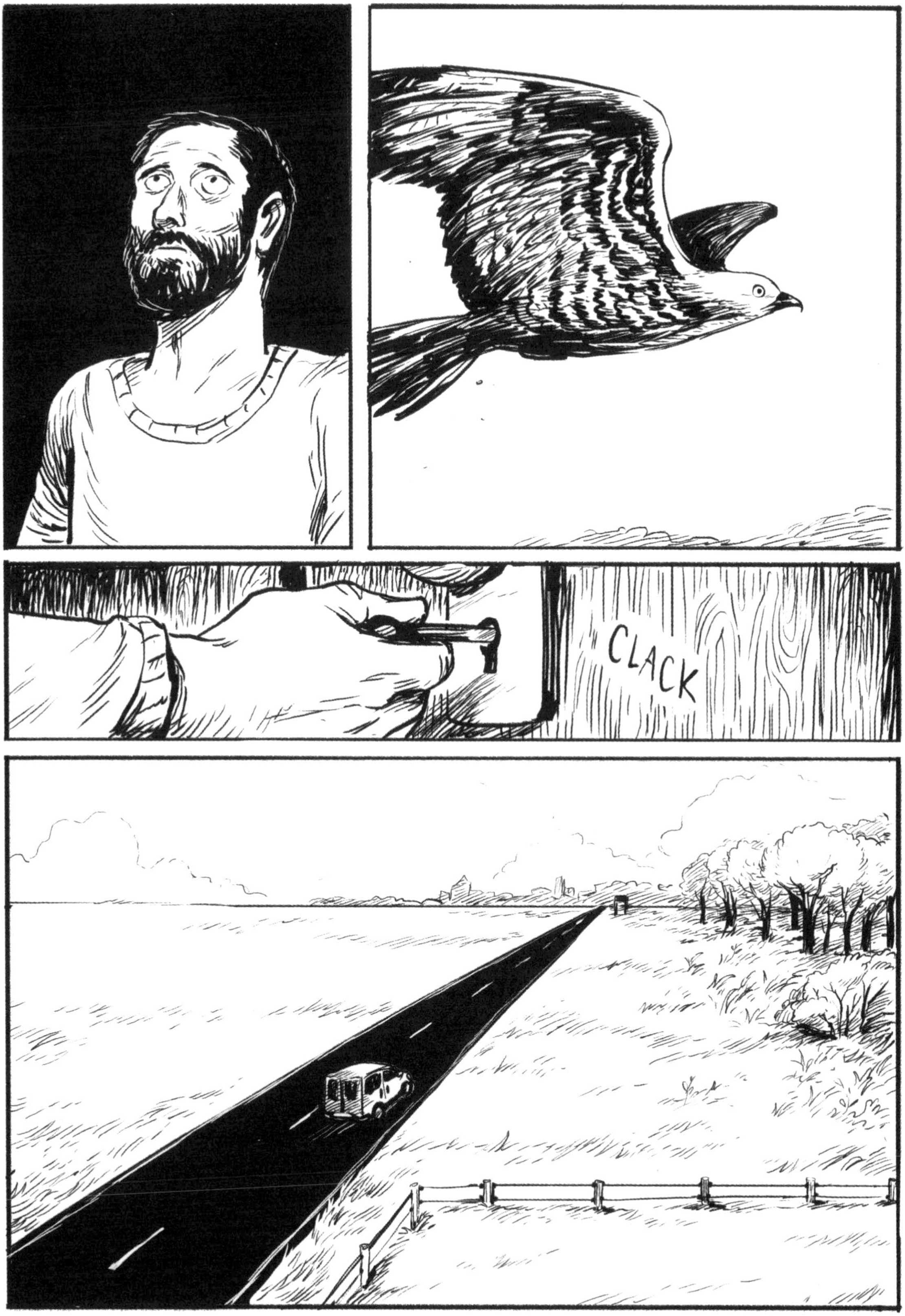
CLACK

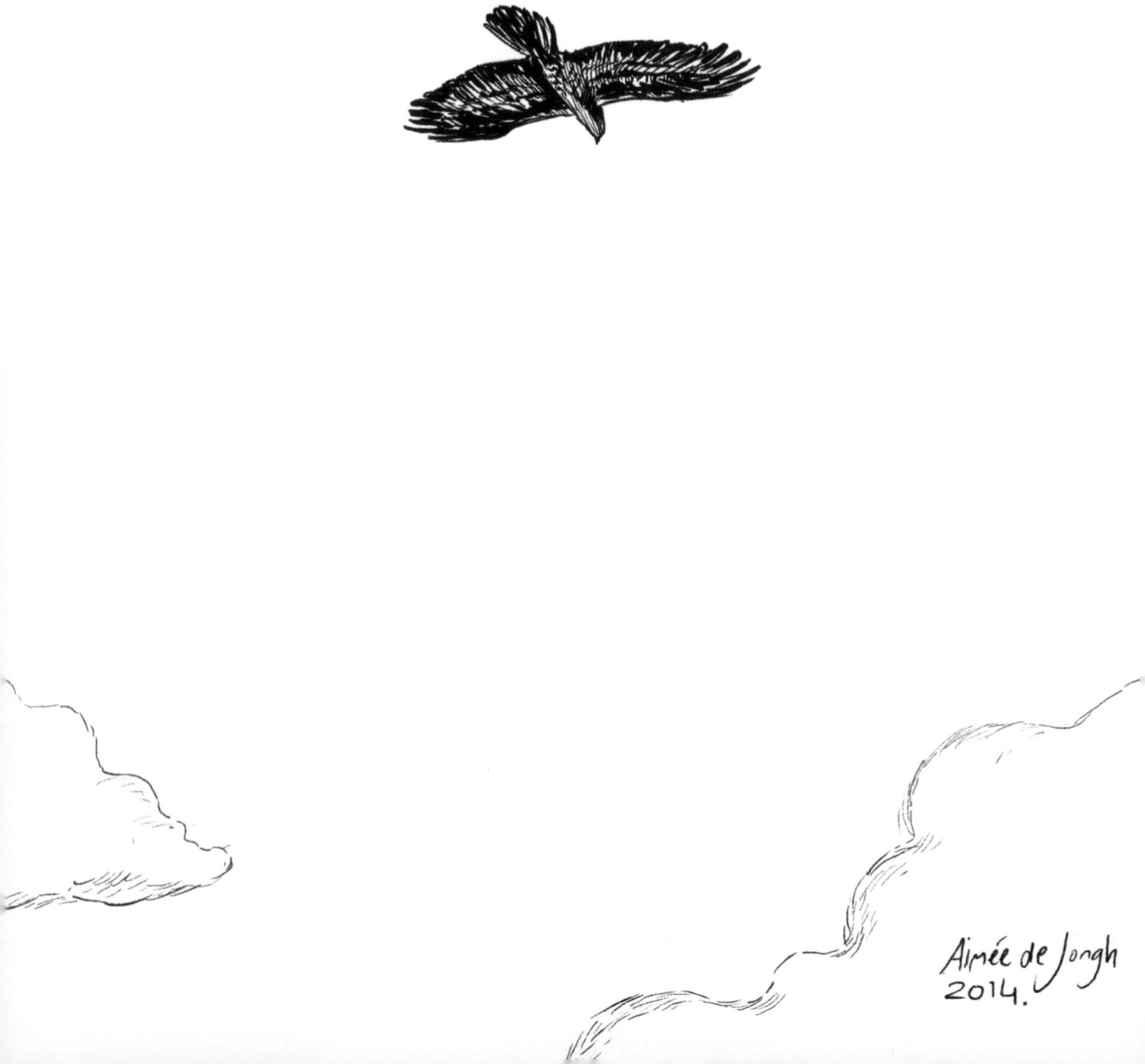
Aimée de Jongh
2014.